ENVIRONMENTAL LAND USE PROBLEMS

ENVIRONMENTAL LAND USE PROBLEMS

A study of northern New Jersey

Summary proceedings of a conference on land use
held at Ramapo College of New Jersey

edited by
JOSEPH LeMAY and EUGENE HARRISON
Ramapo College of New Jersey

MARCEL DEKKER, INC.   NEW YORK

MARCEL DEKKER, INC.

270 Madison Avenue, New York, New York 10016

LIBRARY OF CONGRESS CATALOG CARD NUMBER: 74-79921
ISBN: 0-8247-6219-3

Current printing (last digit):
10 9 8 7 6 5 4 3 2 1

PRINTED IN THE UNITED STATES OF AMERICA

CONTENTS

CONFERENCE PARTICIPANTS

JOSEPH A. ARAMANDA, President, J. I. Kislak Realty Corp.,
Newark, New Jersey
HOWARD S. AVERY, Consulting Engineer, Abex Corporation, and
Civil Defense Director, Mahwah, New Jersey
CAROLYN BASSETT, Chairman, New Jersey State Land Use Project,
American Association of University Women, Northfield,
New Jersey
FREDERICK BAYLIS, Vice President, National Community Bank,
Maywood, New Jersey
DANIEL BERSTEIN, Attorney, Plainfield, New Jersey
PETER BUCHSBAUM, Attorney, American Civil Liberties Union,
Newark, New Jersey
PATRICK CALLANAN, Chairman, Planning Board, Ridgewood,
New Jersey
DONALD CLARK, Planning Director, Bergen County Planning
Board, Hackensack, New Jersey
CHARLES COOPER, League for Conservation Legislation, Teaneck,
New Jersey
PAUL DAVIDOFF, Director, Suburban Action Institute, Tarrytown,
New York
MICHAEL J. DWYER, Attorney, Ridgewood, New Jersey
HENRY EBEL, Suburban Action Institute, Tarrytown, New York
OSCAR EPSTEIN, Chairman, Teaneck Planning Board, Teaneck,
New Jersey
ERNEST ERBER, Director of Research, National Committee Against
Discrimination in Housing, Washington, D. C.
ELLA F. FILIPPONE, Chairman, Passaic River Coalition, Basking
Ridge, New Jersey
RICHARD GALANTOWICZ, North Jersey Conservation Foundation,
Morristown, New Jersey
LIVINGSTON GOODMAN, Mayor, Mahwah, New Jersey
DR. MASON W. GROSS, President, Harry Frank Guggenheim Fund,
New York, New York, representing the Regional Plan Associ-
ation, New York, New York

DR. EUGENE HARRISON, Assistant Professor of Geography,
    School of Human Environment, Ramapo College of New Jersey,
    Mahwah, New Jersey
WILLIAM HARTING, Director, Open Land Data Project, Tri-State
    Planning Commission, New York, New York
MITCHELL KAHN, Assistant Professor of Social Work, School of
    Human Environment, Ramapo College of New Jersey, Mahwah,
    New Jersey
ELEANOR KIELISZEK, Councilwoman and Planning Board member,
    Teaneck, New Jersey
DR. JOSEPH LeMAY, Associate Professor of Political Science,
    School of Human Environment, Ramapo College of New Jersey,
    Mahwah, New Jersey
VIVIEN LI, Youth Advisory Board — Region II, United States Envi-
    ronmental Protection Agency, Ho-Ho-Kus, New Jersey
CHESTER P. MATTSON, Chief of Environmental Programs and
    Planning, Hackensack Meadowlands Development Commission
    Lyndhurst, New Jersey
D. BENNETT MAZUR, Associate Professor of Planning, School of
    Human Environment, Ramapo College of New Jersey, Mahwah,
    New Jersey
LUCIANO MICELI, Miceli Weed Kulik, Landscape Architects,
    East Rutherford, New Jersey
TERRENCE D. MOORE, Executive Director, Newark Watershed
    Conservation and Development Corporation, Newark, New
    Jersey
THOMAS NORMAN, Attorney, New Brunswick, New Jersey
THOMAS M. O'NEILL, Executive Assistant to the Commissioner,
    Department of Environmental Protection, Trenton, New Jersey
DR. RICHARD E. ONOREVOLE, Councilman and Planning Board
    member, Saddle Brook, New Jersey
GEORGE T. POTTER, President, Ramapo College of New Jersey,
    Mahwah, New Jersey
DR. SEBASTIAN RACITI, Professor of Economics, School of Human
    Environment, Ramapo College of New Jersey, Mahwah, New
    Jersey
CHARLES REID, Mayor, Paramus, New Jersey
DR. JEROME G. ROSE, Professor of Urban Planning, Livingston
    College, Rutgers University, New Brunswick, New Jersey
BERNARD SCHWARTZ, Franklin Lakes Planning Board; Vice Chair-
    man, Bergen County Planning Board; Vice President, New
    Jersey Federation of Planning Officials
RICHARD J. SULLIVAN, Commissioner, Department of Environ-
    mental Protection, Trenton, New Jersey

ROBERTA SVARRE, Housing Coordinator, League of Women Voters
of New Jersey, Newark, New Jersey
DR. STANLEY WILLING, Chairman, Division of Business,
St. Francis College, Brooklyn, New York, and President,
Willing Associates, Inc., New York, New York
SIDNEY L. WILLIS, Assistant Commissioner for Planning and
Housing, New Jersey Department of Community Affairs,
Trenton, New Jersey

PREFACE

One of the most pressing problems facing American society today is what to do with the remainder of one of its greatest resources, vacant and, so-called, undeveloped land. The United States possesses some of the richest and most productive land in the world. The competing pressures for developing what is left of the once seemingly inexhaustible supply of land are enormous. These pressures are most intense in the metropolitan areas, and northern New Jersey,* adjacent to the high population centers of the New York City area, is not exempt from them. Its citizens and officials are daily subject to calls for the utilization of vacant space for highways, shopping centers, homes, indus- trial parks, office buildings, and all the other developmental needs of a highly sophisticated modern economy.

These pressures for economic growth are often in conflict with environmental and social values. Northern New Jersey, possessing significant amounts of open land in spite of high population densities, is now developing at what many would con- sider to be a too-rapid rate. Its growth pattern can be described as a decentralized spread of homes and jobs, referred to by many critics as suburban sprawl. Such sprawl has been described as unplanned growth and chaotic development. The axes of growth in this region have developed along major highways such as Route 17, Route 23, and the still uncompleted Interstate High- way 287.

In response to the growing problems of land use in New Jersey, the School of Human Environment at Ramapo College sponsored a conference on March 27 and 28, 1973, to consider the situation and to examine possible solutions for resolving growth pressures in the region. Our idea was to begin to gen- erate an ongoing discussion among members of the community to learn how they feel about what is happening to our land and, more importantly, what should happen to it in the decade to come.

---

*Although many participants defined northern New Jersey differently our focus was centered on the counties of Bergen, Essex, Hudson, Morris, Passaic, and Sussex.

xi

The speakers, as well as the audience, brought a variety of viewpoints and areas of expertise to bear on this very complex problem. The speakers, panelists, and participants included mayors, councilmen, real estate brokers, bankers, businessmen, developers, members of the academic community, state officials, environmentalists, and members of various citizen action groups. This wide diversity was desired because one of the objectives of the conference was to bring together citizens and officials representing different social, economic, and environmental values in order that they could have the opportunity to listen to each other and to begin to understand one another's interpreta - tions of the land use problems facing this society.

It is not necessary for the reader to agree with the various ideas and views expressed by the participants. What is necessary is that he or she recognize that we cannot continue to have uncon - trolled development in New Jersey, as we have in the past, and that all of us must consider and respond to the problems and dilemmas described here.

There were many different values and concerns expressed by those present at the conference. Most of them were well known to us but, in composite, they reflect the dilemmas we face as a humane society, concerned, as we are, with the needs of the human condition and ecological survival.

Advocates of low income housing development are deeply con - cerned about the exclusion of the poor and the working class from various housing areas. Since the movement of American population is away from the city and into low density suburban regions, they cite the moral and constitutional mandate for this society to pro - vide adequate housing for all income groups in suburban commun - ities. They want industrial and residential development to be made more responsible to the needs of lower income citizens.

Local councilmen, mayors, and members of planning and zoning boards tend to be deeply concerned about the need to develop the ratables necessary to provide tax income to pay for increased community services. They are caught, therefore, in a conflict between citizens who want to preserve open spaces and to minimize new expansion and developers who want public approval for development projects that provide the tax money to pay for the services demanded by contemporary middle class America. In the panel discussions, the issue of the property tax, the main source of municipal revenue, was presented as a major obstacle to orderly growth and change.

Environmentalists represent another growing and significant viewpoint that will soon be reflected in all land use decisions. They are highly concerned about the utilization of open space, which can never be returned to its natural state, and the threats to air and water quality. The quality of life that is being produced by rapid suburbanization and by planning which lacks environmental considerations shows evidence of rapid decline and is, in fact, in danger of becoming absolutely unacceptable. In their view, land development and use allocation must reflect consideration of the environmental impact of such development or man's survival will be in jeopardy.

Businessmen also have a distinct viewpoint on the problems of intense land use. They are caught in a myriad of conflicting pressures created by society and technology. From one perspective they are satisfying social needs and wants by meeting the industrial and residential needs of society. At the same time, however, counterpressures are felt from those citizens who object to the negative environmental aspects of such action. The lack of uniform standards among development codes set by local planning and zoning boards has further complicated the developmental process for the business community.

State officials and political leaders have called for the immediate reform of the laws, policies, and regulations shaping the patterns of land use allocation. New Jersey, a state which has always strongly supported local autonomy, is beginning to question whether such a preference can continue, if effective regional and statewide coordination of development is to occur. The pressure for a stronger state role in land use allocation is strong. This emerging state role is manifest in the willingness of the state legislature to approve stronger state authority over coastal wetlands and tidal areas. For example, the Pinelands Protection Act was passed to provide the institutional machinery for possible area-wide planning for a 300,000-acre preserve in south Jersey.

In addition to examining a number of land use issues in terms of their theoretical and specific applications, the conferees presented and extensively discussed feasible solutions to these problems and, in the process, recommended the institution of a number of desirable changes in present land use allocation patterns. A spokesman for the North Jersey Conservation Foundation, a nongovernmental environmental organization, actively engaged in research on open space acquisition and land use

policy, recommended that local planning bodies conduct a natural
resource inventory to serve as a basis for making development
decisions.

Several architects presented their designs for planned communities now under construction in the northeastern United States.
These designs featured cluster housing as an alternative to the
present pattern of spaced housing, which they called wasteful of
the natural environment. They and many other planners and architects have called for a reexamination of the present pattern of
land use allocation which places one family homes on large
acreage because, at the present rate of construction, we will
exhaust the supply of environmentally suitable land much sooner.

Rapid development has increased the problems local governments face in providing adequate municipal services for their
citizens because Americans demand a wide variety of high-quality
services such as education, garbage collection, road construction
and maintenance, adult education programs, counseling services,
etc. The demand for such services accelerates the pressure to
use land in such ways as to maximize its tax revenue generating
potential. While some industries may use land in ways that do
not overburden municipal services and in ways that are consistent
with dominant community values, most of them provide the basis
for political conflict because they require the provision of so
many municipal services that they generate, in turn, a need to
attract still more ratables to pay the ever-increasing costs. On
the other hand, social critics point out that towns which fail to
attract lucrative ratables are severely handicapped in providing
the same variety and quality of social services that successful
towns can provide. Therefore, reliance on the property tax causes
service inequities to develop between different communities. The
arguments and questions raised are many and complex. Perhaps
the main concern of people should be what decisions will provide
the best quality of life for all citizens. This is easily stated but
difficult to do because of the political, social, and economic
conflicts which confront us daily.

One central conclusion repeated by many speakers and
participants at the conference is that we can no longer permit
development to continue in a random, haphazard manner. Our
concern is to find a way to preserve individual freedom of action
while recognizing the overriding constraints of regional needs —
how to do this is a major social and political question.

Social and environmental concerns will no longer allow us
to act as before. Recently Laurence S. Rockefeller, chairman of
the President's Task Force on Land Use and Urban Growth, said
(New York Times, May 20, 1973):

> There is a new mood in America. Increasingly,
> citizens are asking what urban growth will
> add to the quality of their lives. They are
> questioning the way relatively unconstrained
> piecemeal urbanization is changing their com-
> munities and are rebelling against the tradi-
> tional processes of government and the market
> place which they believe have inadequately
> guided development in the past.

The Task Force concluded that more restrictions will have to be
placed on the use of private land. (Task Force on Land Use and
Urban Growth, The Use of Land: A Citizen's Policy Guide to
Urban Growth, New York: Thomas Y. Crowell Company, 1973).

If you are interested in the problem of land use in our society,
and are concerned about what happens to New Jersey, the most
urbanized state in the union, you will find the present report a
valuable guide to current thinking on these issues. The overriding purpose of the conference, and of the report, is to stimulate
discussion on the problems and to aid in the search for both
immediate and long-range policy changes. Many subjects have
been left out because of the broad scope of the topic. Nevertheless, the basic questions have been raised, and the answers
are slowly evolving—sometimes deliberately, sometimes by
rational choice, but, more often, by accident or as a result of
experimentation. Only hard work and commitment can improve
the quality of life here; but, in order to provide future generations
with an environment that fulfills their requirements, the central
question of land use must be framed within a much larger question:
What do you want your state to be? How do you want to live,
and why?

           *   *

The conference was made possible as a result of a grant by
the Northwest Bergen Board of Realtors. Publication of this report
was supported by both the Wallace-Eljabar Fund, Inc., of New
Jersey and the Northwest Bergen Board of Realtors.

We wish to express particular thanks for the strong support of President George Potter of Ramapo College, Mr. Gordon A. MacInnes, Jr., Executive Director of the Wallace-Eljabar Fund, and the directors of the Northwest Bergen Board of Realtors, with special thanks to Theodore C. Cedarstrand, President of the Board. The constant encouragement of Dr. Henry Bischoff, Director of the School of Human Environment, in the planning and implementation of the conference is especially appreciated.

Finally, the participation of faculty and students in the School of Human Environment, throughout the program, helped make the conference a joint community-college endeavor.

Joseph LeMay
Eugene Harrison
Ramapo College of New Jersey

ENVIRONMENTAL LAND USE PROBLEMS

I. INTRODUCTION

In order to provide a basis for discussion, the speakers on the first morning of the conference provided an introduction to the broad, general changes that are now occurring in the New York Metropolitan Region, with a particular emphasis on northern New Jersey. Each of the three speakers represents an institution that is directly concerned with problems that are area-wide, and their presentations provide a regional focus for the remainder of the proceedings. Dr. Mason Gross, former president of Rutgers University and now president of the Harry Frank Guggenheim Fund, spoke for the Regional Plan Association, a private organization concerned with fostering a broad planning perspective for public policy concerning transportation, housing, industrial siting, etc., for the New York, New Jersey, Connecticut area centered on New York City. Dr. Gross spoke of the decline of the city as the center of our commercial educational and cultural life. In emphasizing the interdependence of communities in the New York Region, he pleaded for the necessary rebuilding of our urban centers if both suburban and urban communities are to enjoy a high quality of life. The New York Metropolitan Region, which includes northern New Jersey, is becoming more and more one social and economic system. What happens to one section, such as the cities, affects the other sections as well. Dr. Gross asked the key question for future land-use patterns: "What do people really want to have happen in northern New Jersey?" He asked us to think hard about our system of values and needs for human fulfillment. He noted that the increase of cars will soon be substantially more than the increase in people and asked if we really want to subject our lives and land to such dependence on the automobile. Suburban spread is cited as one of the significant causes of many of our land-use problems. Such spread renders efficient mass transportation difficult if not economically impossible. His questions were certainly central to the problem our society faces with respect to the allocation of land resources. He asked us what we want to do. He pointed out that not only our present process of day-to-day decisions regarding land use but also the totality of human relationships carried on in our physical surroundings needs reexamining.

Mr. William Harting, director of the Open Land Data Project, spoke for the Tri-State Regional Planning Commission. The commission is an interstate planning agency that seeks solutions to transportation and land-use problems of the New York Metropolitan Region covering 22 counties in New York and New Jersey and parts of southwest Connecticut. The commission was established by the three states in 1965. Mr. Harting dealt with the socio-economic statistical patterns that have developed in the region since 1865. He discussed how, in the next decade, land-use pressures will be more intense as population, single family home construction, personal income, and employment will increase. The spread of homes in this region and the dependence on the auto will accelerate at a rapid rate.

Mr. Harting described three broad patterns of movement for industry, population, and commercial centers and presented Tri-State's suggestions for classifying available land into three categories: (1) open land that must be preserved, (2) land capable of supporting clustering of economic development, and (3) land that can support multiple residential patterns, including both cluster housing and dispersed residential development.

The movement from the cities described by Dr. Gross and the area growth patterns depicted by Mr. Harting set the stage for the immediate, pressing environmental problems of growth articulated by the third speaker, Richard Sullivan, commissioner of the New Jersey State Department of Environmental Protection. Commissioner Sullivan's department, which has provided strong leadership for environmental reform in the state, was established on Earth Day, April 22, 1970. It was created by merging all the state agencies dealing with environmental problems into one organization. Commissioner Sullivan described present and future problems caused by rapid industrialization and population growth without overall regional coordination. He cited the need for a viable state role in combating regional environmental problems such as coastal-lands protection, floodplain-area development, air and water pollution, waste disposal, and land-use planning.

He described the property tax as one of the chief obstacles to desirable environmental planning. The burden of the property tax was referred to by many participants at the conference. It forces communities to sanction development regardless of the environmental impact.

In many ways, Commissioner Sullivan developed the theme that while New Jersey is beset with all of the environmental

problems resulting from rapid industrial growth, it is now responding to its problems in a decisive manner. The achievements of the
last few years are numerous:

1. Acts to establish state ownership of riparian lands.

2. Establishment of the Pinelands Protection Council, with
responsibility over an area of 300,000 acres in southern New
Jersey.

3. Establishment of a state authority over construction in
floodplain areas.

4. Establishment of a state authority to oversee construction
in the coastal areas, which include about 750,999 acres.

5. Work on a bill to cover orderly development in the Tocks
Island region, in the northwest part of the state.[1]

6. Work on a pending proposal to create a Skylands Regional
Council.[1]

Thus all three speakers provided an understanding of the
state of change in which we find ourselves and the problems
associated with the uncontrolled growth we are experiencing.

References

1. Both proposals were described in Governor William C.
    Cahill's annual message to the state legislature as follows:

    Tocks Island: Another area of environmental concern is the
    northwest region of the State, which will feel the primary
    impact of the proposed Tocks Island recreation area. This
    is a rural region blessed with scenic beauty, and unlike
    much of our State, is sparsely populated. Governor William
    C. Cahill, Third Annual Message to the Legislature (Trenton,
    New Jersey), January 9, 1973, p. 29.

    Skylands Region: The Skylands Region, in the northern parts
    of Bergen and Passaic Counties, is similar to the Tocks Island
    primary impact area. Primarily a rural, recreational, and
    watershed area, it will be undergoing severe development
    pressure as highways are extended into the area and more
    visitors arrive. The landscape features which attract these
    visitors must be maintained if the environment and economy

of the area are to be healthy. The purity of the water from its watersheds must be safeguarded. Therefore, legislation similar to that recommended for the Tocks Island impact area will be presented for your consideration. It will provide shared responsibility for land use decisions in the Skylands Region. Ibid., p. 30.

WELCOME ADDRESS

George T. Potter

President
Ramapo College of New Jersey
Mahwah, New Jersey

It is a particular pleasure to invite you to this program here on the campus of Ramapo College. The college is beginning to play its role as a member of the community. We have been getting into higher gear to get the college under way for the past $3\frac{1}{2}$ years, since I first came to the state. Our immediate concern was to get the regular academic program established. It gives me a great sense of achievement that my colleagues and I can move beyond the day-to-day complexities of the academic program and into this similarly important area of community service.

I think that it is especially appropriate, too, that in this first example of a community service program here at Ramapo College we are dealing with the important question of land use in northern New Jersey. I think that this was the first problem about northern New Jersey that became clear to me when I came to the state to search for a site for the new college. You may recall that the legislation indicated that the new college would be established in Bergen County, and my first six months as a resident here was directed toward moving around from community to community in exploring the availability of land; exploring the reaction of those several communities to the possibility that a college would be located in their area. Land use was obviously a very significant problem here in the northern part of the state, and in case the fact gets lost sight of, I think it should be remembered that the township of Mahwah was the only township in Bergen County that was receptive to the prospect of the college coming into its area. So, whatever else has happened in Mahwah, I think we should acknowledge that this particular change, in this particular community, was welcomed at the time that we arrived. I hope that they continue to think that we are welcome. Thus far

I don't feel that we have done any harm, and I think we are beginning to do a great deal of good.

I conclude my remarks with a most warm welcome to you. I hope you will learn very much more about Ramapo College in the next two days. I certainly look forward to working with you and your community colleagues in future programs of this kind. I wish you success in the next few days.

II. WHAT IS HAPPENING TO LAND USE IN NORTHERN NEW JERSEY?

A.   A MATTER OF VALUES

Mason W. Gross

President
Harry Frank Guggenheim Fund
representing the
Regional Plan Association
New York, New York

I will not talk about concrete plans or data at all but about some value questions, some philosophical questions, if you like. I am, professionally, a philosopher, and you will have to bear with that for a little while. I am going to try to make you think about some questions that would not normally occur to you.

First of all, I would like to say something about the Regional Plan Association. We consider the region as very much the same region as that viewed by the Tri-State Regional Planning Commission. The area includes, basically, New York City and its suburban areas, plus southern Connecticut and northern New Jersey. We are concerned about the whole metropolitan region of New York, and our basic insistence is that in order to solve problems in this region, you ought to think regionally. One municipality, even one small group, cannot solve regional problems. What is happening in the region is going to affect you, and the decisions you make are going to affect the region. It is best to think these things out beforehand. It is regional thinking that the Regional Plan Association wants to urge upon you. For example, there has been proposed by Governor Rockefeller a new bridge—a long bridge, about 11 miles in length—that will go from Oyster Bay, on Long Island, to Rye, in New York State, on the Connecticut border. Well, that is about as far away from here as you can get, inasmuch as the metropolitan region is concerned. The strong reason given for building that bridge is that the Throgg's Neck bridge and the Whitestone Bridge (both connecting Long Island with the Bronx) are already so crowded, and at times beyond capacity, that they just bog down. Another bridge is needed so that not merely passenger cars but trucks coming from Pennsylvania, for example, can get to eastern Long Island. But they cannot get from Pennsylvania to Long Island without crossing Bergen County. So if the flow of a vast amount of traffic will be made easier by this new bridge, Bergen County is going to be one of those areas affected by it. If you cross into Bergen County, over the George Washington Bridge, and are confronted by that massive stretch of concrete that you see there, and then you begin to realize that this must be extended in order to take care of still more traffic, you will begin to realize what the implications of the new bridge can be.

I also suspect that one of these days someone is going to talk about another bridge across the Hudson, and whether that will be above the George Washington Bridge or below it, I do not know. But again, whatever is going to be done about New York's traffic will have a direct effect on all of northern New Jersey.

May I say right now, partly because of this regional concept, when I first started to think about what I was going to say today, I took your title Land Use in Northern New Jersey not merely to mean this part of northern Bergen County in which we find ourselves today. Partly because I come from Monmouth County, northern New Jersey, for me, comes down as far as Newark, and that is what I think about when I think about all of the problems of land use and so on.

Again, what happens in Newark, and that part of New Jersey, is going to have an effect on what happens in the rest of New Jersey. You cannot get away from your neighbors; what happens in Rockland County, New York, next to Bergen County, what happens across the Hudson from here, and what happens in central New Jersey, all of these things are going to have some kind of effect on northern New Jersey. And whatever you do is going to have some kind of effect on them. Now, you have today a number of predictions on what is going to happen and what some of the problems of land use are going to be.

The question I want you to think about is, What do you want to have happen to northern New Jersey? What are the factors you have to reckon with and how are you going to cope with them? How many of these factors are there? What is the end result of these factors that are going to affect northern New Jersey and what results would you like to see? What is going to happen to them in order that your life styles up here can be as happy as possible?

We are pretty sure that in the next twenty-five or more years the population in the region is going to increase by 25 percent. That is a lower estimate than we have been working with because of earlier census data; more recent data indicate that the birth rate has gone down rather drastically, but still, at least 25 percent seems clear. The number of jobs will increase more than 25 percent in that period of time. And perhaps more striking even than the present population growth, the number of automobiles will probably increase by 50 percent. This, again, is something to contemplate if you think about the future of Bergen County, and so on—the number of automobiles will increase by 50 percent.

If you have been out driving lately around five o'clock in the afternoon almost anywhere in northern New Jersey, try to contemplate an increase in traffic of 50 percent. You must realize that this is going to take an awful lot of thinking, an awful lot of evaluating. Is this what you want? Is this the kind of thing that is desirable? Obviously we want automobiles, but we have a conflict of values here. What is the decision we are going to arrive at? This is the kind of decision we are going to consider.

Now, in all my thinking about northern New Jersey, that is my way of looking at it. One of the most important questions is, What is going to happen to the cities? The cities in northern New Jersey, with the one exception of Paterson,[1] are showing a very rapid decline in population. The people living there have moved out. They moved out, Lord knows where, all over the place, but they are not living there anymore, and the population is going down.

I agree with the idea that it is easier to build on open space than to knock something down. But if you visit some of these old cities, you find that they are being knocked down. There is hardly a major city in northern New Jersey that does not have huge areas in the central part of town where everything is being cleaned out. They talk about building apartment houses or about building new stores in the area, but they have not got around to doing it yet. This goes on as far as Camden, where a huge area of the city is just flat now. All the houses that were there were cleaned out, and the area is simply empty. Many of the open spaces in Plainfield, for example, are being used for parking lots. I suspect that there will be an awful row if they try to build where the parking lots are. But we are tearing down buildings, and we are going to have to consider how we are going to rebuild the cities in a more satisfactory way than we have been doing lately.

Because I think that the most important thing that is happening to civilization here in New Jersey, which affects us all, is the disappearance of the cities.

I have to remind you that the city has been, throughout the entire history of western civilization, the place where our culture has developed, and it has been so right up to our present generation. That statement still is true, but it is showing signs of being weakened at the moment. The city has represented modern civilization to us. There has been a steady migration from scattered communities into the cities, and lately, with the need for large populations on the farm being less important than it used to be, the migration into some cities throughout the country has been increasing. In fact, there is still a great deal of immigration to the cities but not enough to balance the emigration of those who previously lived there.

But just think what these cities have been. In the first place, they were where the jobs were concentrated. You went to a city to get a job. If you wanted to get away from the farm, and the backbreaking life that farm life can mean, and wanted steady employment, you went to a city. There was a variety of jobs, and you were surer of earning a living there than outside the city.

In the second place, it has always been the place where our finances have been managed. For good or evil, this is the place where banks have developed, where all kinds of financing has taken place; you don't find this in the small communities. The cities have been the center of financing, coming finally to downtown New York, the center of the financial structure of the whole country. More than that, this is where commerce has grown up, not merely where the factories grew up but where interchange was. It has been the center of our great diversity in trade, bringing together goods from all over the world for the American populace to enjoy. But more than that, in the city, and only in the city, has it been possible to develop great libraries, great museums, good art galleries, developed orchestras, and with orchestras I would include the best jazz banks. The theater is a city thing; the ballet is a city thing. Many, many colleges and universities have developed in the city. It has been the center of medical care, in the form of great and high specialized hospitals. These are the things that have made the city great and made it grow. This has been where American civilization has progressed and grown.

If the city collapses, what is going to happen to these things? We are seeing it happen right now. Let us take one example that I used, namely the symphony orchestra. Symphony orchestras all over the country are going broke. There just isn't support for them in the cities, as there used to be.

People talk about it being dangerous in the city at night, and that is why they don't go to the concerts that they used to go to. Symphony orchestras then play to half-full halls. This is true not only in the smaller cities in the country; it is true of the New York Philarmonic; it is true of the Metropolitan Opera House. The support is not there, and they are going broke. I am told that unless federal support is stepped up considerably, and there is very little sign of that, we have just about seen the end of ballet in this country. We can't afford it anymore. People are not there, they won't go to the cities; they will not leave their suburban homes to go to the cities to support the ballet.

If our cities are not thriving, then all these cultural and artistic enterprises will continue to fall apart. Last year, the New York Public Library, one of the greatest public enterprises in the world, had to go out screaming for emergency funds from the public. They just simply did not have money to pay their bills; they were just going to have to close down some of their branches. It is almost impossible to believe that this could happen to such a well-publicized institution as the public library.

This is one of the results of what is called "spread city" or "scattered city." People just are not supporting the old city, and the great institutions that have grown up there are dying from lack of support.

I think we feel in the Regional Plan Association that we have got to persuade the people who live in the cities, the business-men, and the people generally, that they must redevelop these cities. They have got to keep their populations there, and they must develop environments where people can live happily and richly.

Now one of the things we were able to persuade them about was not to scatter the new meadowlands area with office build-ings. Office buildings belong in cities; that is where you can get your employees, where you can concentrate them and get them organized and so on. This is a very good thing. Manufacturing is dropping in the area, and we can expect a tremendous increase in the number of office workers—a great concentration of them in the cities is fine but scattering them throughout the countryside is not.

One of our main objectives is to try to make people, when they plan and when they start to think regionally, to think of what the cities have got to be because unless they do, the cities will collapse, in a tremendously important way, and civilization in this part of the country will collapse with it. I just don't know what is going to happen. What do we do now, if we don't go to concerts and theaters? We sit at home and watch TV. We listen to our stereo, for example, and we think how wonderful it is to listen to these orchestras right in our own homes. But, you know, these orchestras are not going to be there if we don't give them better support. They are going to fold. So don't think that the stereo is a substitute for a real live symphony because there won't be any real live symphony orchestras unless they get the support they need.

We are in really desperate cultural shape, and people in a civilized community like northern New Jersey ought to take these things very seriously indeed. We are right on the edge of a rich cultural area, but we are not making use of our cultural advantages and we are not giving institutions the support that they so desperately need. And support requires concentration; it requires concentration of people in places called cities.

I am very much encouraged by what is beginning to happen in the city of Paterson. There is a group in Paterson that is trying to get under way a new town development there, in the city itself, to bring Paterson back and to give it life. It has been increasing, not significantly but still increasing, in population and this, I think, is a very significant development indeed.

There is a similar growth by what I think they call a new town in an old town in the community of Jamaica, on Long Island, in New York City. Industry there and the government have gotten together and have tried to rebuild an exciting kind of center, a metropolitan center within that part of the borough. They are not only getting new offices to come in and settle there; they are also rearranging the department stores in their relation to subway stations. They have persuaded the State and City to open a college there, York College, and they are beginning to develop relationships to the schools. All in all, it has become a very lively place.

There is another center in downtown Brooklyn; it is coming to life and beginning to realize what it is in danger of losing and what it is capable of becoming if concerned groups can get together. It does not require governmental planning, but it does need a great deal of imagination and energy on the part of the citizens in that area. If they will get together and start to plan it, it is amazing how much support is available to them and how much they can do.

I say we have got to have the cities developed. One thing that has become current nowadays, and this is frequently done by all our congressmen, is to scream for more money for mass transportation. It is a little hard to know what this is all about because the kind of building that we are doing now is the kind of building that almost certainly cannot be served with mass transportation. If you are going to spread your houses all over the countryside, then there are not enough buses to come to pick people up because they cannot afford to do so. Unless you are going to have some totally different scheme, such as completely free government-supported mass transportation and forget the cost, it just isn't going to be possible to service such dispersed populations. You may just as well forget it. In order to have mass transportation, you must have concentration. If our cities are going to fall apart, and you are going to spread everything all over the countryside, it will be impossible to have any kind of mass transportation at all. Even the trains won't be able to do it because they go to cities. So if the cities fall apart, there won't be the possibility of serving the populace by trains. But we are always demanding better transportation. Now if it cannot be done by mass transportation, then what is it going to be? Apparently it is going to have to be done by highways! Highways mean not only more cars but also a greater demand everywhere for more parking places.

Believe me, after being president of Rutgers University, which is located in three cities, I can tell you that the parking problem is one of our most serious problems. They say that whenever the association of urban colleges meets anywhere in the United States, no matter what topics they have on the agenda, before the first day is over, they are all talking about parking. Parking is that one insolvable problem, as far as colleges in the city are concerned. But this parking problem is going to get much worse as this increase of 50 percent in the number of cars becomes a reality.

You must think about your parking problems as well as your highway problem. Obviously, what we have got to have is greater concentrations of people who are serviceable by mass transportation.

Open Space

One of the main objectives of the Regional Plan Association has always been the matter of trying to preserve open space. We have a plan that we are trying to develop and sell to people like yourselves, and others all over the country, for the creation of a great connection of open spaces throughout the length of the Appalachian Trail. We wish to see if we cannot create an enormous park, several miles wide, along the more than 2000 miles of the trail, in order to keep open space within a reasonable distance from our great concentration of population. But if you manage to do that, then you must plan where you are going to put the growing population so that they won't be crowding into that area.

I might remind you that the Regional Plan Association really started and pushed through that scheme, which I hope is going to work, called the Gateway National Park, which includes the Sandy Hook peninsula, some of Staten Island and Breezy Point, on the western extreme of Long Island. It is a fascinating park development as a recreational area for the people in the concentrated areas of New York and New Jersey. The only problem that hasn't been solved yet is how do you get there because if any number of people went by road they wouldn't get there. The road would become blocked, and there would be no movement of traffic at all. They can get there by boat if someone can figure out how to do this without incurring too great an expense for the whole thing.

I think what we are really talking about in New Jersey, on Long Island, in Westchester, and even up in Connecticut is this business of what has been referred to as leapfrogging. This is a situation in which a community, for certain reasons, will preserve a certain area from development and the developers will respond by jumping over it. They will go further on out and develop an area beyond the protected one, and pretty soon you have a tremendous development. You have to think about what some of these developments are like.

There is a fascinating one called Twin Rivers, which is just outside of Hightstown (N. J.). I don't know how many hundreds of apartments are there, but it is compact, it does not waste space. Hightstown is nowhere. It has one great advantage. It is on exit eight of the New Jersey Turnpike, and I imagine that is the reason why Twin Rivers is there. Because every morning people get into their cars and swirl onto the Turnpike and go somewhere else. As far as one can see, there is no particular reason, except exit eight, why anyone should live in Twin Rivers. It is no an attractive piece of land at all, and the houses are not particularly attractive. They are all right, I suppose, but there is nothing that brings you there; there is no particular appeal to that place at all. I think those communities are like the old apartment houses in New York that instead of being ways of bringing people together are designed to keep people apart. If you live in a New York apartment house, the last thing you want to do is to get to know the people who live on the same floor with you; you avoid that absolutely. I suspect that is what this new community of Twin Rivers is like. You do not want to become a prisoner of the other fellow who lives in the house; you avoid him like the plague.

But what reason is there, what kind of satisfaction is there, what kind of community life is there, when the only reason for being in a place is to get on the Turnpike and get away from there. It seems to be a very curious type of community we are building there, so unlike the old community life in our larger towns and cities. The two situations can hardly be compared at all. I think are going about impoverishing our lives because we are not really thinking about what we want most in this world; we are settling for something less altogether too quickly.

We were talking about Mahwah. I had an earlier experience about the region of Mahwah. I came up to this area one Sunday morning in June when they were building a connection from Route 17 onto the New York Thruway. I got to a point on Route 17, which was about five lanes wide at that point, where all traffic had to converge on one muddy road to get on the Thruway because the connection had not been completed. You can see what happens in that kind of thing. We sat there for hours in the blazing sun, just as miserable as you can be, and the curious thing was that nobody was complaining at all. There were lots of kids playing around in the backs of cars; even the dogs were not barking. Not a horn was honked. Nobody tried to push ahead of anyone else.

We just sat there, quietly benign. It seemed that the reason for this calm was that we didn't care whether we were stuck there or not. We were not going anywhere in particular. All we wanted to do was to get away from where we had been, and we had accomplished that already. We knew we would have just as bad a time when we returned at night, so why be worried about it now.

It is this kind of existence that the automobile has made possible for us. It is a wonderful type of life. If you have a radio, you can listen to a soap opera, and that's real rich culture. What kind of life do you really want? These are the kinds of things a planning group has got to think about along the way. What kind of life do you want to have? What kind of existence? Don't simply say we have land and how are we going to use it? The question is, How do you want to use it? What kind of community are you going to have? What are your values going to be? These, I think, are the really important questions.

The series, Choices for '76, is designed to elicit value responses on major planning issues from citizens throughout the metropolitan region, and every television station in the whole region is presenting it; there are nineteen of them, and this is the only time that all of them have gotten together on one program series. I hope that groups in this area will watch it and discuss it. You can obtain ballots listing the alternative choices presented, and we want you to indicate what you believe are the best choices of all the possibilities offered. The choices are based on values: What do you really want? What are you willing to pay for? This is the kind of a thrust we want to generate. We don't want small planning groups to decide what you want. Once you make it clear to your government what you really want, your government listens. Until you do that, they are going to flounder along as they always have, hoping to find the solution that will cause the least trouble.

We are trying to get people to think about what they really want their communities to be. How much do you really want to be the slave of, the prisoner of, the automobile? How much of this scattering do you want, with all the loss of cultural life that comes along with it? How much of that are you willing to take? Are you willing to see the cities really collapse, bringing down so much that has meant the essence of American cultural life, and Western culture in general, with them? How much are you willing to see, and how much are you willing to do about it? These are more important questions now than ever before. And I think that because the population rate is going down, we may have a chance to accomplish some of these things. At one point we thought things were going too fast for us but now we may have a chance to re-establish some control over our future. Please go at it with all the force you have at your command.

Reference

1. The population of Paterson rose only slightly within 1960-70. This change was from 143,663 in 1960 to 144,824 in 1970. Population Characteristics in New Jersey, Department of Conservation and Economic Development, Trenton, N.J.

B.   A QUESTION OF STATISTICS

William Harting

Director
Open Land Data Project
Tri-State Regional Planning Commission
New York, New York

This conference is pleasing to me because it shows concern by you over what is happening to your area. I would like to commend the college for sponsoring this conference in order to bring the problems and possible solutions to the forefront.

All planning agencies have assembled facts to aid them in the planning process. The Tri-State Regional Planning Commission has been gathering information since its inception back in 1961. In 1963 it undertook several major surveys; among them was an extensive land-use survey, including a transportation study of rail, bus, and taxi, goods movement, and general aviation. It recently has acquired most of the computer tapes of the 1970 census. The findings from all these sources are available to our technical family, that is, the various county and state agencies, municipal governments, and to the general public as well.

In talking about what is happening to northern New Jersey, I thought I would break it down into two primary components: one about people and the other about land.

First let us take a look at the people side. The counties of Bergen, Passaic, and Rockland (N.Y.), at the turn of the century, had about 300,000 people, and half of them, 155,000, lived in Passaic County. This was primarily due to the textile mills there (mainly in Paterson). By 1935, the area's population had reached 835,000 people. In those 35 years, Passaic County's population had doubled to 309,000. Bergen County's population had increased by five times and surpassed Passaic by 100,000 people. Its population then was 409,000. Populations in Rockland County, in that same time period, doubled, while populations in Sussex County increased by about a third. By 1960 the population in this area had surpassed one million people. From our 1963 survey we

23

determined the population density in terms of persons per square mile. We discovered that the Paterson-Passaic-Clifton area still stands out as having a higher density than most of the region. And, of course, there is a concentration of population in southern Bergen and Passaic counties. Population will continue to grow nationally, as well as regionally, and we expect no significant change at the regional level from that observed at the national level.

When we are considering what is happening, we should examine the household size, that is, the number of people per household, or per housing unit. For the last several decades, since 1940, there has been a downward trend in the number of people per household. We, as most other planning agencies, expect that this trend will continue. According to the 1970 census, the population per household in Bergen, Passaic, and Rockland counties was 3.07 persons per household. The Tri-State Planning Commission's projection is that the region's per household size will stabilize at around 2.7 persons.

In the 1970 census there were 530,000 housing units in this area accommodating the region's now 1,600,000 people. Of these 530,000 units, 304,000 were single-family units, that is, 57 percent of all the housing units were single-family dwellings. It is expected that, at capacity, this region will contain 892,000 housing units.

People have to work, and they travel to work. In our 1963 survey we found the concentration of employment is greater than that of the population in general, and Manhattan has the greatest employment concentration. Along with population, you can expect employment to grow. Again, you will not see any significant change between the region and national trends.

When people have money, one of the things they do is buy a car. If you live in a one-family house, and your income increases, the probability of having more than one car is very great. If you live in a multifamily structure, the probability of having one car is less, and the probability of having two cars is considerably less. If you have a car, you make trips; in our planning vernacular this is called the daily vehicular travel. Most of the trips you make are to home or to work. We anticipate more cars, and this means more trips; in fact, we anticipate a substantial increase in the number of trips. To accommodate the trips you need highways. The map above shows Tri-State's interim highway plan, with expressways marked. (See Fig. 1.) These are limited access routes that are designed to form a network, or pattern.

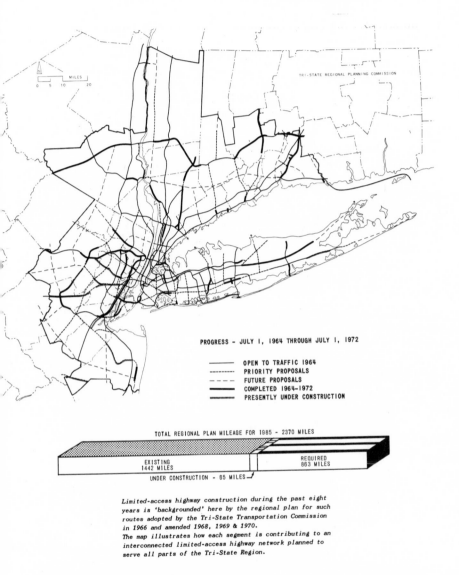

PROGRESS - JULY I, 1964 THROUGH JULY I, 1972

————— OPEN TO TRAFFIC 1964
--------- PRIORITY PROPOSALS
– – – FUTURE PROPOSALS
━━━━━ COMPLETED 1964-1972
▰▰▰▰▰ PRESENTLY UNDER CONSTRUCTION

TOTAL REGIONAL PLAN MILEAGE FOR 1985 - 2370 MILES

EXISTING
1442 MILES

UNDER CONSTRUCTION - 65 MILES

REQUIRED
863 MILES

*Limited-access highway construction during the past eight
years is 'backgrounded' here by the regional plan for such
routes adopted by the Tri-State Transportation Commission
in 1966 and amended 1968, 1969 & 1970.
The map illustrates how each segment is contributing to an
interconnected limited-access highway network planned to
serve all parts of the Tri-State Region.*

FIG. 1.   Freeway status map.

This highway plan is presently being updated and revised. Since
1966 some of the roads that were scheduled for planning have
already been built.

People also travel by rail but not in the same quantities.
The next maps (Figs. 2 and 3) depict this region's passenger rail
traffic net and Tri-State's suggestions for development priorities.

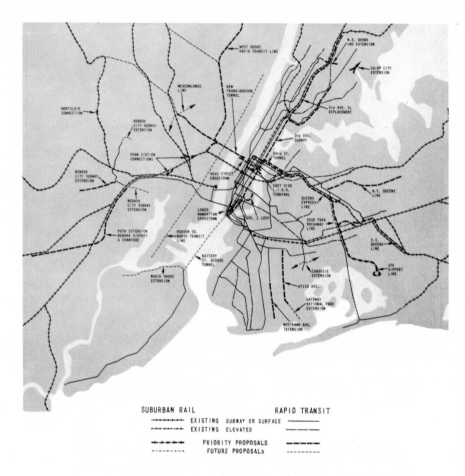

SUBURBAN RAIL   RAPID TRANSIT

+++++++ EXISTING SUBWAY OR SURFACE ————
++++++++ EXISTING ELEVATED   ————

++++++   PRIORITY PROPOSALS   ——————
--------   FUTURE PROPOSALS   --------

FIG. 2. Central area.

How Was the Land Developed?

Back in 1900, as with the population, developed land was concentrated around the harbor area. Again, there was intensive
development around the Paterson-Passaic area. By 1935 we
started to spread out. It is interesting to note that the development followed the railroads. By 1962 we were getting into spread
city. By this time the auto was becoming a vital force. It made
people very mobile. People did not need to stay near the railroads
anymore, and we are now experiencing a filling in of relatively
unpopulated areas.

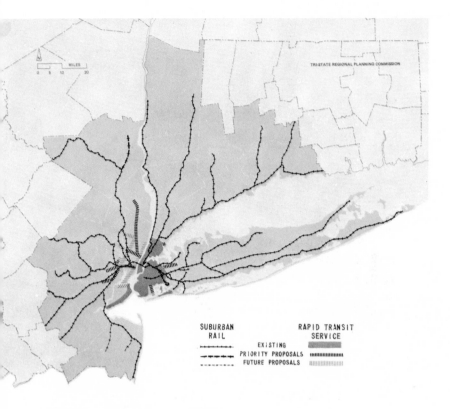

FIG. 3.   Regional transit plan.

In our 1963 land use survey we studied the building densities encountered in the region. This value is based on floor space. In the Bergen-Passaic-Rockland County area there are 601 square miles of land. In 1963, 334 square miles, or 56 percent of that area, was developed. The remaining 44 percent was still available for development. In 1970, according to our updated land-use survey, 386 square miles were developed, or 64 percent. The rate of development is about 1 percent per year. The developed area may be broken down into land-use categories: 167 square miles for residential uses; 46 square miles for nonresidential use; 50 square miles for streets and highways; 85 square miles for recreational and park use; and 38 square miles for watershed, military, and other specialized uses. There still is 215 square miles, or 36 percent of this area, as yet undeveloped. A central question of this conference is, What do you want to do with that area?

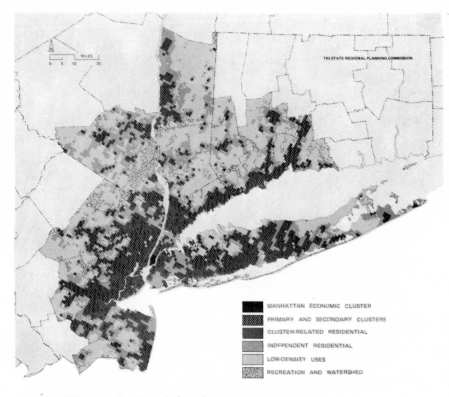

MANHATTAN ECONOMIC CLUSTER

PRIMARY AND SECONDARY CLUSTERS

CLUSTER-RELATED RESIDENTIAL

INDEPENDENT RESIDENTIAL

LOW-DENSITY USES

RECREATION AND WATERSHED

FIG. 4.   Regional development plan.

Most of the development that will occur will take place on
land that is currently vacant. Areas that are already in urban use
will probably become more densely settled. But it is easier to
build on vacant land than it is to tear down something and rebuild
it. Land is still available for development throughout the metropolitan area, but Tri-State, being a regional planning agency,
has proposed a regional development guide to help bring about
orderly growth. In order to generate guidelines for development,
we have established a series of land-use categories (see Fig. 4):

    1. Manhattan economic clusters.
    2. Primary and secondary clusters.
    3. Cluster-related residential.
    4. Independent residential.
    5. Low-density uses.
    6. Recreation and watershed.

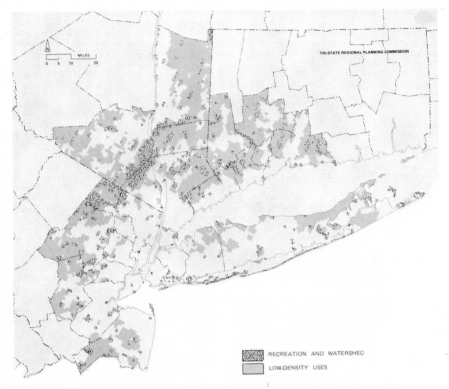

RECREATION AND WATERSHED

LOW-DENSITY USES

FIG. 5.   Open lands.

Figure 5 shows those areas that we feel should be preserved
as open land. Open lands may be divided into two categories:
recreational and watershed areas and low-density uses, still
predominantly open.

It is our judgment that for purposes of efficiency and better
planning control, economic development should be clustered.
This would also place residences and community services where
the jobs are. The creation of three residential activities categories: (1) cluster-related residential development; with high-
density residential areas located next to economic clusters;
(2) independent residential areas; and (3) low-density residential
areas, which would include those squares that we saw in combination with the open land map. (See Fig. 6.) When all of the
maps shown are combined, we believe that they represent a workable
able development plan for the Tri-State area.

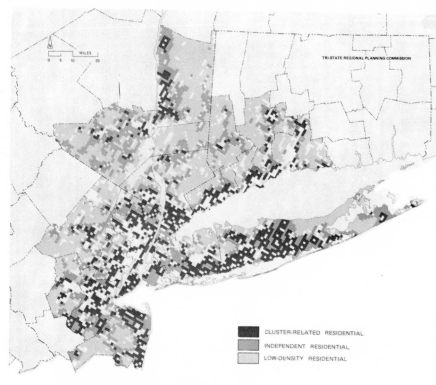

FIG. 6.   Residential activities.

Remember, land is a limited resource and, once developed, can seldom be returned to the open-land categories. A plan is more than maps; it contains long-range goals, and it has short-range priorities. Tri-State monitors and adjusts to this area's change because a good plan is designed to accommodate public preferences so long as they do not work to the unfair disadvantage of others. We believe that private and public action, in combination, can lead to a pattern of land use that will best serve the general welfare.

C. A SURVEY OF POLICIES

   Richard J. Sullivan
   Commissioner
   Department of Environmental Protection
   State of New Jersey
   Trenton, New Jersey

When most people talk about the environment, they talk in terms of pollution—dirty air and dirty water. We have it around us; it is part of the conspicuous evidence of the environmental neglect of the past decades. It is quite understandable that people would try to identify whether the environmental reform movement is making progress, or not, by whether or not the dirty air and dirty water are getting cleaner and whether they are getting cleaner fast enough. I can report, although that is not my purpose in being here, that once in a while something good happens in the environmental business, and we are making some progress in cleaning up these two aspects of the problem. The air is getting cleaner faster than the water for a collection of reasons that I find fascinating, although I am not responsible for the progress. One reason, for example, is that most of our dirty air comes from privately owned chimneys, and we seem better able to impose the sanctions of remedial statutes upon private parties than we do upon government, which happens to operate most of the liquid-waste-disposal facilities.

   I was briefly involved in water-pollution control around the year 1950, but I was not further involved in that area of the environment until 1967. I was astonished to find, when I returned, that they were building the same old secondary treatment plants that represented commonplace technology 17 years before. They were building them on larger tracts of land and with more attention to landscape and pretty administration buildings, but the technology was almost the same. We are talking about local governments being unwilling to build up-to-date sewage treatment plants. The same old plans were off the shelf. We find consultants apparently

31

unwilling to innovate for their clients because they are required to meet a certain standard.

In contrast, during that period there were fantastic changes made in air-pollution control. This was due to the influence of state and federal legislation and to the fact that industry, with its ingenuity, was coming forth with innovations in technology that could solve 90-95 percent of the air-pollution problems that could not be coped with ten years before.

It is also a curiosity to me that a lot more money has been put, by the state and by the federal government, into the state program to clean the air than into any program to clean the water. As recently as two years ago, the federal government provided $300,000 to pay for the program to enforce efforts for water purification; and $1,800,000 for air purification, six times more.

I can assure you that the problems are at least of comparable difficulty. The reasons for this continuing disparity are due more to legislative accident than to logic. With extra state and federal funding in the past two years, the state agency that handles pollution problems has grown from 35 people to 94. Maybe, with expansion, we can begin to cope with many of the issues that are our direct responsibility.

A final illustration that contrasts the two is the enormous difficulty in persuading municipalities to group together in such a way as to facilitate the construction of a regional facility to dispose of all the liquid wastes in that region. It is much more efficient to handle wastes on a regional basis than for each town to attempt to deal with its own. Even where the region can be defined in terms of topography, population density, the kinds of waterways that traverse it, etc., I assure you that it is a lot easier to define the region than to get the seven, or eight, or fifteen towns that comprise it to join together for action. I see progress coming here, but it is very painful. I think additional legislative authority will have to be invoked by the state, or the pace of regionization will not keep up with regional needs.

There is a whole lot more that has to be done with dirty air and dirty water; much of this involves enforcement. Enforcement has been stepped up greatly in the last few years in response to what we think the public wants. And there will be more invocation of the penalties called for in the statutes; more penalties, larger penalties, etc. This is what I have characterized as the environmental law-and-order syndrome, the belief that the environmental issues that face us in New Jersey are a product of a lack of enforcement. Those who have the responsibility to enforce must be vigorous and persistent; then we will get back to the clean air and water of the good old days. I think that those who fail to conform to standards should be dealt with as sternly as the law allows, if we are going to take the problem seriously. I am more concerned, however, that even if we do crack down on violators, and even if all the pollution atrocities in New Jersey are eliminated or brought fully under control, it is possible that all of our progress will be overcome by the urbanization of our state through a lack of a strong system of controls in the land-use field.

I would say that the crucial environmental issue facing New Jersey in the future will not be pollution enforcement; it will be in the way we manage our resources. Are we willing to put the energy and the money into the recycling of solid waste? I think we are on the threshold of acquiring facilities in the state to do just that; to do it at the disposal site. This is also true for the sewage sludge that ends up as an environmental contaminant instead of going back into the ecosystem as it should and will if we are willing to devote the resources to the task. The environmental horror of the month, as someone has characterized it, in the belief that this is a case of cyclic public attention, is the energy crisis. The way in which we use our limited resources says a lot of what we think about our environment and will have an important effect on the environment's character in the future; that may be an even more overriding concern than whether or not there is enough to meet the need.

But the most important resource that we have, in terms of the character of the environment, is the land that we think we own but of which we are only temporary custodians. In my own judgment, about 60 percent of the rest of New Jersey is in undeveloped form: much of it from here to the Delaware River; much of it in the southern region of the state. If we develop the rest of New Jersey under a system that has our insane dependency on the property tax, then, in my judgment, there is no hope that our environment will have a character that I believe the public wants. I don't say this to make the contention that local officials cannot make wise land-use decisions; they can. We are certainly no smarter in making decisions than they are. The local officials are on this dreadful fiscal treadmill of the property tax. The people that are required to make decisions as to what gets built where are also required to figure out where they are going to get the money to run the government next year. This puts them in such a fundamental conflict that we see evidence throughout New Jersey of environmentally silly uses of the land.

It is obvious to me that people have other demands that have to be met. This environment is for us and not just for the trees and the rabbits. People have got to have places to work, places to live. We don't think that the houses that they will inhabit have to be built on the coastal marshes, however. And we don't think their shopping centers have to be built on the floodplain of the Passaic River, to give two illustrations of the point I like to make.

This may suggest some interference with home rule, which is anathema to some. If we are to accept the traditional pattern, with continued handwringing over the problem of unwise land use and "is it not terrible, " no one is going to do anything to protect our environment. In my opinion, however, after years of doing battle in bureaucracy, it is more than possible to do something besides wringing hands. I think it is possible to do something about the environmental problem, as well as all the other problems, if we are willing to make the attempt. If certain characteristics of the present system impede that kind of progress, then we should attempt to change those characteristics.

I think the attempt to change is being made in a way that is not fully recognized by all of those who share our concerns about where New Jersey is going in the future. For example, in 1970 the legislature decided, by a slim plurality but it decided, that the state should control the future use of about 250-300,000 acres of coastal wetlands. That was a direct intrusion by the state, giving it exclusive responsibility, in the interest of essentially giving protection to a substantial portion of our state. And it was done! Five years earlier, in my judgment, it would not have been possible to find a sponsor for legislation of that kind. The sensitivity of the public has evolved enough to encourage these changes, and the elected representatives have been responsive enough to do things, because they think their constituents want them done, that they would not have attempted a short time ago.

The Hackensack Meadowlands Development Act is another illustration. While this was not done essentially for environmental reasons, it was done in the interests of orderly development. It established a single agency over 18,000 acres of real estate in the expectation that that development would be more sensible than if it were done by 14 municipalities, individually,

in isolation, given all the pressures the officials of those communities constantly are under.

We have taken a new view, in our agency, of what to do with
the riparian lands that are owned by the public. These are lands
that are affected by the tides twice a day. Nobody knows how
many acres of land there are in this category. The state, even
though it has owned these lands on behalf of the public since we
became a state, has never defined the extent of its ownership or
its claim of ownership. This fact has led to all sorts of terrible
confusion with respect to the real-estate aspects of it alone, to
say nothing of environmental consequences.

I don't know what is to become of it all, but we decided that
this laxity in exercising authority was irresponsible. The courts
have informed us that they also believe that our inaction was
irresponsible, and we have moved forward, just in the past two
weeks, with the first publication of maps, which we in the department have recommended to the natural resources council for adoption, setting forth our claim to the public's interest in tide flow
lands. We published seven maps: one dealing with those lands
that used to be meadow in the Elizabeth-Newark area, and are
now all paved over, and the first six maps depicting our claim of
ownership in the Hackensack Meadowlands. Between now and
August, we will publish the rest of the maps governing the Hackensack Meadowlands. In each case, on the basis of all information we could discover and with the use of new techniques
mastered in the course of mapping the coastal wetlands, we will
claim what we think the public owns and we will relinquish claim
to what we think it does not own. The burden of proof will be
upon the state because we are not seeking to upset title. I am
sure that those who are dissatisfied, and there may well be some
who will disagree with the state's representation of claims here,
will take the matter to court. In my judgment, that's where such
claims belong. We hope it does go to court, and the judge can
look at the techniques, the information, and the decisions made
by the state and make an objective decision, on the part of the
public, as to whether we did our job correctly or not. We look
forward to that.

Apart from this, however, for environmental reasons, we
think it is unwise for the state just to be in the mail-order land-
sale business with respect to riparian lands, a procedure that
has characterized this program for decades. This process has
resulted in the selling of lands that have environmental

significance for very low prices, making possible unwise types of development, including some of those lagoon communities along the shore. We don't think that should be done anymore because those lands are held in public trust. They should not be conveyed unless there is some obvious public benefit and unless the environmental consequences of their development will be minimal.

There is another bill that the legislature enacted as an experiment. It adopted a bill establishing the Pinelands Protection Council to cover that ecologically unique tract of 300,000 acres in the southeastern portion of our state. The council doesn't have any legal authority; it can only bring to public scrutiny any major developments proposed for that region in the hope that this public exposure will cause the developments to be carried out with as much sensitivity to the environment as possible. The council is also charged with developing a comprehensive land-use plan for the whole area, irrespective of municipal boundaries. I think it is a constructive experiment because it is an attempt to deal with the same issue that brings us together today, and I hope it is a success.

A couple of months ago, the legislature adopted a bill that allowed the state to share land-use controls over the floodplains with local governments; this probably amounts to another 250-300,000 acres of our land. The bill was passed in the interests of public safety. We cannot continue to build on river floodplains because they were designed by God to be flooded. When we build there, anyway, the water that used to go there in time of flood now flows downstream, into another town and into somebody's living room. I cannot think of a case more graphic than this, where land-use controls being vested exclusively with the municipality are bound to fail to serve the public interest.

Environmentally, we regard floodplains as special kinds of lands, too, and we like to see as much of these properties protected as possible. The current legislative argument for its protection is embodied in bill number 1429, sponsored by Assembly Speaker Thomas Kean. This bill would provide for the review by the state of all major facilities (by major facilities we mean anything from a 25-house subdivision on up) built on what we would define as the coastal zone; this would include all land encompassed by a line running from Sandy Hook, around Cape May, up to the head of tide at Trenton, and going inland whenever necessary to embrace those lands that surround the headwaters and the estuaries of our important streams and rivers. This coastal zone bill covers about 750, 000 square miles, which is about one-fourth of the total area of New Jersey, and would require the development of a comprehensive land-use plan for the entire region. Such a plan would, of necessity, take into account the special character of coastal lands.

We don't think New Jersey's policy should be to discourage industries. I made the point before that people have other needs besides environmental protection, but we don't think that, with or without a super port, we should put heavy industry in those regions that are now successfully devoted to a recreation-oriented economy. However, we think it is possible that land-use pressures will get to be so great that this is exactly what people will try to do. Our number-one priority among the environmental bills now pending before the legislature concerns this issue. A couple of months ago I really wondered whether the legislature was ready for this kind of involvement in the land-use process. I thought, perhaps, that it was not, and we did have some nega-tive testimony at the public hearings. One legislator from the coastal region said that if this bill passed, he would introduce a bill of his own, taking the words "liberty" and "prosperity" off the state seal [laughter]. He was really trying to convey a mes-sage to the anonymous bureaucracy in Trenton that they should come down to south Jersey, having screwed up the north, and tell the southerners what to do with their property. There is a tempta-tion to go along with that philosophy, except that if we permit the inevitable process of free-enterprise land use to proceed in the south as they did in the north, we will get the same results. And then, we will be going in with after-the-fact correctives instead of trying to do some land-use planning in the first place.

We hope the bill will pass. There is other legislation dealing with the environmental impact of major projects, and maybe one of these will also pass. The governor will soon issue an executive order directing that all state projects must go through the full environmental impact statement process, so that at least our credentials will be is good order before we begin bossing other people around.

The next two bills that will come along are directly related to where we are this morning. Unfortunately, the college, as I recall the geographical definition, is a little too far east to be embraced by the bills, but it will be in their backyard. These are two pieces of legislation that have been drafted by us and will be recommended to the governor before this week is over.

The governor has already announced public support for these bills in principle. One will call for a sharing of land-use decisions between state and local government for the Tocks Island impact area, a region up in the northwest quadrant of our state that would, in the words of Governor Cahill, be subjected to intrusive and tawdry development should a very large dam be built at the Tocks Island site. The impact area comprises about 30 municipalities, some of which don't even have zoning ordinances, let alone comprehensive development plans. As a matter of fact, Governor Cahill has said, among other things, that legislation of this kind should be enacted to protect the area even if the dam should not be built at all.

Similarly, we are recommending, actually we are reviving a recommendation in different form, to provide for the same kind of decision sharing between state and local government for the Skylands Region. This region covers an area of about 500 square miles, starting at Mahwah's western boundary and going across the state until it touches the Tocks Island impact area.

So in these two bills we are talking about a thousand square miles, or a seventh of New Jersey, up in the rural wilderness area of our state. We are aware, and do believe, that certain kinds of protection should be provided for this magnificent landscape, and we hope to be able to put our beliefs to work. I am hopeful that this legislature will enact all three bills. Not that enacting bills will make dreadful problems go away; but they will pave the way for a system that can better balance the needs of the public for material goods and shelter against the constraints imposed upon that kind of development by the available resources. In my opinion, the constraints imposed on development by inherent characteristics of the land, or by inadequate water supplies, or by inadequate waste-disposal facilities, given the technology that we have, were not fully recognized in the past. It does nothing, in my mind, to lament environmental problems unless we, despite the myriad obstructions and impediments to environmental progress, try to do something about them.

As your responsible bureaucrat in this area, I sure mean to try.

III. PROBLEMS OF GROWTH

A. ASPECTS OF NEW JERSEY'S PHYSICAL GEOGRAPHY

Dr. Eugene Harrison

Assistant Professor of Geography
School of Human Environment
Ramapo College of New Jersey
Mahwah, New Jersey

Underlying much of the discussion found in this volume is a basic appreciation of the significance of the physical environment, but the natural laws operating in the region are frequently assumed as given or understood. However, a brief review of some of the elements involved should preface a study of the area's potential land-use pattern.

The last major ice sheet left the upper portion of the region only about ten thousand years ago. For this reason, in many ways this region is extremely young and subject to relatively rapid processes of change associated with geomorphically young landscapes.

Some of the rivers found here are fairly young, although some of them are the inheritors of valleys that were carved out by rivers that flowed through the area before the glacier covered it. In addition, most of the valleys found here were reworked by glacial and periglacial activity. When the glacier retreated from the region, it left a great deal of debris behind. This material covered the valley floors and is actively worked by rivers today. The significance of these facts about the nature of the covering of river-valley floors comes from the fact that our use of the land found in the river valleys should involve an understanding of the constraints on land use that they suggest. In particular, it must be understood that the land is subject to action that will affect its use as an anchorage for construction.

When rivers are active in downwardly cutting their channels to establish a concave upward profile, the most efficient cross-sectional shape for the transport of water and sediment, they

tend to form fairly straight watercourses in homogeneous rock.
(In areas in which the rock is not homogeneous, there is a tendency for the water to carve its path along the lines of least
resistance.) In this stage, the valley floor is completely filled
with the stream. After the generally concave upward profile is
established, the river's energy is partially diverted from vertical
cutting action and the streams begin to cut laterally. In this
process they carve out the valley floors that men find most desirable for development. Eventually, the valleys become quite wide,
and the streams occupy only a small part of the entire space that
they have carved out. The chief thing to keep in mind is that the
rivers have not ceased their work simply because man has occupied some of the land they are not currently shaping.

Throughout geologic time, the rivers tend to move back and
forth across their valley floors, continually lowering their local
base levels and widening their valleys. When we begin to en-
croach on the areas closest to the rivers, we must be aware that
they are most likely to be reworked by the rivers again, and
possibly in the near future. This is an aspect of the consideration
of floodplain encroachment that is often overlooked. Certain general
facts must be recognized. The first is that when rivers begin to cut
laterally, they tend to meander, thereby increasing the river's overall length and slowing the water down. However, river meanders do
not remain fixed in space; they tend to be widened on their outer curves
and fill in their inside curves. In this manner, rivers tend to drift
sideways, exposing flat land on one side and cutting into the steep
valley walls on the other. In this process, the meanders drift downstream as well, so that over a period of years different meanders
will cover the same section of the river. The rapidity of the
movement of the meanders and the widening of valleys is usually
dependent on the resistance to erosion of the rocks being worked.
In areas in which valley floors are covered by unconsolidated
glacial material, rivers can rework their bed areas and shift with
greater ease than they can in areas of exposed hard rock.

For the developer and the zoning boards, this factor should
be of prime importance because the land close to the river is
highly susceptible to undercutting.

It must also be recognized that rivers will handle the amounts
of water entering according to principles of natural law. In an
undisturbed state, if a river receives more water than can fit between its banks, the additional water and sediment carried along
with it will flow over the sides of the banks. Most of the sedi-

ments will be rapidly dropped as the water coming out of the stream loses its velocity, and mounds of water-sorted debris (natural levees) will be left along the stream banks. If this natural flooding condition is prevented from happening by the placement of walls along the river's edge, the amount of water being transported downstream will continue to increase, and the potential flood hazard downstream will be increased. Flooding is a natural safety valve for a river. If a river cannot release excess water as it accumulates, the pressure of water volume will increase, and the point at which the river finally releases its overflow will receive more water travelling at greater velocity, thereby increasing the amount of damage inflicted.

In terms of regional-development plans, the role of flood hazards is crucial. When one town decides to build artificial levees along the river in its jurisdiction, it is threatening the communities downstream because it is removing some land from flood-discharge accessibility.

The soils in these flood-prone lands are also significant. They serve the function of absorbing large amounts of overland flow of water coming into the river, and they even out the flow of water into the river over time by releasing it to the river through underground flow throughout the year. For this reason, land in the floodplain is important because it cuts down flooding by absorbing some of the flow of water during periods of precipitation and by maintaining a base flow of water in the rivers through the rest of the year, through subterranean feeding of streams from the water table. When lands along the river are covered by artificial, nonporous structures, they no longer have the ability to impede the overland flow of water; in fact, they may cause this movement to be accelerated. In addition, these lands can no longer serve their storage function as well as previously. They will not lose their entire function as storage areas as long as the water table is not lowered so far as to fall below the river bottom, but they will certainly decrease in their significance as storage areas for the stream.

As rains fall, some water is directly absorbed by the earth if the ground surface is porous, or it moves downhill over the earth to the nearest stream. As more and more of the land is covered by nonporous surfaces (houses, roads, parking lots, etc.), the amount of water flowing into streams over the surface increases, even if the amount of rainfall has not increased over previous periods. This will cause streams to flood much more frequently.

If artificial levees are also constructed, constricting the river to its present channel and not permitting any overbank discharge, the volume of water being transported downstream increases extremely rapidly. With an increase in volume, the ability of the stream to do work increases, too. This means that the stream can carry on its process of reworking the land with greater effectiveness, cutting down weak barriers or reworking unprotected bank areas with great rapidity.

Throughout the state, the nature of the bedrock and the overlying soil must be carefully analyzed before land-use plans can be finalized. Where the bedrock is porous, it is an important source of subsurface water either by drainage into streams or by supplying water to wells. Such bedrock must be used with care because it is possible that use of the land in a given area may contaminate the water supply of lands farther down the slope of the bedrock. This factor is of utmost importance in major recharge areas. If such areas are used for solid or liquid waste disposal, the subsurface water supply of many communities might be affected. Such points must be constantly analyzed when any new type of land use is planned. It is possible that the community making a change in land use will not be adversely affected by its action, but if any other community is affected, the practice involved should be brought to a halt. Regional planning of land use is, for all these reasons, absolutely essential.

B. PANEL

ENVIRONMENTAL CONCERNS REGARDING
ECONOMIC GROWTH

Chairman: Eugene Harrison, Assistant Professor of Geog-
           raphy, School of Human Environment, Ramapo
           College of New Jersey, Mahwah, New Jersey

Members: Ella Filippone, Chairman of the Passaic River
           Coalition—A Watershed Association

           Vivien Li, member of the Youth Advisory Board,
           Region II, of the U. S. Environmental Protection
           Agency and Environmental Specialist to the
           Planning Office of the City of Newark Division
           of City Planning

           Charles Cooper, Legislative Agent of the League
           for Conservation Legislation, the acting coordi-
           nator of the Hudson Environmental Coalition, and
           a member of the Steering Committee of the Save
           the Meadowlands Coalition

           Carolyn Bassett, Chairman of the New Jersey
           State Land Use Project of the American Associ-
           ation of University Women and member of the
           Atlantic County Citizens Council on the
           Environment

1. Introduction

The building of highways, the construction of office complexes,
industrial parks, and shopping centers, and the increasing use
of open space for housing and industrial needs have placed enormous burdens on the environment. Physical growth has meant
loss of water-storage capacity, increased flooding, air and water
pollution, loss of open space, and destruction of wilderness areas
and wildlife. The members of this panel analyzed the issues and

45

articulated the fears of the many citizens who are concerned about the consequences of continued growth in New Jersey.

Mrs. Ella Filippone described how water-resource management must fit into a plan for balanced development. Miss Vivien Li showed a series of slides illustrating the nature and the magnitude of the pollution problem in this part of New Jersey. Unfortunately, it was not possible to reproduce Miss Li's presentation in this volume. Mr. Charles Cooper discussed the problems involved in protecting the Hackensack Meadowlands and presented a prepared paper for inclusion in this volume. Finally, Mrs. Carolyn Bassett discussed parallel environmental problems that are being encountered in the southern part of the state.

2.   How Does Water-Resource Management Fit into a Plan for
     Balanced Growth?

Ella F. Filippone
Chairman
Passaic River Coalition
(A Watershed Association)
Basking Ridge, New Jersey

New Jersey's appetite for economic development seems to be
insatiable. Each year thousands of acres of open space and farmlands are eliminated and replaced by office buildings, houses,
shopping centers, and parking lots. Yet many local officials continue to argue for more commercial and residential development
on the assumption that unconditional economic growth will provide a wider tax base for their communities and grant financial
relief for soaring property taxes.

Uncontrolled and unplanned development ruins the landscape
and contributes to a declining quality of life. Even if aesthetics
are considered of secondary importance, a point has been reached
where the economics of conservation can make more dollars and
sense than the economics of growth. With special attention to
aesthetics, the economic appraisal has always been rather blurry;
however, if we combine the effects of pleasing surroundings with
those of mental health—peace and quiet—a value can be placed
on open space, parks, and proper landscaping, and if we go far
enough, on the value of a tree.

All of our values are computed in terms of dollar value. We
have not, until just recently, begun to think about placing a value
on clean air, clean water, a tree, or the intrinsic values of a
floodplain. More and more the facts show that development costs
a town more money for more services than the amount of new tax
revenues flowing in from additional development. In particular,
whenever more houses go up, more services—more road maintenance, snowplowing, water and sewage lines, and schools—must
be provided. The inevitable result: up go property taxes to pay
for these new services.

Balanced Growth

We hear a great deal these days about balanced growth. If we were to ask two people, I am sure, we would not get the same interpretation from them. According to the Report of the National Goals Research Staff, "Toward Balanced Growth: Quantity with Quality":

> Most present-day pronouncements on regional development and population distribution invoke the criterion of "balance." That term turns out to mean a rather wide variety of things, though it usually connotes avoidance of extreme concentration or specialization of population. To some, balance means primarily curbing the growth of large cities and helping small towns or farms to survive. To others, it means a more equal pace of growth among regions, cities, and size-classes of urban places. To others, it means a more even dispersal of industrialization and greater diversification and self-sufficiency for the economies of individual regions and communities. To others, balance refers primarily to population mix: that is, the degree to which different racial or socio-economic categories of people are distributed similarly, in an "integrated" pattern, as opposed to disparate "segregated" patterns. [1]

Possibly to an environmentalist, balanced growth means the reordering of priorities so that all aspects are considered within development and/or change. For example, in the Lake Tahoe Basin, within the land-use ordinance, there is the requirement of filing a "land capability report." This report, submitted by the applicant pursuant to the order, should contain information concerning the environment and use capacity of the lands within and adjacent to the proposed development and the probable effects of proposed land uses and land coverage. It states:

> With respect to environmental and use capacity, the Report shall contain detailed information (as prescribed in guides, if any issued by the Agency) concerning topography

and slope; geologic conditions and hazards, soil properties, capabilities, and limitations; surface and ground water conditions; vegetation characteristics; and related environmental facts pertinent to the property.

With respect to the effects of proposed land uses and land coverages, the Report shall contain detailed maps and other information concerning grading, planting, revegetation, landscaping, drainage, and other means proposed to avoid the environmental problems characteristic of the site; a preliminary site plan showing lot lines, roads, and buildings; a statement as to the impact of the proposed uses on educational facilities, fire and recreational facilities, and commercial services and facilities; and a statement as to other off-site implications of the proposed uses (such as the availability of water, power, and sewage treatment.)[2]

In the case of the development of a large industrial complex, it should also be necessary to show the impact on surrounding communities since employees do not always reside in the community that obtains the new, large ratable.

As we proceed to interpret "land capability," we begin to head in the direction of appraising land for the highest and best value. Where should we build our homes? recreational facilities? schools? How many people can this land sustain? Such questions are being heard more and more often in all quarters.

Floodplains in New Jersey

The floodplains of New Jersey, whether in the Passaic River Watershed or in the Hackensack, are considered the most valuable real estate in the country. There are parcels of land that have an undeveloped, unimproved appraised value of anywhere from $5,000/acre to $100,000/acre to $120,000/acre. Within these appraisals, however, are not factored negative incentives toward development, and it will be within the not too distant future that the formula will arise to re-evaluate this type of land.

It will be through the activities of multidisciplinary teams that this will happen.

Let us explore the benefits of a floodplain, which to date have no economic dollar value. A floodplain serves as an aquifer to recharge the underground water table, the basic source of water supply for the state. Over the past 10 years, the water table under Morris County has been dropping, thus leading to a need to find additional sources of water supply for a growing region. Therefore, we could certainly begin to place a value on a flood-plain which serves as a fresh-water acquifer. The Horstman Dump case, which has recently been heard by the N.J. Division of Water Policy and Supply and the Public Utilities Commission (PUC), is an excellent example of lack of understanding toward a flood-plain/fresh-water aquifer.

Horstman's Dump is located in East Hanover Township, on Pinch Brook and Black Brook, which are tributaries of the Whippany River, a major tributary of the Passaic River. Horstman's Dump is approximately 11 acres in size and accepted garbage from many municipalities and other sources throughout New Jersey. The Water Policy and Supply Council of the Division of Water Resources is supposed to monitor such facilities; however, several violations were apparent when the site was inspected. The PUC has juris-diction over sanitary landfills in New Jersey; again, no surveil-lance had taken place during the 4-5 years of operation. The garbage lay uncovered for days according to testimony of residents. When a storm raised the water level, the water that rose contained leachate and debris from the dump. The residents appealed to the state of New Jersey; Sandoz-Warnder, a pharmaceutical manufac-turer, joined in the action because they have eight wells on which they depend for water supply for their production processes. After a hearing before the Water Policy and Supply Council, a decision was rendered, signed by DEP Commissioner Richard J. Sullivan, which permitted an encroachment of 125 feet from the center line of Black Brook and 50 feet from the center line of Pinch Brook. In the summary, wherein is a section entitled "findings of fact," we find:

> A sanitary landfill is presently being con-
> structed . . . The 1903 flood reached an
> elevation greater than 181. 0 in the vicinity
> of . . . property, while the flood of August
> 27-28, 1971, known as Doria, reached
> El. 179. 0 in the same vicinity . . . At least

six floods have approached El. 179.0 in the
area since the flood of Doria.

> Prior to the placing of fill within. . . property,
> approximately one-half of said property was
> marsh land and constituted an integral part
> of the flood plain. The subject property rep-
> resents approximately 1.8 percent of the
> flood plain that is available upstream of it.
> The filling in of any part of a flood plain
> contributes to the loss of flood storage area.
> The filling in of said flood plain when com-
> pounded by other fills will have an adverse
> effect on future floods.

> One thousand cubic yards per day of com-
> pacted refuse is being placed within the
> applicant's property. Testimony was given
> as to the expected life of the sanitary land-
> fill in relation to various possible encroach-
> ment lines. Such testimony, however, is
> not relevant insofar as the present appli-
> cation is concerned. [3]

How anyone can accept the latter part of the statement is
unbelievable since we know that when a landfill has been placed
over a marsh, the leachate will contaminate the underground
areas for many decades to come. The facts are clear: garbage is
being placed in a floodplain in an area in which underground
aquifers are being used. The dump has been burning from time
to time, as all such structures do. The granting of this encroachment permit sets a precedent for the rest of the Passaic River
floodplain/marshes. A determination must be made regarding
priorities in this case since we must dispose of our garbage, but
we must, at the same time, protect our fresh-water supply. From
a purist point of view, all garbage should be removed from this
floodplain; however, the question then arises as to where it
should be placed.

To answer this question, we would have to involve ourselves
with a management program with in-depth efficiency uses for the
processing of garbage and use, which is not the purpose of this
paper. Back to the floodplain: it serves to clean water and air
through the various types of plants, etc., that exist there naturally. What value do clean air and clean water have as their

contribution to the health of $3\frac{1}{2}$ million people? Again, we are beginning to monitor mortality figures where deaths occur (a) directly from respiratory diseases or (b) as a result of a respiratory disease prior to the onset of a coronary (for example). We are beginning to note health problems during various climatic conditions. Once some of this data is processed, we can begin to place a value on the ability of plants to cleanse. It gets very close to the value of a human life—which is almost limitless in expected value. Ask yourself: How much is my life worth? If I had all the money in the world, what value would I place on myself? Life is the most precious commodity any of us has. A healthy floodplain contributes substantially to the health and well-being of the public and therefore should remain undeveloped in the "public interest." Another function of a floodplain is that it acts as the nursery for the countless microorganisms that make up the ecosystem under which we live—many thousands of little organisms on which higher life forms feed, which eventually make up the food chain, of which man is the highest creature. When we limit the variety, which pollution does, a floodplain or marsh is no longer viable. This entire structure is critical to an ultimate productive life for all humanity.

What do we do then? Should we preserve all floodplains? How do we define such land? Within the Passaic River Watershed because the Central Basin was once a glacial lake, we find extensive marshes and floodplains. There are those who feel this land is too valuable to set aside for open space. However, let us approach this quest from a more scientific direction. Again, borrowing from the Lake Tahoe experience:

> A Stream Environment Zone—A required land strip on each side of the stream bed necessary to maintain existing water quality. The width of the stream environment zone shall be determined by on the ground investigation. Investigation shall consider, (1) Soil type and how surface water filters into the ground; (2) The types and amount of vegetative cover and how it stabilizes the soils; (3) The slope of the land within the zone and how significant it is for retaining sediment from reaching the streams. The intent of maintaining the Stream Environment Zone shall be to preserve the natural environment qualities and function

of the land to purify water before it reaches
the stream. [4]

The Lake Tahoe ordinance further prohibits any kind of intense
impact in a stream environment zone or 100-year floodplain. Within
the state of New Jersey, we presently have a law that prescribes the
delineation of the floodplains, but forceful stoppage of any encroachment or development must be acted on in the future. In
this regard, many organizations have joined the Passaic River
Coalition, the watershed association, when they called for complete and absolute termination of encroachment, building, and
development on floodplains in the public interest.

Furthermore, those structures that are in such land areas
should be removed so that future life and property are not lost.
The economic cost (one-time) will be high; however, the need for
continuing insurance, construction, and maintenance of structures
will not be necessary. Over the long term, removal of homes in
floodplains, especially, will be most worthwhile.

Water Resources and Land-Use Planning

The concept of combining efficient water-resource management
practices with regional land-use planning is a simple one to
understand and to advocate but difficult to apply. At the theoretical level sophisticated systems-analysis models have been
designed for urban and regional water management.

While water resources are usually considered in regional-
development plans, they do not form the basis of the plans.
Water supply and waste management are normally just elements
of plans, but they do not shape the plans. A few exceptions have
been found, such as metropolitan Toronto, where a regional-
planning process has been established that uses water supply
and sewer facilities, as well as other public-works investments,
as an administrative device to implement a land-use plan that is
based on utility-service principles. The Research Triangle Region,
North Carolina, has also developed a regional guide based on
plans for water supply and sewer facilities. [5]

Metropolitan Toronto

The metropolitan system of government of Toronto came into
existence because of a water shortage in this rapidly growing
suburban area and because of severe overloads at existing

sewage-treatment plants. Lake Ontario serves as the source of water supply and as the recipient of effluent for the Toronto area, and therein lay the problem. (Sounds very much like the Passaic Basin.)

Most of the municipalities were inadequately served with sanitary drainage and sewage-treatment facilities. A large portion of the population in the outer suburbs were served by septic tanks that were unsatisfactory at the typical subdivision densities because of the soil conditions. Sewage-treatment plants were overloaded and at times only removed half of the suspended solids. As a result, the partially treated effluent caused pollution in the lake, thereby endangering the water supply.

The Metropolitan Corporation established the supply of basic services within its area of 240 square miles and, equally important, had the ability to regulate urban development over a surrounding area twice as large again, for a total of 720 square miles.

Among the established development principles, which apply to the total planning area, is the policy that permits private water supply through individual wells and private sewage disposal through septic tanks only where development takes place at low densities. These low densities are limited to areas in which such development will not preempt land required for future growth at urban and suburban densities. In effect, a service area was established within which future metropolitan growth is provided for; beyond that area only rural type of development will be permitted. In addition to the use of the water and sewer plan to define the limits of urban growth, the public-works program of the Metropolitan Corporation implements the staging of urban development. Since development can only proceed on serviced land, the municipality's financing and construction program for public works—water mains, sewer trunk lines as well as other community facilities—act as guides for the location of urban development.

The Toronto experience demonstrates that water-resource-development policies are effective only if used in concert with enforceable land-use plans and land-use controls.[6]

Passaic River Watershed

Experience gained from other areas of the world should be applied to land use/water-resource management in the most densely populated part of the United States, one of the leaders in the world!

Development principles have to be tightened to include drainage on site. Consideration must also be given to flora and fauna on the site. Studies of a parcel of land being developed for residential use must also consider, among other things, the ability of this small or large parcel of land to hold the water where it falls. Within the scope of Planned United Development or cluster zoning, or any other form envisioned by planners and architects, keeping the water somewhere on site is becoming mandatory in the Passaic River Basin. It can be done through various means: retention or detention ponds of various design, dry wells (large and small), and open-space management are but a few ways to consider within the planning process.

Future development and redevelopment are part of the complicated societal issues stressing northern New Jersey daily. Whether corrective action is possible often underlines the most ideal plans of professional and citizens alike. Let us close this discussion, therefore, with questions regarding the feasibility of any project.

1. Technical Feasibility: Can it be done? Is a potential course of action within the realm of possibilities given existing knowledge and technical capabilities.

2. Economic Feasibility: Is it worth doing? Will the expected benefits to be derived from any course of action exceed the expected costs including the cost of other opportunities foregone? (Study Army Corps Proposal II-B for the Passaic River, February 1973.) If this criterion cannot be met, a course of action will leave people worse off rather than better off.

3. Financial Feasibility: Can sufficient revenues be generated with reference to a proposed program of action to cover expenditures? Where products may not be marketable under normal marketing conditions, the financial feasibility of water-resource-development programs may depend on funding from tax revenues or the development of politically imposed pricing mechanisms such as user taxes, user charges, etc. Efficiency in water use should also be advocated. If we had to pay the true cost of clean water (which we feel is not in the too distant future), we would not be so wasteful.

4. Legal Feasibility: Is a proposed program of action lawful? Is the proposed program within the legal competence of an entrepreneur to undertake on his own authority?

5. Political Feasibility: Can the appropriate decisions be sustained? Conditions of political feasibility may affect decisions

bearing upon financial and legal feasibility in the sense that the authorization of a project and the appropriation of funds may be subject to a continuing series of decisions to sustain its operation. In a most general sense, a political system is concerned with the allocation, exercise, and control of decision-making capabilities among people. [7]

Control of water to secure maximum supply and control at costs determined the economic situation is the engineering problem, and that problem is solvable, we have always been told. Ahead of the engineering accomplishment is the engineering of people. The decision of the community at large must be made. For accomplishment, its public body, its semipublic water organizations, and its individuals must unite in teamwork to pool, rearrange, and compromise existing interests, to legislate, and to create a competent organization to carry out the engineering solution. [8] This has never been done in the Passaic River Watershed — perhaps with the concern for land use, water-resource management, and the many organizations that have been established during the past few years, we are on that threshold.

References

1. Report of the National Goals Research Staff, Toward Balanced Growth: Quantity with Quality, Washington, D. C., July, 1970, p. 157.

2. Environmental Problems of the Lake Tahoe Basin, Hearings before the Subcommittee on Air and Water Pollution of the Committee on Public Works, United States Senate, 92nd Congress, 2nd Session, August 21, 1972, Brockway, Calif., p. 225.

3. Hearings, Water Policy and Supply Council, N. J. State Department of Environmental Protection, March, 1973.

4. Environmental Problems of the Lake Tahoe Basin, p. 235.

5. Water Resources Policy and Population Change, National Water Commission, Contract NWC 71-016, Washington, D.C. October, 1971, p. 73.

6. Ibid., pp. 73-74.

7. V. Ostrom and E. Ostrum, Legal and Political Conditions of Water Resource Development Land Economics, Volume XLVIII, Number 1, February, 1972, University of Wisconsin, Madison, Wisconsin, p. 1.

8. California Department of Public Works, Division of Engin-
    eering and Irrigation, Santa Ana Investigation, Flood Control
    and Conservation (Sacramento, California: Bulletin Number
    19, 1928.)

3.   Fumbling in the Meadows[*]

Charles Cooper
Legislative Agent
League for Conservation Legislation
Teaneck, New Jersey

The concrete and steel facade of mid-Manhattan gazes emotion-lessly westward toward a struggling marshland that may soon share its fate. The Hackensack Meadowlands, northeastern New Jersey's last metropolitan space resource, is swiftly and inexorably headed toward glorious urbanization, with scarcely a whimper of protest from a public unaware of the issues or stakes involved. For the environmental movement, those stakes are especially high, and the precedents set in Jersey's meadows can heavily influence land-use planning across the country for some time to come.

For most New York metropolitan area residents, familiarity with this substantially open area (roughly the size of neighboring Manhattan) extends only to the knowledge that some 42,000 tons of garbage are dumped there each week. More recently, the decision to develop a multimillion-dollar sports and racing complex as a home for the New York Giants has focused additional attention on the district. However, few realize that this is but one visible manifestation of the state's economically opportunistic yet environmentally shortsighted "master plan" for the region.

Through unexpectedly massive input at a series of public hearings on that "master plan" late in February, the environmentalists have succeeded, at least temporarily, in giving the Meadows issue its greatest public visibility to date. On successive evenings a broad spectrum of professional ecologists, urban planners and concerned citizens produced overflow crowds in the hearing chambers and forced the scheduling of additional sessions to accommodate a total of nearly 100 witnesses. Such testimony as that contained in a nine-page telegram cosigned by Eugene P. Odum, director of the Institute of Ecology at the

[*]Reprinted from Environmental Action, April 1, 1972, pp. 11-13.

University of Georgia and five of his colleagues, has substantiated the feeling among local environmentalists that this land-use
battle is one which must of necessity now enter the public forum
at the national level. Dr. Odum, author of the internationally
known textbook, Fundamentals of Ecology, stated that the plans
for a new city in the Meadows appeared "ecologically unsound."
An examination of what has led many to that same conclusion
must begin with a historical perspective.

That portion of the Hackensack River basin known as the
Meadowlands District has historically resisted urban sprawl that
characterizes the surrounding communities only by virtue of the
expense involved in taming its wetlands for developmental purposes (drainage and fill). By 1968, advances in the "state of the
art" of profitably constructing revenue-producing industrial and
commercial facilities—popularly known as "tax ratables"—made
the Meadowlands ripe for development in the eyes of the 14
municipalities within whose boundaries the district is contained.
Sensing a potential goldmine, the state legislature passed Chapter 404 of the laws of 1968, the so-called "Meadowlands Act."
It provided for the orderly (hence more financially efficient) development of the Meadowlands district under the aegis of a new
state agency called the Hackensack Meadowlands Development
Commission (HMDC), to which the wishes of the 14 municipalities
were subordinated.

Within the text of this 1968 legislative mandate is the key
to understanding the current mismanagement of the Meadowlands
for it speaks primarily of industrial, commercial, and residential
development that "can no longer be deferred" and, in the same
sentence, of the ecology of the area that must be "considered."
Quite naturally, the various stages of the "master plan" of the
HMDC, particularly the "Comprehensive Land Use Plan" recently
in hearings, reflect the priorities as emphasized in the act. Environmentalists, who might rejoice at the comparatively progressive
concept of regional planning as opposed to chaotic municipal
competition for ratables, are faced in this case with a poor second
choice.

Specifically, the plan proposes that an industrial urban complex with some 400,000 inhabitants coexist—presumably peace-
fully—with some 1,500 acres of "marshland conservation" in a
20,000-acre tract. A city, no matter how aesthetically zoned,
has heretofore placed inevitable demands on the environmental
carrying capacity of a region. This region, even with the

undeveloped Meadowlands within, already carries a population of some 10,000 persons per square mile, a density more than 2.5 times that of Hong Kong. In designating areas wherein urban-open space preservation (and creation) should receive top priority, metropolitan New York City, including northeastern New Jersey, could well head the list! Yet a state noted for an abundance of urban decay, as evidenced by Newark, Paterson, and Jersey City, has chosen to divert the energies of repair and rehabilitation away from these recognized areas of crisis into the elimination of potential greenspace and the establishment of another metropolis.

The 60 colorful and expensive pages of the HMDC's "Comprehensive Land Use Plan" are carefully designed to impress the reader with the philosophy of environmental compatibility apparently inherent in the commission's proposals. However, after extensive study of the plan and conversations with HMDC members and staff, such groups as Environmental Action, Friends of the Earth, National Audubon Society, North Jersey Conservation Foundation, New Jersey Citizens for Clean Air, Sierra Club (North Jersey group), and the N.J. branch of the American Society of Landscape Architects agreed that the current plan negates the major environmental priorities of this already overburdened metropolitan region.

One such priority is the existence within the district of some 5,400 acres of potentially viable salt marsh. New Jersey has expressed recognition of the irreplaceable values inherent in such ecologically superior systems and their natural capacity for flood control through the progressive Wetlands Act of 1970. However, for reasons that must be interpreted as political and economic in the face of readily available scientific evidence to the contrary, lands under the jurisdiction of the HMDC were the only ones in the state specifically denied the protection of the Wetlands Act. The testimony of the marsh ecologists from the University of Georgia, some of whom assisted in the structuring of the Wetlands Act, affirmed that far more than 5,400 acres is conceivably threatened by the priorities implicit in that denial.

Urban residents, for many of whom improved air quality is becoming a necessity, may well take alarm at the admission by both HMDC and the Environmental Protection Agency (EPA) that a federally funded air-quality study now under way will only reveal which variation of the HMDC plan will result in a minimum of further degradation in regional air quality. Since EPA's basis for funding was to utilize the results in planning future urban developments, environmentalists might wonder if worsening air quality will therefore remain ideologically compatible with such development in EPA's eyes.

Similarly, it seems that these "regional planners" have ignored the most basic concept of sound environmental design, that water is the unifying ecological reality. Unable to regulate omnipresent pollutants entering the Hackensack River from the Raritan, Hudson, and Passaic Rivers—all of which empty into the same Newark Bay tidal system—the Commission still claims that water quality is the key to success of its plan. HMDC has likewise been unable to account for sources of potable water to meet the needs of the 400, 000 additional future inhabitants of the district. In fact, a recent report by Rutgers University and the Army Corps of Engineers predicted severe drinking water shortages for the region by the 1980s.

Faced with the recognizable lack of environmentally responsible means of generating electric power, as well as an existing situation characterized by frequent brownouts and blackouts, the HMDC plan makes no provision for supplying its new city with electricity. Claims that a giant incinerator will supply power seem hollow in the light of the Commission's prediction that it would burn itself out within 11 years, and environmentalists look with concern upon a recent plethora of half-page ads by Public Service Gas and Electric Company proclaiming that New Jersey needs nuclear power "now."

An agency charged with regional planning within sight of the New York City skyline might seem an ideal mechanism for the promotion of a much-needed model of total urban transit. However, HMDC can only speak of the need for mass transit and then hope that it will emerge, for the commission has neither the power to implement nor, apparently, the desire to actively advocate such a system. Instead, its plans and those of the Sports Authority necessitate the daily movement of thousands, in large part through expansion of highways and automobile use, two aspects of modern urban life most symptomatic of anti-environmental planning.

Finally, there is perhaps no region on earth in which the problems of solid waste management have yet reached such overwhelming proportions as in the Meadows district. The HMDC was mandated in 1968 to accept some 30, 000 tons of garbage per week from 128 municipalities—forever. That "flow" of solid waste will approach 54, 000 tons per week by 1975 should the commission continue to accept it. Indications are that it will and further complicate the situation with refuse from the new city. Aside from public lamentations, HMDC's only proposal to date has been the world's largest incinerator, which could accommodate 30, 000 tons per week for 11 years.

Even as the "Comprehensive Land Use Plan" demonstrates evidence of the environmental irresponsibility in development of a Meadows city, the sports complex and incinerator proposals reflect what many consider a disturbing attitudinal trend at the state level that may result in a series of even less acceptable environmental compromises. The sports and racing complex has been personally packaged by Governor William Cahill as the project that will "make New Jersey Number One. " So anxious was the governor to assure the New York Giants football team of the state's unalterable commitment to provide them with a home in the Meadows that he chose to ram through the safely Republican legislature a "Sports Authority" bill in near record time last spring. The bill specified the creation of an autonomous agency lacking public accountability and even independent of the state's own HMDC, with powers of bonding and eminent domain and the express purpose of creating and managing a sports mecca in the Meadowlands. The original legislation not only lacked so much as a reference to environmental factors, but failed as well to specify what portion of the Meadowlands the authority is to control. Hastily generated shock waves from such groups as National Audubon Society and the North Jersey Conservation Foundation stimulated minor restructuring of the bill to specify a 750-acre tract and token vagaries about consultation with the New Jersey Department of Environmental Protection (DEP). However, the ease with which HMDC's planning power was overridden, despite a public facade of harmony, caused substantial dismay to those who looked upon the commission, if not its plan, as an institution with some potential for environmental protection.

Opponents of Meadowlands development are consistently faced with questions concerning the best alternative land-use plan for the region. Environmentalists, as well as HMDC's chief of environmental programs, have agreed that restoration of the Hackensack salt marsh for controlled recreational and educational purposes would be the most ecologically responsible course of action. Areas of the district degraded beyond the possibility of marsh restoration by the abuses of dumping and spot development afford the opportunity for the creation of selected facilities compatible with increases in the quality of life in the New York metropolitan area. Specifically, these sites could provide space for experiments in total resource recovery systems of solid waste management, mass-transportation terminals, active-participatory recreational centers, and water-treatment facilities. Developmental energies and finances tuned to the creation of jobs, housing and even sports complexes, could best be reapportioned to such areas as Paterson and Newark that cry for repair, not the additional competition from a shiny new city in the Meadows.

However, the economic and political realities of implementing these priorites for use of the Hackensack Meadowlands must serve as a harsh example for the future of regional planning. The apparent need is for modification of the current Commission or creation of a more comprehensive planning authority capable of managing such broad-based factors as transportation and water quality. It would seem possible to create such an authority in one of four ways: intermunicipal cooperation, state legislative (and executive) mandate, interstate cooperation, or federally legislated and executed land-use policy. The municipalities of the Meadows district have dedicated themselves to such intense competition for tax ratables that the only partial point of agreement among them is the pursuit of joint legal action by ten of the fourteen, challenging the state's claim to title over the Meadowlands. Interstate cooperation between New Jersey and New York remains only in the wishful thinking stage, as competition for sports franchises seems to take precedence.

While the cost of retaining the Meadowlands as open space in a state with virtually no broad-based revenue source other than a property tax remains a roadblock to restructuring a regional mandate through the state's legislature, a recent turn of events has suddenly created temporary access to this decision making process. On March 8, 1972, the justices of the state supreme court confronted representatives of the Cahill administration with the opinion that the 1968 Meadows Act is unconstitutional, forcing Cahill to seek amendments designed to avoid such a declaration. Environmentalists now perceive the first real opportunity to reorient plans for the Meadows and the equally real probability of an attempt by Cahill to squeeze minimal amendments through the Legislature in a manner similar to last year's Sports Authority power play. At the time of this writing, a major battle appears imminent in a legislature more politically balanced than last year's and more responsive to a public aroused by the recent HMDC public hearings.

Environmentalists might well devote increasing effort to the Meadows as a federal issue. Specific federal involvement in the

Hackensack Meadowlands will continue to come about through such programs as the air-quality study, a $300 million Corps of Engineers flood-control project, and Housing and Urban Development funding. Thus an avenue exists, at least through the environmental impact statements required of federal agencies by the Environmental Policy Act of 1969, for bringing land misuse to the attention of decision makers at the federal level. While financially unpressured federal agencies might respond with protective measures for the Meadows, a decidedly worthwhile achievement would be the enactment of land-use controls responsive to the environmental problems created by such ostensibly attractive plans as that of HMDC. The greatest danger to the environment will not be the implementation of variations on the "Comprehensive Land Use Plan," but in permitting such to occur without focusing widespread public attention on the backwards techniques of resource analysis promulgated by the overdevelopment of irreplaceable urban open space and wetlands.

Environmentalists and others previously engaged in active criticism of the HMDC plan now find themselves faced with a threefold task. They must simultaneously continue to maximize the public visibility of the issue, delay implementation of the HMDC plan without fostering chaotic spot development by private interests and promote a detailed and environmentally responsible alternative land use plan for the region. That alternative is currently being devised by a group known as "Young Environmental Designers" at the Livingstone College campus of Rutgers University, with maximum cooperative participation by the urban-environmental coalition. Suggestions with the potential to broaden the scope and credibility of the plan are being actively sought. They, along with expressions of anger, concern, or sympathy may be sent to 844 River Road, Teaneck, New Jersey 07666. If New Jersey's open space is sacrificed in silence, who will speak when they come for yours?

4.   Parallel Problems in Southern New Jersey

Carolyn Bassett
Chairman
New Jersey State Land Use Project
American Association of University Women
Northfield, New Jersey

In considering the environmental concerns linked to economic growth, we should recognize at the outset that although we may isolate certain factors to study them in depth, or for purposes of discussion, all the factors in an environment are interrelated. I have selected the topic of water and sewage disposal to illustrate some of the ways in which sudden growth can cause problems in a community, but I could equally well have chosen housing, highways, or the disappearance of open space.

I have lived in Atlantic County for the past six years, and most of the remarks that I will make will be from my knowledge of this county and two of the adjacent counties, Ocean and Cape May. These three counties have many qualities in common: They are all resort-oriented areas that have enjoyed sizable amounts of undeveloped or agricultural land once you leave the highly developed strip bordering the Atlantic Ocean. All are experiencing rapid expansion. Ocean County is the fastest-growing county in the state, and although Atlantic County only grew 9 percent in the last ten years, some of the communities within the county are experiencing phenomenal growth: Egg Harbor Township increased by 80 percent and Somers Point grew 70 percent in the same period. Cape May County grew 23 percent as a whole.

As the population increased, many problems began to develop. In the area of sewage, the island communities had used sewage-treatment plants that provided primary treatment for the sewage and then pumped the treated effluent into the back bays. While the population was small, this method was satisfactory, but as summer visitors swelled the load to be handled, the treatment plants sometimes resorted to pumping the sewage into the bays without any treatment, and boaters have observed fecal material floating in the water. Not only is this unsightly, and a deterrent to aesthetic enjoyment of the waterways, but it has led to the closing of thousands of acres of shellfish waters due to pollution. A news release from the Department of Environmental Protection on March 21 of this year states that 5,426 acres have been closed, double last year's closings.

On the mainland, septic tanks have been the prevalent method of dealing with sewage. This worked fine when homes were widely spaced, but as more areas began going to quarter-acre lots, the ground could not absorb the discharges. Further adding to the problem was that many new homes were built in marshy or low-lying areas. Again, bay areas and streams became polluted, and in some cases the well water has been contaminated by septic tanks. Many lagoon developments in Ocean County also rely heavily on septic systems.

All three of these counties draw their water supply from an aquifer known as the Cohansey Sand, which extends under the vast undeveloped acreage of the Pine Barrens and the western areas of Atlantic and Cape May Counties. This aquifer has the ability to supply a population of much greater density than is currently projected, but some areas are experiencing difficulty because municipal wells have been placed too close to one another, and Cape May County has had some cases of salt-water intrusion, while Avalon is pumping fresh water into its wells during the winter to handle the increased demand over the summer. Extensive development over the recharge area of the aquifer could jeopardize the water supply in these counties.

Each of the three counties has a regional sewerage authority, but not one has corrected the situation satisfactorily. The Department of Environmental Protection has placed a ban on construction in many of the seaside communities until the sewage-treatment facilities are able to handle more homes. The department has also required that homes using a septic system be at least 10 feet above sea level, a requirement that has slowed down lagoon development.

Currently, Atlantic County is engaged in a controversy over the Regional Authority's proposed ocean outfall pipe, which would extend a couple of miles into the Atlantic and discharge second-arily treated waste. Some environmental groups would like to see tertiary treatment, using a spray field, employed. Various municipalities are also bickering about how much of the bill they will be required to pay.

If these problems are ever resolved, we will have a whole new crop: where to lay the trunk lines and where to locate the pumping stations. It has frequently been seen that just as development follows highways, which it has in these three counties, development also follows sewer lines, especially when the land is not suited to septic systems.

The problems that have arisen over sewage and water as these counties have grown illustrate some of the basic conflicts that occur when an area experiences a growth spurt. First, new people are coming into the area from diverse backgrounds and with diverse aims. In most cases, little attempt is made to discuss the attributes of a desirable community, and growth develops without any plan. Second, there is a tendency to continue to do things by old methods, even though conditions may have changed radically. This tendency is reinforced by the home-rule concept, which makes it difficult for communities to work together for their mutual benefit. Third, there is a polarization of opinion where builders and realtors frequently find themselves lined up opposite conservationists and environmentalists. In some cases, there may be irreconcilable differences, but usually I feel that we want the same things: a quality of life that we cannot achieve if we disregard nature. If we contaminate bays and beaches in a resort area, we are killing the goose that lays the golden egg. Very often the economic gains that we have been pursuing so fervently turn out to be a chimera: the new homes require more services, which raise the tax rate; the new industry requires outlays of money to clean up its pollutants.

New approaches are needed to solve our problems. The answer does not lie in refusing to act because population pressures make even inaction have a detrimental effect. We need to recognize that we are an integral part of nature; we can only push her so far before she rebels. I think that we will have to take Ian McHarg's advice and begin to "design with Nature" so that both man and the environment of which he is a part will prosper.

C. FLOODING AND EARTHQUAKES IN RELATION TO
    LAND USE IN NORTHERN NEW JERSEY

    Howard S. Avery
    Consulting Engineer, Abex Corporation
    Director, Township Civil Defense & Disaster Control
    Mahwah, New Jersey

Several hundred natural disasters occur every year in the United States. Most of these are related to wind, water, snow, and ice. In certain parts of New Jersey flooding and earthquakes are important elements affecting land use.

Flooding

Flooding and its attendant damage has been severe in the Passaic River basin in recent years. This damage is the result of building on floodplains. Such hardship could be avoided by reserving floodplain areas for recreational and wildlife uses that survive floods with minimum damage.

One reflection of the economic burden of flooding is the prohibitive cost of flood insurance. Only recently has such insurance come within the average person's means (because it is federally subsidized at taxpayers' expense) through the National Flood Insurance Program. To qualify the residents of a community for such insurance, an ordinance must be in effect to prevent building on the flood hazard area.

It is not easy to define the hazardous areas with precision. Gauging station records, identified high-water marks, aerial photographs at flood crest times, and topographic maps can be used together if they are available. A community should arrange a more precise survey to define land elevations (that are close to streams) within one or two feet in terms of sea level datum.

The highest known water level within a fifty-year period has been used as a basis for predicting maximum floods. However, this tends to neglect the upstream development in recent years. Houses, large one-story industrial buildings, shopping centers, roads, and parking lots have substituted quick-runoff surfaces for the natural water-absorbing ground cover. If the rain and weather conditions of one of these earlier reference storms were to be repeated in the present, the flood levels and damage are likely to be greater because of the accentuated quick runoff.

It is also wise to avoid building on or along tributaries to the main streams, particularly if they flow out of mountainous areas and have steep gradients. The steep streams can become raging torrents, causing damage from their velocity effects in addition to flooding. Highway U.S. 202 was blocked in 1971 when a bridge was wrecked by one of these torrents.

Besides the permanent streams that drain them, mountains have established side-hill drainage lines for quick runoff. These normally dry beds and gullies can also be impressive torrents during a storm. What may not be generally recognized is that disturbance of side-hill ground cover by construction activity may alter a drainage pattern, or erosion of a denuded area may start a new drainage line.

All development upstream increases the flood hazard downstream. Besides this, in mountainous areas accentuated erosion from development carries much mud and silt downstream, to slowly fill up the catch basins above dams and perhaps to modify the floodplain of main river valleys. The point to remember is that the sedimentation and the erosion that cause it increase with the slope of the side hills.

Earthquakes

Earthquakes in northern New Jersey are a less generally recognized hazard than flooding. Nevertheless, they do occur and are potentially destructive. Fortunately, most of them have been small, and because of a lack of public awareness they may escape notice.

Earthquakes are associated with faults. A fault, in the geologic sense, is a fracture in the earth's crust, with displacement of one side of the fracture with respect to the other and in a direction parallel to the fracture. The surface along which the dislocated masses have moved is called, when not notably curved, the fault plane. Tendencies toward crustal movement slowly build up enormous stresses, which may be in either tension or compression. At first solid rock deforms elastically under such pressures, but when the resulting stress exceeds the elastic strength of the rock, then fracture occurs, the movement or slippage relieving the stress. Earthquakes are the manifestation of the slipping and elastic rebound of the stressed rock.

The maximum shaking and destructive effects of earthquakes appear in loosely consolidated rocks, gravels, and soils saturated with water.[1] Thus structures built on floodplains with a high water table are particularly vulnerable to earthquakes. Restriction of building on floodplains with intent to avoid flood damage also has the effect of protecting against earthquake damage.

There are many faults in North Jersey. The geologic map of New Jersey[2] shows eleven major faults in a cross section across the state from the Hudson River to the Delaware River. This section is about 56 miles long and roughly parallels the N.Y.-N.J. border that trends northwest and southeast.

What is probably the largest of these crustal fractures is usually called the Ramapo border fault. Among readily accessible references that mention it are Widmer's The Geology and Geography of New Jersey[3] and Schuberth's The Geology of New York City and Environs.[4] Some years ago it was mapped from Stony Point, New York, on the Hudson River to Peapack in the vicinity of Bernardsville, New Jersey. More recently it has been traced across the Hudson River and studied in more detail.[5] In New Jersey it separates the Precambrian igneous and metamorphic rocks of the Ramapo Mountains from the much younger Triassic sediments and intruded diabase of the Newark series. The trace of the fault plane runs along the southeastern edge of the Ramapos. This plane dips perhaps sixty degrees to the southeast.

The Ramapo fault has an unusually long history, possibly going back to late Precambrian or early Paleozoic time some 600 million years ago.[5] However, most of the recognizable displacement probably began in the Triassic Period between 180 and 225 million years ago. Since then, the movement on the fault plane is believed to have exceeded ten thousand feet according to Schuberth.[4] Other estimates range as high as 30,000 feet. The relative displacement of the Triassic sediments is downward in relation to the crystalline Ramapo Mountain rocks.

A fault plane can be a zone of weakness and fragmentation of rocks along a fault further make this more subject to erosion than the less disturbed rocks alongside. Such erosion along the fault line has controlled the course of the Mahwah River in Rockland

County, New York, and that of the Ramapo River from Suffern, New York, to Pompton Lakes, New Jersey. The floodplain of the latter is largely covered with Quaternary deposits of stratified glacial drift from the Wisconsin glacial epoch (perhaps 15 thousand years ago) of the Pleistocene, and river sands and gravels that conceal the exact location of the fault plane trace.

The presence of the Ramapo Fault, the known relation between fault movement and earthquakes, the fact that earthquakes have occurred in New Jersey and have been felt by residents in the vicinity of the Ramapo Fault, all indicate that seismic activity should be considered in land-use planning. Such planning will require some insight into the magnitude of the danger.

For Northern New Jersey it is not possible to predict when the next significant earthquake will occur, how frequently earthquakes will occur, or when they will be dangerous rather than trivial. However, it can be predicted with virtual certainty that there will be future earthquakes.

It has been estimated that annually over a million earthquakes strong enough to be felt occur around the world. Most of these are not recognized by the public even if they are felt since, if small, they simulate the vibrations of a passing truck. About 220 major shocks and about 1,200 other strong earthquakes occur per century. The obviously high risk areas are in other parts of the world, but there is no assurance that northern New Jersey or the metropolitan area will experience only mild quakes. After 200 years of quiet, Charleston, South Carolina, had a very destructive earthquake in 1886, so strong that it was felt in New Jersey. The following is an authoritative statement by Carl Kisslinger of the Cooperative Institute for Research in Environmental Sciences at the University of Colorado:

> Although the number of large earthquakes east of the Rocky Mountains is much smaller than to the west, the much larger areas of high intensity for a given magnitude in the East makes the long-term risk, in terms of potential damage to property and loss of lives, roughly as great as in the West. [6]

The less severe shocks occur nearly everywhere over the earth. These are the kind that seem likely for and have occurred in northern New Jersey. There are official records of earthquakes associated with the Ramapo Fault for November 30, 1783 (3 shocks in 5 hours); January 4, 1885; January 31, 1885; April 1, 1947; September 3, 1951; October 13, 1962; December 20, 1962; November 30, 1964; and May 21, 1966. There was another quake on August 17, 1953, that was not attributed to the Ramapo Fault but that was felt in the area. The shocks in 1783 were felt from New Hampshire to Pennsylvania. The Rockland County earthquake of 1951 was felt over an area of 5, 500 square miles. [7]

Two systems of rating earthquakes are used. The Mercalli Intensity Scale is subjective and based on human perception. The rating steps run from I to XII and are given in Roman numerals. The Richter Scale of earthquake magnitude, which is in terms of the energy involved, is based on instrumental records from seismographs and is given in Arabic numerals. The San Francisco earthquake of 1906 had a magnitude of 8. 25; the Ramapo Fault quake of 1951 a magnitude of 4. 4. In relation to planning, a reasonable prediction for northern New Jersey would be 5 on the Richter scale and intensities up to VI or VII on the Mercalli scale but with greater intensities close to the fault-line trace.

With an intensity of VII, damage should be slight in buildings of good design and construction. There is a considerable literature on earthquake-resistant construction, [8] and it is no more than prudent to take advantage of it and follow the guidelines when building in northern New Jersey. If a Richter 5 quake is adopted as the basis for design in the general area of northern New Jersey, where loosely consolidated rocks, gravels, and water-saturated soils are involved as with the floodplain of the Ramapo River, it would be better to design for a Richter 7 magnitude because of the greater vulnerability of structures on such terrain.

Caution should also be used in crossing a fault line or traversing a floodplain adjacent to it with gas, water, sewage and drainage pipes, or electrical cables. These can be broken by an earthquake, with considerable community hardship resulting. If a quake were strong enough to start fires and break water mains at the same time, the effects could be catastrophic. The Immaculate Conception Seminary in Mahwah, New Jersey, in recent years has had a number of otherwise unexplained breaks in its water pipes; its location is near the Ramapo Fault and a branch fault that is believed to trend north and south.

Slumps and landslides can be initiated by earthquakes. On hillside slopes where the soil has layers of weakness or incipient slippage, where it can become unstable from excessive water absorption, or where it forms a relatively thin layer over smooth bedrock, there is always the danger of a slide if the slope exceeds the stable angle of repose. Freezing and thawing or waterlogged soils from excessive rain as well as earthquakes can trigger slides. Thus it is prudent to avoid building on or below areas that have these potential slide conditions; a hilltop location is much better than a side hill.

Summary

Encroachment of floodplains by buildings has been responsible for much expensive damage during floods. Upstream developments that have substituted quick runoff surfaces for water-absorbing soil accentuate flooding conditions. The obvious remedy is to avoid building on floodplains, reserving them for recreational and wildlife use. Ordinances to restrict such buildings are necessary if communities are to benefit from the National Flood Insurance Program. Tributary streams, particularly from mountainous watersheds, should also be avoided because of their flood hazard.

Earthquakes are a less well recognized hazard, but they do occur along the eastern seaboard. They are associated with movement on geologic faults. There are a number of such faults in North Jersey, of which the well-studied Ramapo border fault is probably the largest. It is active and is associated with a number of officially recorded earthquakes, of which one in 1951 had a Richter magnitude of 4.4 and was felt over an area of 5,500 square miles.

Remedial action involves the use of earthquake-resistant design and construction, avoidance of loosely consolidated rocks, gravels and soils saturated with water as a building base, and avoidance of building on slopes that are potential landslide hazards.

In northern New Jersey a reasonable design expectation is a Richter 5 magnitude earthquake, which can be increased to 7 magnitude as a safety factor for building close to an active fault.

References

1. C.K. Leith, Structural Geology, Henry Holt, New York, 1923.

2. J.V. Lewis and H.B. Kummel, "Geologic Map of New Jersey," (1910-1912); revised 1931, 1950, Department of Conservation and Economic Development of New Jersey.

3. K. Widmer, The Geology and Geography of New Jersey,
    Vol. 19, The New Jersey Historical Series, Van Nostrand,
    Princeton, New Jersey, 1964.

4. C. J. Schuberth, The Geology of New York City and Environs,
    The Natural History Press, Garden City, New York, 1968.

5. N. M. Ratcliffe, "The Ramapo Fault System in New York and
    Adjacent Northern New Jersey: A Case of Tectonic Heredity,"
    Geological Society of America Bulletin, 82, 125-142 (1971).

6. C. Kisslinger, "Seismology" (an annual review), Geotimes,
    18, No. 1, 30 (1973).

7. R. A. Page, P. H. Molnar, and J. Oliver, "Seismicity in the
    Vicinity of the Ramapo Fault," Bulletin of the Seismological
    Society of America, 58, 681-687 (1968).

8. "An Earthquake Reading List" compiled by William A. Sansburn,
    California Mineral Information Service, April and July 1965
    (A Publication of the California Division of Mines and Geol-
    ogy, Vol. 18, Nos. 4 and 7), Ferry Building, San Francisco,
    Calif. 94111.

D. PANEL

PRESSURES ON LOCAL PLANNING AND ZONING BOARDS

Chairman: Donald Clark, Planning Director of the Bergen
County Planning Board, Hackensack, New Jersey

Members: Charles Reid, Mayor of Paramus, New Jersey

Oscar Epstein, Chairman, Teaneck Planning
Board, Teaneck, New Jersey

Bernard Schwartz, Franklin Lakes Planning Board;
Vice Chairman, Bergen County Planning Board;
Vice President, New Jersey Federation of Planning
Officials

1. Introduction

Each of the panels focused on an area of concern to different sec-
tors of the populace. The panel on planning and zoning boards
consisted of individuals who have been members of such local
boards over the past decade. They represented an impressive
amount of experience in handling local responses to proposals
for land-use changes from builders, environmental organizations,
and housing groups. Their discussions presented a composite
picture of the pressures and difficulties to which local boards are
now being subjected on a daily basis.

Donald Clark, planning director of the Bergen County Planning
Board, chaired the panel. He indicated that the pressures of economic and population growth were the root causes of local dilemmas.

Mayor Charles Reid of Paramus, New Jersey, saw the pressures
as inevitable since the available supply of land has decreased
while the principle that each man has a basic right to own and
develop property is still highly valued by society. He also cited
the property tax as one of the main causal factors for pressures.
That local revenues are based on the property tax has caused
municipalities to increase their efforts to attract industry and
commerce in order to provide themselves with sufficient ratables
to obviate the need to raise tax rates. In addition to economic

77

pressures, Mayor Reid cited the impact of social pressures being brought to bear on groups responsible for making planning decisions.

Oscar Epstein, chairman of the Teaneck Planning Board, agreed with Mayor Reid but asserted that economic pressure is the sole determinant of all the other pressures. He noted that the desire to make a profit from land holdings leads many to conclude that material quantity is more important than quality of life.

Planning boards are caught between those who wish to change land-use patterns and those who wish to preserve the status quo. The pressures resulting from fiscal zoning are enormous because they lead to pressures for still more development. He described the process as one in which newly developed properties generate such a large demand for town services that, in many instances, they cause the municipality to spread its available resources even more thinly than before, thereby reducing the quality of life in the community. Not surprisingly, he finds no long-range benefit from fiscal zoning.

Mr. Epstein also noted that conflicts may exist between local zoning and planning boards, with the former sometimes taking a more liberal view with respect to permitting development. The courts, he has found, have become arbiters in this tug-of-war between environmental and social needs.

The final discussant, Mr. Bernard Schwartz, is a member of the Franklin Lakes, New Jersey, Planning Board and is vice-chairman of the Bergen County Planning Board. In addition to discussing many of the pressures mentioned by other panelists, Mr. Schwartz examined possible solutions. He proposed that the state higher educational system provide information and data on land-use issues to local bodies. Furthermore, he observed that stricter laws governing land-use allocation may be necessary if we wish to set aside more land for parks. Finally, he noted that we must be prepared to pay the cost to preserve green spaces, and we must implement this decision.

The articulation of problems and solutions by those involved in the grinding work of decision-making should provide the concerned citizen with insights into the complexity of the issues placed before local bodies involved in making land-use-allocation decisions.

2.   The Land Ownership Dilemma: An Overview

Donald Clark
Planning Director
Bergen County Planning Board
Hackensack, New Jersey

The pressures of growth that we are now feeling in the northern
New Jersey area are caused by many obvious factors. If your
community is located near an area of large-scale economic activity, you are going to feel pressures emanating from that area; if
you are near an efficient transportation system, you will feel
added pressures; if you are near an area of outstanding natural
beauty, you will also feel the pressures. This will occur more
and more frequently. Even when your community is fully developed, you will feel the pressures. Because your land has been
used up does not mean the end of pressures. You then go into
the redevelopment cycle. The pressures go on forever. You have
them from individuals who want to partake of the good life; they
want open space. You certainly have pressures from entrepreneurs
who are out to make profits. These, then, are some of the pressures built up at the local level.

We can see future pressures in the projected population
statistics for this region. The Regional Plan Association has
indicated that by the year 2000 we will be adding about 25 percent more population to the New York Metropolitan Region. The
population of the six northern counties (Bergen, Essex, Passaic,
Morris, Sussex, and Hudson) in New Jersey will increase from
3.3 million to 4.3 million by the year 2000. While Bergen County
will increase about 28 percent in population, Essex County (which
contains the city of Newark) will only increase by 6 percent.
Essex is now 90-95 percent built up. The largest increases will
be in the counties located further out, such as Morris and Sussex,
both of which will double in population. (The population of Sussex
County is expected to increase from 78,000 in 1970 to 123,000
in 1975.) From 1960 to 1970, Bergen County absorbed 1,600 to
1,700 acres of vacant land yearly. In the same decade, the population in Bergen increased by about 10,000 per year. However,

since 1971-72, the increase has dropped to about 5, 000 per year. We are in the inner ring of the New York Metropolitan Region, and the growth we had been experiencing is now moving farther out.

The old development cliché of the chamber of commerce, that "bigger is better, " must now be examined and reappraised. It's not size that we are concerned about but the quality of our environment—the quality of life. If they are not now the criteria for growth, then they soon will be.

I think the pressures that your town will be experiencing will not only be material pressures involved in how to handle the applicant who wants to build, and the ensuing pressures to rezone, you must also respond to the pressures to provide for the maintenance of the quality of life expected by the people in your area.

3. Historical Roots

Charles Reid
Mayor
Paramus, New Jersey

Land use has been a concern of all societies throughout recorded history. The ancient Roman Empire had land-use control and zoning as far as residential communities were concerned. The Romans also had the first sewer system.

In our history, land was particularly controversial in the Far West. We know about the conflict between the sheepherders and the cattle barons. Land was developed along our waterways because that was the only means of transportation. When we built the railroads, land use followed. We always have had an abundance of land, and this has enabled us to fulfill most of our needs.

In early history land ownership was the main source of wealth; it still is to a great extent. We measure a man by the land he owns. Ownership of large acreages is the mark of a wealthy citizen; it means a man has stability. We have traditionally taxed a man on his holdings. Part of the American dream is that each man has a right to own his particular parcel of property. This dream has become a basic right. Now we are well spread out, and there is not enough land for all. The suburban sprawl is a reflection of this great American dream.

Those who have developed property holdings want to preserve them. People are concerned about their individual holdings. This view is giving way, however, to the feeling that there is a general responsibility to the community in the use of land. We no longer have the Puritanical attitude that a man's land is his own.

Zoning to control land use was simplistic at first. Now zoning is highly sophisticated. Residential, commercial, and residential zoning have become quite complex.

We now have fiscal zoning because of the increase in population. All funds at the local level come from the land. This means that industry and commerce have to be attracted to the community to reduce the taxes levied on the individual home owner.

Other countries have zoning problems also. In England, land prices are much lower. They have a land-use law that controls the use of land far more stringently than in the United States. Prices are controlled. The national land-use law stipulates the use of land; for example, it is very difficult to convert farm land into residential acreage.

In addition to economic pressures, we have the social pressures generated by the aspirations of blacks. Their present goals of home ownership were our goals twenty years ago.

We also have environmental concerns. We have a conflict in writing laws controlling our environment because we are concerned about impinging upon individual freedom: to what extent do the new laws impinge upon the traditional right of a man to use his property? We are still a capitalistic society. People buy a home and land and anticipate making a profit on them.

There is a great deal of discussion about centralized planning. The Regional Plan Association has been in the forefront in proposing centralized planning. While regional plans are necessary, such proposals impose upon local concerns and needs because they do away with the neighborhood concept. We now realize that there has to be a balance between home rule and centralized planning.

We are very jealous about our property, and we lack proper concern about the future. We always want the law to apply to the other fellow and not to us. This is basic human nature.

In summary, most of our pressures are economic ones; they are based on: our interpretation of the great American dream, our tax structure, and our individual lack of concern for the welfare of our fellow man unless it affects us.

4. Social and Economic Factors

Oscar Epstein
Chairman
Teaneck Planning Board
Teaneck, New Jersey

To be on the planning board you have to have a thick skin. The pressures are sometimes overt and sometimes very subtle. They are both regional and local. There are pressures from those who make money and want you to act according to their interests. The economic factor, as Mayor Reid indicated, is the prime determinant of most kinds of pressures. There are those who want you to do something so they can make some money, and there are those who are concerned that what you will do will cost them money. In other areas these same people are very civic-minded, but, when it comes to land, their only concern is to make money.

A good planner is one who has his head in the clouds and his feet on the ground.

The quality of life is becoming very important to us even though very few people have been brought up on this philosophy. As society becomes more affluent, people will be more concerned with what they see and hear. They will be concerned with the factor of whether the land is giving them a better life as well as how much money they are making from it.

Many towns have used zoning to exclude blacks. The people of Teaneck realized that this was a foolish and ultimately impos- sible thing to do. The black population of Teaneck is now 15 per- cent of the total population, and there have been no great problems as far as zoning is concerned. The quality of the people coming in is just as high as before, preserving the community's quality atmosphere. We found that being frightened has no purpose.

Planning boards do not make arbitrary changes that are harm- ful to the citizens. After all, planning-board members are resi- dents of the town. They have the same values as other residents. They are not going to rezone the town if there is significant oppo- sition. It is not always easy to sit on a zoning or planning board and do a very good job. The people who come before you are your

friends and neighbors. You have to make decisions. Sometimes
they don't favor your neighbors or friends. We have had some
terrible battles on rezoning. But after it is done, there are few
complaints. Planning boards do make mistakes, however.

The purpose of public hearings is to give the people a chance
to talk to the planning board. We rarely hold executive meetings
concerning matters to be taken up at a public hearing, so that our
minds should not be made up until the public is heard. This procedure has worked out well.

Fiscal zoning is the most troublesome kind of zoning in the
country. I have found that most fiscal zoning is not beneficial to
the community. Those towns with the greatest numbers of ratables
usually have the highest taxes. If ratables were the sole answer,
the citizens of New York shouldn't have to pay any taxes. When
you fiscally zone, you bring in the problems that cost most in
services. You estimate the police and fire services required by a
new project. At first you conclude that a project is fiscally profitable. What you don't see are the pressures that are brought to bear
on the community. For example, when a shopping center is constructed, traffic pressure from residents and nonresidents going
through the town increases substantially. The formerly adequate
streets are no longer adequate. Streets must be widened, and
property must be condemned. Other streets wear out more rapidly.
You may need more police because of the increased population.
As you can see, there are many hidden costs of fiscal zoning.

The courts also play an active role in land use. Planning
boards and the courts must agree on the definition of oversize
zoning. The courts have to decide on the extent of the need for
adequate breathing space, for parks, and whatever else is necessary for an adequate life. The courts must balance environmental
needs with social needs. In Loechner v. Campoli, the court ruled
that a planning board cannot turn down a subdivision plan solely
on the basis of the amount of frontage and square footage. The
court ruled that you had to grant a subdivision, subject to a variance by the board of adjustment (zoning board). We have found
that the board of adjustment frequently grants a variance when
properties are to be built on undersized lots. We do not agree
with the Loechner v. Campoli ruling because footage requirements,
if they are not excessive, can have valid zoning purposes.

5. A Search for Solutions

Bernard Schwartz
Franklin Lakes Planning Board
and
Vice Chairman
Bergen County Planning Board
Hackensack, New Jersey

We have not done very much planning. The title of the panel is,
in a way, a criticism of the way we have acted. We have dealt
mainly in terms of crisis, rather than in terms of the future. Now
we are concerned about the environment because we all have
more time; leisure time permits us to think about a different set
of values.

There are two types of pressures: those that are upon us and
we can't walk away from, and those that are not readily apparent.

The most immediate type of crisis comes from the pressure of
people who want to develop their land. We all want to develop
our land in the most profitable way. The planning board must look
at the proposal from the view of the benefit of the community. We
have a problem in balancing the equities. The owner has a right
to develop his land, yet there is a community interest.

We also have the problem of fiscal zoning. Revenue pressures
force us to make all kinds of wrong decisions. It may seem great
to have that plant on the main road, but we don't know the impact
that such a plant may have on the community ten years hence.
We don't know what provision of services to that facility will add
to the running costs of the town. In addition, we have the pressure of keeping the taxes down.

We have problems caused by public utilities that advertise
to attract industry and people to the state. There is a continuous
cycle: we have to have more industry, to support more people, to
bring in more industry, etc.

In response to such pressures there are a lot of tools that
would help the zoning-change applicant and the community. We

can look at cluster zoning for a solution. For example, out of 100 acres of land you could leave 50 to 60 acres open. There is a bill now in the state assembly concerning cluster zoning. One of the problems of cluster zoning is who is going to maintain the vacant space? Will it be the town or the home owners? Cluster zoning has been used successfully. You can take 60 percent of the land and leave it vacant for a park and thus protect it for perpetuity.

One thing the state legislature should do is to give Rutgers University some money to do the following: (1) to provide a clearinghouse of information and data on land use that is available to everyone so that local people, applicants, members of planning and zoning boards, can get all the information they need from one source. They could find out what has been done anywhere; what information is already available in Idaho, or Arizona, or anyplace else. (2) Another thing they ought to do is to establish a research facility so that if there is information that is needed by the environmentalists or by other data bank users, with respect to development standards, the college could attempt to provide it.

We have an applicant in Franklin Lakes who wants to take the crest off a hill in order to build. This is soil mining, but the question is whether this is good or bad. He wants to take down many trees, but many residents feel that these trees are important to the area. We have to develop standards that will benefit both the individual and the community.

We have to establish some new standards of professionalism for planners. Most planning experts in this state have qualifications that can be described as "have briefcase, will travel." There are very few who say "I only represent developers," or "I only represent planning boards." Some will appear before a planning board and take one point of view and then go before some builders and take the opposite point of view. A planning expert is not supposed to be an advocate of a particular point of view. We need to develop some expert information in these areas.

With respect to fiscal zoning, we need some kind of tax reform that will change the equation. We need tax reform from a planning point of view and from a social point of view.

On my list there are really three important questions:

1. How many people can the land really hold? How many people can we allow to live in the state of New Jersey? There must be reasonable limitations.

2. How can we preserve enough green space in terms of conservation and recreation to ensure that New Jersey will be a desirable place to live?

3. How are we going to provide much-needed housing for our citizens? How do we provide housing for the have nots without taking unfair advantage of the haves?

We must plan ahead in the areas of population, housing, and open space!

The federal government has made us work on green-space plans. A county planning board now cannot get money from the federal government unless it comes up with an open-space plan. The question gets down to economics. In our society, most of the land is owned by someone. Most people will not give up their land for a park or green space unless they are paid for it. Another question we must answer is whether we should buy land for parks now or thirty or forty years from now. On the matter of when to purchase green space, I would say that there is the same urgency with respect to this problem as there is to population pressure. We must interest people in solutions, but they resist anything different. Members of planning boards must provide leadership in the search for solutions.

6.   Selected Questions by Other Participants

What is the minimal size for cluster zoning in a town?

Mr. Schwartz: There is no precise number for the cluster concept. In Hawaii you find five one-hundred-thousand-dollar homes on one acre which anyone would live on. The best source of information is the National Association of Home Builders.

Mayor Reid, are you aware of the problems that local mayors have had with the Hackensack Meadowlands Commission? They claim that the state is usurping their powers. The commission has come out with its own zoning plan. Do you feel that the state should have set up such a commission?

Mayor Reid: Mayors are concerned about the loss of their own fiscal ratables. This is the problem we discussed before. I happen to think the Meadowlands program is a fiasco. But it is the lesser of various evils. The projected development will create a new city. This will only increase the urban problems of Jersey City and Newark. It will create a new market, at the sacrifice of the old markets, and add to the decline of the cities rather than stimulate their rejuvenation. I would argue for open space. My first choice would be not to have the development program at all. My second choice is that development should be controlled. My third choice is to have the status quo—that is, leave it to the towns to develop as they see fit.

Mr. Epstein, would you discuss the Hackensack River proposals?

Mr. Epstein: Regarding the Hackensack River Project, this has finally been begun, but it has been discussed since the turn of the century. Around 1906, Cornelius Hart spoke about damming the Hackensack River and developing parks alongside of it. The need for this project is greater now than it was then, but nothing was done about it for sixty years.

Several years ago, several communities started talking about damming the Hackensack River and building parks along the riverfront. There were tremendous pressures from the towns involved, as well as from local industries, not to go ahead with the project. Rather than use the river area for recreational purposes, they prefer to use it for ratables.

Hopefully, in three years we will have a river that is dammed and dredged. We will have boating and fishing. A few years ago we got many polluters to stop polluting the Hackensack River. We hope that, eventually, the water will be clean enough for swimming.

E. PANEL

IMPACT OF THE TAX STRUCTURE ON LAND USE POLICIES

Chairman: Sebastian Raciti, Professor of Economics, Ramapo
College of New Jersey, Mahwah, New Jersey

Members: Eleanor Kieliszek, Councilwoman and Planning
Board member, Teaneck, New Jersey

Patrick Callanan, Chairman, Planning Board,
Ridgewood, New Jersey

Dr. Richard E. Onorevole, Councilman and
Planning Board member, Saddle Brook, New Jersey

Henry Ebel, Suburban Action Institute, Tarrytown,
New York

1. Introduction

Because the property tax is a primary source of revenue to local
governments, land taxation has profoundly influenced the development of American cities. At the turn of the century, communities
vied with one another for commerce and industry by offering com-
petitively low tax rates. While this brought the cities badly
needed revenue and an increase in jobs, most of this growth
occurred with little preparation or planning. Many towns were
soon dependent on a few or single firms and many more found
their streets congested by trucks and crisscrossed by railroads,
their air polluted, and in general a gradual deterioration in their
quality of living. All too often this cycle was completed when
the manufacturer also found the conditions in the city so intoler-
able that he, too, sought new areas to relocate his operations.
Thus began a pattern of declining ratables followed by rising tax
rates as older cities sought to maintain or increase revenues.
While the situation of our older and larger cities is quite familiar,
little is often known about the problems faced by smaller or newer
communities, also in need of revenues and also almost totally
dependent on land as a source of this revenue.

This situation is quite common in northern Bergen County where the tremendous growth of the past decade has placed a great strain on public facilities. How to obtain badly needed revenue is a vital question hotly debated at many town council meetings. The panelists who discuss this issue of land use and tax policies provide interesting and quite different approaches to the problem. Dr. Richard Onorevole, a councilman from Saddle Brook, stresses an approach of land development that maximizes revenues. Mrs. Eleanor Kieliszek, councilwoman from Teaneck, disapproves of land use being dictated by revenue needs and urges instead that tax reform relieve the towns and cities from the pressure of land development dictated by revenue needs. Mr. Patrick Callanan, from the Ridgewood Planning Board, urges some tax reform but argues that resistance to much land use and development is often due to a poor presentation of the issue by community leaders. Finally, Mr. Henry Ebel, of the Suburban Action Institute, reports on a study that purports to show the basic inequity of the present system that allows individual communities to determine local tax rates. This system, he argues, intensifies the current self-defeating situation whereby older cities must raise rates to make up for lost ratables and newer communities allow their vacant land to be developed for industrial parks, shopping malls, and highways in an effort to attract more ratables. He argues instead for a uniform land tax set by the state, with the state collecting and disbursing those revenues to communities according to their population size and need. The ensuing discussion with members of the audience upheld the view that tax reform is an essential part of proper land use.

2. Open Land Ratables

Dr. Richard E. Onorevole
Councilman and Planning Board member
Saddle Brook, New Jersey

I want to address myself to several questions: (1) our particular philosophy in this area, (2) why taxes are so crucial, (3) the services required by our citizens, (4) the major question of how to pay for town services, and (5) future needs.

The concept and philosophy that we face in the United States is one of individual freedom, of the right of a person to do what he wants with his property as long as it is within reason. It must be noted, however, that our definition of "within reason" is becoming more restricted as the nation becomes more urbanized.

In New Jersey, with a total population of over seven million, Bergen County ranks second in population, with over 900,000 people. (Essex County, the most populous county in the state, has about 932,000 people.) Bergen County has a population larger than that of eleven states and is confronting problems of population density, traffic congestion, and a growing demand for municipal services.

Municipal services are provided, mostly, through use of the property tax. The Supreme Court ruled that the property tax is an equitable method of providing for such services as education, public safety, public works (for water supply, street maintenance, etc.), and recreation, but the costs of these services, and the demand for them, are expanding. Our problem, then, is how to use the community's property in such a way as to generate revenues to provide required services yet preserve some open space.

Saddle Brook, New Jersey, is mainly a residential community whose residents moved directly to Saddle Brook from Hudson County and New York City. Partly because of the lack of established site improvement standards, the planning board permitted the first developers to build houses very close to the front footage of property lines and to build warehouses and factories without any setbacks. Until the ordinances could be rewritten, the planning board had

had very little authority, outside of persuasion, to ask for provision of parking facilities, green areas, buffer zones, trees,
and the like. (Even if you legislate the provision of these particular requirements, it does not necessarily mean that an area's
standards will come up to those preferred by members of the
ecology movement.)

Before we used different zoning techniques, we permitted
the construction of large structures that created two types of
drainage problems, lack of ground infiltration and increased overland flow, and which provided only minimal financial benefit to
the community. For example, one particular firm, covering twelve
acres, contributes $42,000 a year in taxes, a reasonable amount to
pay based on a 1972 assessment of $3.60 per $100 of evaluation.
On the other hand, if we take twelve other acres near this plant,
we see how different land uses (hotels, motels, and office buildings) can generate much larger tax revenues. The second area is
located near the Garden State Parkway and Route 80 and produces
an annual tax yield of $340,000. You cannot always construct
high-rise motels to provide high tax yields, but if a community
can zone its property so as to get the greatest possible yield for
each developed parcel of, say, twelve acres, and can keep twelve
other acres open for recreation purposes, for flood control, and
for ecological balance, then the town may be moving in the right
direction.

The point I would like to make is that we can provide adequate services for the community (quality education, health,
safety, and recreational services), and we can pay for these
things by using the land in ways that will give us the best possible tax yields from the smallest amounts of developed space.

3.   Problems Inherent in Fiscal Zoning

Eleanor Kieliszek
Councilwoman and Planning Board member
Teaneck, New Jersey

I serve on the town council of Teaneck, a town that has a population of 42, 000 distributed over a land area of five square miles.
Teaneck has a budget of 20 million dollars, 12 million of which
go to provide for education, with the remainder being used to
provide other municipal and county services.

I joined the council after serving on the P. T. A. , the League
of Women Voters, and the Planning Board. When I had to make
decisions that involved fiscal zoning, I did so with the assumption that I would do it properly. I would not make planning or
zoning decisions on the basis of the tax structure because we are
not permitted, under the law, to zone for fiscal realities; I would
vote to zone and plan according to the statutes. As you know,
however, you get worn down, and then you must deal with realities. Their problem of a heavy tax burden was solved, partially,
by bringing in more ratables (with the assistance of several major
highways in that area).

My view is that I am not willing to live with that kind of
fiscal reality any longer. I feel that the property tax has as great
an influence on how a community zones and plans as the topography of that community or the location of highways; perhaps it
has the greatest impact. Even highways are located on land that
can be obtained at the lowest possible cost. Land that has a high
tax potential generally will not be used for highways. Therefore,
when Route 80 came through Teaneck, it was constructed through
a county park; that was the cheapest way to do it.

If we look back at the controversy over the location of Ramapo
College, this site was chosen because the land was available at
low cost. It was not constructed in Hackensack, where the ratables are high. (The city of Hackensack wanted the college built
elsewhere because it has enough of its ratables tied up in county
buildings, and it did not wish to lose more ratables in exchange
for the new college.)

In Teaneck, a town that is almost entirely developed, with only 40-50 developable acres remaining, our problem is how to acquire more ratables. Almost all of our community is covered with one-family houses. It is good, attractive housing on reasonable-sized lots, with frontages from 50 to 100 feet wide, but if we continue to look to the property tax as our principal source of revenue, we have no place to go. We added only 2 million dollars of new assessments to a total of 461 million in assessments in the last year. Perhaps our community will have to begin to plan for redevelopment; we could take advantage of the location of local highways, such as Routes 80 and 4, to add new ratables to the new community. However, we feel that it is unpleasant to develop the community further solely for the purpose of continuing to provide the services that a town traditionally gives. We don't feel that dense development is the answer for every community, though, undoubtedly, there are places for dense development. It may well be that because highways are passing through Teaneck, we will be led to zone or to rezone the area to permit high-density uses at the junction of the two highways. We may be able to do this as a short-run solution to our financial problems, but we cannot look to that sort of answer for the long-term solution. Sooner or later high-density development brings with it high cost, and then you start on the round robin again.

We should look to the state legislature for another form of taxation, one that will take over the burden of the cost of educating our children. We provide a good environment for families to bring up children. Why should we change that? Just in order to take care of our tax problem? I believe that the legislature should come up with a form of taxation (other than the property tax) that would provide for education so that we can conduct our town planning in a way that is humane. If this is accomplished, we won't have to view each subdivision as bad for the community because it will add children to the school population.

I also would like to say that we must work for the proposed community planning law. Although I believe that some communities, and Teaneck is one of them, have handled this problem as well as they can, there are others that, because of the press of their own fiscal problems, are creating problems for other people; they need the guidance of state planning laws. I look forward to a time when a town must present its master plan to a state agency for review. State guidance as to the density we should have in communities like Teaneck, Hackensack, and Ridgewood would be helpful. Is it best for high-rise locations to be in

Fort Lee and Hackensack? There should be some way that we can take a more broad and rational approach to planning so that those of us on the local level would be free to do what is best for our own community, while still considering the needs of Bergen County and the state of New Jersey. I am for change and not willing to stick with things as they are.

4.   Tax Reform and the Community

Patrick Callanan
Chairman
Planning Board
Ridgewood, New Jersey

There are a number of ways in which this subject of tax structure could be approached. The previous speakers have focused on two of the factors as they relate to housing. I am going to examine another area that is impacted because of the effect of the tax structure on land-use policies. I feel the most significant impact is observed in a community such as Ridgewood, which is a community that does not have some of the problems faced by Teaneck.

The present tax structure rests on revenues from real property and creates a heavy tax pressure on those individuals with fixed incomes. This problem is particularly significant in a period when school and other municipal costs rise sharply. These individuals now make themselves heard in the voting booths, in an election year, and at school and town meetings. They are not about to listen to anything new in the way of innovations, because anything new costs money. They are not about to spend money on something that will benefit the future when they can barely afford to support present school and municipal costs. On the other hand, the planning boards in various communities have the responsibility to plan for the future; in many instances, this involves initiating innovations in land-use policies. People do not object if new land-use policies involve rezoning for business purposes or for some other use, especially if the rezoned areas do not border on their property and produce an increase in ratables that will generate more tax revenues.

But the clash that I want to refer to takes place when the planning board concludes that it must provide more land for municipal and school uses. (I am referring to those land-use policies that require that communities acquire land for recreational purposes, school-expansion purposes, or for parking uses.) Such decisions cost money, reduce ratables, and generally fly in the face of those people in the community who oppose any increase in expenditures.

My question to you is how can this conflict be resolved? It is easy to say that a broad-base tax that relieves us of the burdens of the property tax is the answer. In my opinion that is not the whole answer. Any community that looks to such a tax structure for an answer to its financial problems is making a serious mistake. I feel that the answer lies in the ability of the planning board to put its methods across to the public. In fact, it is an educational process that can best be accomplished by periodically reviewing where the town was, where it is now, and where it should plan to be in the future. I think people in the community should be brought into the future plans of the community and understand the reasoning and the projections that led the planning board to decide on the specific land-use policies that are being presented to them. I don't propose that this will convince everyone that future planning should not be negated in favor of present tax savings, but it will, if done properly, make some of those who are interested enough to review the planning boards' deliberations more amenable to land-use proposals that will tend to increase the tax structure but will provide the town with many future benefits. This sort of community-education problem exists in Ridgewood, and Ridgewood's situation is typical of that in many towns in Bergen County.

The League of Women Voters recently prepared two reports for the village of Ridgewood. One report compared Ridgewood's recreation and park facilities with statewide guidelines and concluded that the village must devote more land to recreational and park use. Many people in our community, however, feel that we do not need additional recreational and park facilities; we have yet to develop what we have. The other report dealt with senior-citizen housing and attempted to identify property that will serve the needs of senior citizens who can afford high-, moderate-, and low-income housing. From a practical point of view, such housing must be constructed by a nonprofit organization or by the municipality itself. Yet neither of these nonprofit organizations would pay taxes.

The school board also finds itself short of land when it compares its present land holdings to statewide formulas. The school board, therefore, would like to see more land developed for school uses (which would further decrease taxable property in the community).

Another report, by a consultant on traffic and parking requirements for the village, pointed out that there is an absolute need

for additional land for parking. Finally, the state wants to con-
fiscate 16 acres of prime ratable land bordering on Route 17 for
an overpass. (We think this proposal is totally unnecessary.)

Now, consider these five requests in view of the fact that
Ridgewood is a totally developed community with what some
people already consider a high tax rate. A recent survey of all
residents indicated that they wanted to maintain the residential
character of the neighborhood, and a good majority also wanted
some senior citizen housing. Approximately 16 percent of our
residents are 60 years or older, and many have fixed incomes.
And now a recreation committee has come out with its conclusions
that we have set aside an inadequate amount of land for recreational purposes. How is this issue to be resolved? I think this
is the clash that exists. But I think we have the answer; we have
already begun to distribute a questionnaire with which we have
involved the people from the beginning. We are reviewing our
master plan, and we intend to present it to our citizens. With
citizen understanding and cooperation, we believe that we can
create a master plan that will be balance and that will solve the
town's problems while staying within the financial and political
limits of the community. I think rationality is the only solution
to the problem of the impasse on tax revenue and land-use policy.

5. The Taxation of Industrial and Commercial Property
   in the State of New Jersey

   Henry Ebel
   Suburban Action Institute
   Tarrytown, New York

Suburban Action is very active in zoning matters such as those
now being challenged in Mahwah. We are also instrumental in
the Madison case, which is now being decided in the New Jersey
Supreme Court. I have just completed a study, under the sponsor-
ship of SAI, based on the facts obtained from computer print-outs
done by an economist at N.Y.U., Professor Immanuel Tobien. The
findings come from the compilation of data from each of the state's
567 municipalities. A summary of the report follows.

The conclusion that emerges from this study is that the present system of taxing industrial and commercial property in the
state of New Jersey is an inequitable one. It is a system that
has turned the taxing power over to the state's 567 municipalities
and that has therefore given birth to 567 tax policies. It is a
system that encourages these municipalities to war against each
other through the use of the tax rate and other incentives to attract industrial and commercial ratables to their borders. It is a
system that has already divided the state into "have" and "have-
not" municipalities, that has deprived New Jersey's most populous
municipalities of the funds needed to serve their residents, and
that has turned over to a select number of affluent suburban towns
a disproportionate percentage of the state's tax resources.

The Property Tax in New Jersey

New Jersey relies on local property taxes as a source of governmental financing to an extent matched or exceeded by few other
states. Local taxes on industrial and commercial property account,
on a statewide basis, for approximately one-third of all property
taxes collected. However, analysis by counties shows that taxes
on industrial and commercial property can account for as little as
19 percent and as much as 61 percent of all property taxes.

Industrial and commercial ratables are clustered in the northernmost and, to a secondary extent, in the southernmost counties of the state—those counties, in other words, that are part of the New York and Philadelphia metropolitan areas. However, even within these counties there exist, by virtue of the state's entirely localized administration of the property tax, profound disparities between one municipality and another in their valuations of industrial and commercial property (ICP).

An analysis of ICP valuations per capita of population reveals that the state's eleven most populous municipalities have ICP valuations averaging $18,213 for each resident. A similar analysis of ICP valuations per capita in 16 of the state's newer and rapidly developing suburban municipalities reveals an average of $84,600 for each resident. In 1970, the eleven largest cities held 18.7 percent of the state's population and 61.3 percent of its nonwhite population. In the same year, the 16 suburban municipalities analyzed held 5.1 percent of the state's population and 1.7 percent of the state's nonwhite population. While the eleven cities held 15.8 percent of the total ICP in New Jersey, the 16 municipalities held 17.1 percent.

The distinction between the older cities and older industrial suburbs on the one hand and the newer developing suburbs on the other is true not only for their ICP valuations per capita of population but for the rate at which they tax industrial and commercial property. In the state's eleven largest cities, the ICP tax rate in 1970 averaged 7.6 percent. In the 16 suburban municipalities analyzed, the rate averaged 2.2 percent.

In order to determine as clearly as possible the impact of ICP tax rates on the state of New Jersey, the state's 567 municipalities are divided into ten deciles of 56 municipalities each. Decile I includes the municipalities with the lowest ICP tax rates in the state, and the deciles run sequentially to Decile X, which contains the municipalities with the highest ICP tax rates. Study of the deciles reveals that the municipalities with the highest tax rates in the state contain a quarter of the state's population, and that these same municipalities have the lowest per-capita valuations of ICP in the state.

Moreover, the deciles establish a clear correlation between the rising population of a municipality and the likelihood that it will appear in a high-tax decile. Of the 84 municipalities with populations above 20,000, 15 appear in Decile X, 11 in Decile IX,

12 in Decile VIII, 10 in Decile VII. The number of populous
municipalities decreases steadily to a total of 2 for Decile I,
which contains the municipalities with the lowest ICP tax rates
in the state.

The deciles establish a clear correlation between a low
municipal tax rate on ICP and municipal affluence as revealed by
a high per capita valuation of ICP. Of the 25 municipalities with
the highest per capita ICP valuations in the state, 18 appear in
either Decile I or II.

However, analysis of the 91 most affluent municipalities in
the state, defined as those with per capita ICP valuations of
$30,000 and above, reveals a high positive correlation between
small municipal size and ICP tax wealth. Of these 91 municipalities, 62 had populations below 10,000 in 1970, and 15 had
populations between 10,000 and 20,000. Small suburban municipalities with fewer than 10,000 inhabitants thus account for 68
percent of the ICP-rich municipalities in New Jersey. At the same
time, these 91 municipalities have the lowest ICP tax rates in
the state. Twenty-six of them appear in Decile I, 25 in Decile II,
12 in Decile III, and 11 in Decile IV.

Analysis of municipal tax collections in 1970 similarly reveals
the fiscal imbalance in the state; 16 rapidly developing suburban
municipalities, containing 5 percent of the state's population,
succeeded in collecting more than a third of the amount collected
by the state's eleven largest cities, containing 15 percent of the
state's population. They succeeded in doing this despite the fact
that the ICP tax rate in the eleven largest cities was 345 percent
higher on the average than the rates they themselves were levying.

Finally, this study establishes a correlation between rising
ICP tax rates in New Jersey's municipalities and rising tax rates
on residential property. However, in the wealthiest municipalities
as defined by per capita holdings of ICP, the ICP rate is kept significantly lower than the rate on residential property in order to
maintain the power of the municipalities to attract additional
industrial and commercial ratables. In the ICP-poor municipalities,
the rate levied on ICP exceeds that on residential property as a
result of political and humanitarian considerations and despite
the ruinous impact of this differential in encouraging the out-
migration of industrial and commercial ratables.

Population and Job Movements in New Jersey

The second and briefer portion of this study establishes the extent to which the patterns of taxation and ICP location analyzed to this point coincide with the patterns of residence for the state's social, racial, and income groupings.

The increasing concentration of the state's nonwhite and nonaffluent population in the center cities and the movement of relatively affluent whites out of these cities to suburban municipalities is shown through a study of U.S. Census Bureau figures for 1960 and 1970.

The sixteen rapidly developing suburban municipalities whose ICP tax valuations have been extensively examined showed a total population increase of 31.9 percent in the period from 1960 to 1970, considerably greater than that for the state as a whole. In both 1960 and 1970, however, their share of the state's nonwhite population was identical: 1.7 percent.

Finally, attention is paid to the extent to which the movement of ICP from center city to affluent suburb is a movement not only of tax resources but of blue- and white-collar jobs. Analysis of employment patterns in the Newark SMSA from 1947 to 1967 shows a consistent pattern of job decline in the center city and job growth in Newark's suburban ring.

Recommendations

The study concludes by recommending:

1. That a uniform statewide tax should be imposed on all industrial and commercial property located within the borders of New Jersey.

2. That the rate of uniform statewide taxation should be established at the median rate obtaining in the state's 567 municipalities. In 1970, the median rate stood at 3.22 percent.

3. That under a uniform statewide system, the state should collect taxes on industrial and commercial property and that disbursement of the taxes collected to the individual municipalities should take account of two considerations: (A) the total population of the municipality and (B) the service needs of that population.

The recommendations are analyzed at length in terms of their direct and indirect consequences.

Particular attention is paid to the political feasibility of a reform in New Jersey's system of taxing industrial and commercial property. The conclusion is that such a reform is eminently feasible. At a time when a family of four living in a home assessed at $62,000 can, if both children are attending municipal schools, be defined as a "welfare family," the number of disadvantaged municipalities in the state of New Jersey is steadily increasing. The imbalance in the distribution of ICP ratables is affecting a growing percentage of the state's white and formerly affluent citizens. Under these circumstances, the myth of a solidly white/suburban opposition to nonwhite/center-city problems has very little substance. If there is a municipal "class war" in New Jersey, it is between the "have" and "have-not" municipalities, and the latter now include a growing number of suburban municipalities. The time is ripe for tax reform in New Jersey.

F. PANEL
    VIEWS AND CONCERNS OF THE BUSINESS COMMUNITY

Chairman: Stanley Willing, Chairman, Division of Business,
           St. Francis College, Brooklyn, New York and
           President, Willing Associates, Inc., New York,
           New York

Members: Joseph A. Aramanda, President of the J. I. Kislak
           Realty Corp., Newark, New Jersey

           Frederick Baylis, Vice President of the National
           Community Bank, Maywood, New Jersey

1. Introduction

This paper was presented by Mr. Joseph A. Aramanda, president
of the J. I. Kislak Realty Corp., one of the largest real-estate
firms in New Jersey. The purpose of the panel was to articulate
the concerns of the business community and to describe its perception of the various problems regarding land use. The panel
chairman was Dr. Stanley Willing, who is president of Willing
Associates and a faculty member of St. Francis College in Brooklyn, New York. The other discussant on the panel was Mr. Frederick Baylis, vice president of the National Community Bank,
Maywood, New Jersey.

    Mr. Aramanda's presentation reflected the business commun-
ity's view of the problems to be faced when planning for industrial
expansion in the cities and suburbs. His main theme was the
lack of, and the strong need for, regional planning in the state.
Noting the obsolescence of many community master plans, Mr.
Aramanda cited the need for a regional approach to land-use
planning.

    Another concern was the lack of development on vacant indus-
trial land in the cities. He inferred that we are not taking advantage of our land resources in the cities. With the movement of
business out of many New Jersey cities and the pressures of

growing costs of land in the suburbs, this view is certainly valid and tends to focus on the future significance of urban vacant land areas for industrial and residential development. Land costs in the suburbs may force us, as a society, to turn back to development in the urban core.

Although many Bergen County communities are exceptions, he found that, in general, businessmen are not being consulted on the problems of raising revenues for local municipal services and the updating of zoning laws and regulations in most New Jersey communities.

2.   Regional Growth and Local Government

Joseph A. Aramanda
President
J. I. Kislak Realty Corp.
Newark, New Jersey

I very much appreciate the opportunity to appear on this panel, and I am certainly most impressed at the scope of this two-day conference on land-use planning and development. The choice of the conference's theme—Land-Use Planning and Development—indicates how greatly our attitudes toward New Jersey's environmental resources have changed from being mainly a matter of private interest to one of public concern. Quite frankly, I doubt if this conference would have been considered feasible ten or even five years ago.

What has happened since then, of course, if that—for one reason or another—the public has come to redefine living values. As a result, ecology, which is precisely defined as the study of the relationships between organisms and their environment, has become a household word, connoting the preservation and enhancement of our total land supply.

In the process, "save the environment" has become the slogan to rally many enthusiastic and well-meaning people in support of many particular causes and special interests. Unfortunately, the aims of all these efforts often seem to be at odds one with another because, except for conferences such as this one, there has been little effort to define terms, let alone reach agreement on land-use goals.

What precisely is meant by land enhancement or land improvement? How and for whom is the environment to be saved? And what are the costs involved—not just in dollars but in human values, social needs, and civic responsibilities?

Mayor Kenneth A. Gibson of Newark has said that wherever the cities of America may be headed, Newark will get there first. The same might be said of New Jersey as regards the environmental concerns of the entire country.

The smallest of the Middle Atlantic states, New Jersey is now the most densely populated of all states, even though two-thirds of our total land area remains farmland and forest. We are fortunate to have a very healthy economy with growth expectations that are based on a sound foundation of diversified business and industry. In addition, as is especially evident in the Bergen County communities, many of our towns serve as the suburban bedroom for New York and Philadelphia.

Industry is also moving into our suburbs, or seeking to do so. In the past three years, New York City has lost more than one quarter million jobs in both manufacturing and nonmanufacturing industries. New Jersey has gained more than its proportionate share—evidence of the belief by business that this state is a good place in which to live and work.

Yet our own "big six" cities are suffering from a variety of urban ills—decaying and inadequate housing, declining business, crime, disease, and staggering welfare problems. Despite the prime market for industrial space that exists in this state, there is a substantial amount of inner-city industrial space that is either underutilized or empty. In any consideration of environmental needs and problems, we should certainly remember that urban acreage is also a vital part of our total land resources.

Quite simply, our challenge, as both concerned private and corporate citizens of New Jersey, is to relate the growing, competitive demands of our population for residential, commercial, and industrial property to an ever-diminishing supply of available land. And we are attempting to meet this statewide challenge with a municipal home-rule philosophy that seeks to deny the urgency for a correlated regional approach to land-use planning. Even within the context of municipal home rule, many communities are unable to take effective measures for beneficial growth because their freedom of action is limited by carefully developed, overly detailed, and outdated master plans that are, in reality, unworkable in terms of the actual pressures of change.

The 1970 national census disclosed that more Americans now live in the suburbs than in central cities. In this respect, Bergen County might well serve as a case history for the nation. The 70 municipalities of Bergen County have a total population of 900,000, yet only 5 of these communities have more than 30,000 residents. With only 3 percent of the state's area, this county now houses 13 percent of its population—an increase of more than 120,000, or 15 percent, since 1960.

As every suburban homeowner is painfully aware, property taxes tend to rise with the population. Obviously, more people require more municipal services such as schools, fire, and police protection and waste collection and treatment—and the provision of all of these services must be based on each municipality's ability to raise revenue. As a result, New Jersey, which takes pride in having no state income tax, must admit to bearing one of the heaviest real property tax burdens in the entire country. Of all these expenses, school costs are, far and away, the highest single item. The Supreme Court's decision, last Wednesday (March 21, 1973), upholding the property-tax financing of public schools will not prove to be a boon to the homeowner, either. The suburban resident of an essentially middle-income town experiencing a rapid growth in population may not have to assume any of the burden of educating the children of the inner cities, but he will not obtain any relief from his own rising school costs from more affluent communities.

Because of the burden of local property taxes, many communities in New Jersey have sought to control their growth rate by means of stringent zoning that, in effect, becomes a competition to exclude on the part of neighboring towns.

In theory, every community recognizes that one realistic solution to the fiscal ills accompanying growth is to increase the total amount of municipal revenue. In theory, communities also recognize that new business and industry represents a sound means of increasing revenue by developing new ratables. Nonetheless, these same communities more often than not adhere to outmoded planning concepts and zoning codes that effectively prevent entry into the town of the businesses that can provide new sources of tax money. Even those that are willing to tolerate industrial acreage evidence little, if any, interest in providing room for housing to be occupied by the workers employed by the new business neighbors.

Certainly the problems of regional growth and the pressures of change they generate can be resisted on a short-term basis, but only on a short-term basis. Eventually, change must come in response to new orders of priorities—and the decisions by state and federal courts that establish these priorities.

I am sure that you are all aware of the class-action suit now pending which seeks to upset the zoning codes of four representative New Jersey municipalities. Whatever the disposition of the suit, the pressures for change resulting from growth in population and industry are not likely to lessen.

Change, however, can be managed so that its effects are mainly beneficial. It is the management of change that becomes the crucial factor in the continuing development of our land resources. For effective management of change to occur, individual municipalities must recognize the impact of regional growth and, beyond that, admit that there is nothing sacred or eternal in their existing master plans.

In any well-managed business, the line of products or services is under constant review by management to assure that what the company makes or provides meets the changing tastes and needs of its customers. No manufacturing method or marketing plan, however perfect it appeared to be at conception, is considered to be the final word.

Considered in terms of a business enterprise, the municipality's product is the quality of life it provides its residents. In order to assure that this quality remains acceptable and available at a reasonable cost, local governments should adopt the practices of business management and subject their master plans to review in light of the realities of changing needs. The analogy of municipal government to business management is certainly a reasonable one in terms of the skills required and costs involved. The operating budgets of almost all of New Jersey's middle-sized communities is equal to the cost of running a fair-sized business.

After all, the concerned homeowner is also an employee or the member of profession, even though he may not always remember that this dual interest exists. Still, if we believe in the value and efficiency of the management skills used in business, then we should also believe in the usefulness of their application to the day-to-day affairs of the communities in which we live.

Yet it is all too rare an occasion for a municipal government to seek the advice and counsel of its business community in the review or development of such major items of interest as zoning laws and means of generating revenues. In the case of a major city, for example, the expertise of resident bankers, realtors, and manufacturers might well prove useful in attracting new business to available, empty industrial space, thereby creating new jobs where they are needed. By the same token, the views of the business community and industry should be sought by planning boards charged with the responsibility for allocating land in response to the needs for residential, commercial, and industrial space.

Fortunately for the future, there are in this state many examples of communities in which local government has responded positively and imaginatively to the impact of changing trends in population growth and industrial expansion. By admitting the need for change and by management of change while it is still practical, these communities have taken major steps to assure their future viability.

In Bergen County itself, for example, there are 27 industrial parks. The locations of these parks have been chosen to provide the new industrial neighbors with convenient access to transportation without disruption to the residential sections of the communities. The towns obtain new ratables that will grow as the parks are developed, while the presence of new industry stimulates the economy in which the local merchants operate, and this increase in purchasing power benefits adjoining communities as well.

This is growth planned as it should be, with attention given to both immediate and future needs and with the basic recognition that flexibility must be built into all planning if the community's own well-being is to be assured. Without this flexibility and without municipal cooperation on a regional basis there can be no effective development, let alone enhancement, of our remaining land resources.

G. PANEL

THE SUBURBS AND LOW-INCOME HOUSING

Chairman: Mitchell Kahn, Assistant Professor of Social Work, School of Human Environment, Ramapo College of New Jersey, Mahwah, New Jersey

Members: Ernest Erber, Director of Research, National Committee Against Discrimination in Housing, Washington, D. C.

Roberta Svarre, Housing Coordinator, League of Women Voters of New Jersey

Peters Buchsbaum, Attorney, American Civil Liberties Union, Newark, New Jersey

Paul Davidoff, Director, Suburban Action Institute, White Plains, New York

Summary Report

Mitchell Kahn
Assistant Professor of Social Work
School of Human Environment
Ramapo College of New Jersey
Mahwah, New Jersey

This panel considered the issue of low-income housing in the suburbs from a number of related viewpoints. These included need, home rule, the legal basis, and the moral imperative. In addition, various solutions were discussed. Among these were regionalization of zoning, reforming of the local tax structure, subsidies to builders and consumers, fair-share formulas, rehabil·itation of inner-city housing, and housing allowances.

The Need for Low-Income Housing in the Suburbs

The impact of suburbanization is readily seen in the 1970 census data. As Mrs. Svarre pointed out in her presentation, a plurality of Americans now live in the suburbs. Some 36 percent of the American population lives in the suburbs, while 34 percent lives in rural areas, and 30 percent lives in the central cities. Perhaps of greater significance is the exodus of business and industry from the city. Over half of the jobs in the 15 largest metropolitan areas in the United States are located in the suburbs. A Regional Planning Association study indicated that of the one million new jobs that were created during the years 1960-67 in the New York Metropolitan Area, some 75 percent were in the suburbs. Those jobs that were created in New York City proper were of the professional and management type, which required greater skills and education than those possessed by the average low-income person. Mrs. Svarre referred to a study sponsored by the City of New York that found that over 80 percent of management level personnel stay with a company after it moves its plant or headquarters from the city to the suburbs, while over 75 percent of the nonexecutive personnel leave the company. The suburban housing situation is one of the prime reasons for this occurrence. As Mr. Erber pointed out in his opening remarks, housing opportunities for families earning less than $12,000 annually are

decreasing. For people with very low incomes, housing possibilities in the suburbs are minimal. It has become apparent that the
private housing market is not responding to the growth of business
and industry in the suburbs. There were 70,000 new jobs created
in Westchester County between 1960 and 1970, while during the
same period only 35,000 new housing units were built. Jobs
increased at a rate of 2 to 1 over new housing starts. The manifestation of what a Suburban Action Institute report called "the
suburban lock-out effect" is becoming obvious. The harshest
effects of this process fall on low-income people in the inner
city. Without suitable housing opportunity in the suburbs, they
benefit little from the job expansion there.

The exodus of industry from the cities to the suburbs also
has negative effects on the cities. A number of speakers noted
that there is a biracial social structure developing in the United
States. This was officially recognized by the Kerner Commission
when it noted that this nation is becoming two societies; one,
which is white and suburban, and the other, which is inner-city,
black, and poor. The migration of industry to the suburbs is
exacerbating this process. Suburbs, in their quest for tax ratables,
are shrinking the cities' tax bases.

The effects that this process has on cities can be seen
clearly using the example of Newark. First, the exodus of industry necessitates a rise in the property tax. In Newark this is now
in excess of $9 per $100 of assessed value. Thus, a person own-
ing a $30,000 home must pay $2,700 a year in property taxes.
Needless to say, this encourages middle-income people to leave
the city for the suburbs where, in most cases, the property taxes
are less than half of Newark's. Newark, increasingly deprived
of industrial tax ratables and a large middle-class, has become
insolvent. With 40 percent of Newark's population living at
poverty level or below, there is a greater need for social-service
expenditures without the additional income to meet them.

There is also an inverse effect that is created when Newark
residents who work in the suburbs cannot find housing there.
Mrs. Svarre described this sharply when she stated:

> Only 88 of the 5,000 workers at the Mahwah
> Ford plant actually live in Mahwah and can
> take advantage of the good schools that Ford's
> taxes provide. I think we'll accept the fact
> that capital and labor combine to provide the

> product that ends up paying taxes to Mahwah.
> Over half of Mahwah's school taxes are paid
> for by industry. Mahwah made the decision to
> invite industry in. Mahwah made the decision
> to zone its land into one- and two-acre devel-
> opments. Newark had nothing to do with any of
> these decisions. Yet Newark has to find the
> tax dollars to provide education and essential
> city services for the families of nearly 1, 000
> Ford workers. This is called the "spill-over
> effect" of local zoning. One town is stuck with
> the consequences of another's decisions. [1]

The suburbs cannot solve all the cities' problems on inequal-
ity, poverty, racial segregation, and fiscal crises, but the evidence offered here demonstrates that there is a substantive
relationship between these problems and suburban affluence. It
is also evident that the suburbs can help alleviate them with
more flexible housing practices regarding low- and middle-income
housing.

The Limits to Home Rule

Over 150 years ago, the French diplomat Alexis de Tocqueville
noted that much of the strength of American democracy was rooted
in the decentralized and highly participatory local governments
that he observed in the late eighteenth and early nineteenth cen-
turies. Although local control and decentralized government are
ideals that have always been esteemed in the United States, there
is little question that they suffered a decline in the twentieth
century with the growth of corporate enterprise that, in turn,
necessitated the growth of big government. In land-use policy,
however, local governments have continued to play a significant
role. In the suburbs, home rule has been used to exclude minorities and low-income people. What are, and what should be, the
limits to home rule? The following discussion of this issue is
extracted from Paul Davidoff's presentation:

> Home rule is a basic ingredient of American life.
> As our nation grows larger in population, our
> society becomes more organized and controlled
> by private and public centralized bureaucracies.
> It becomes harder and harder for the individual
> to feel he is a part of the agencies that govern

his life and his opportunities in his community.
We have witnessed in the past decade a very
strong revolt against centralized power with the
demands for decentralized control of the schools,
and of course we have seen in the suburbs a
very strong advocacy of the mainenance of
local home rule. Citizens should be able to
control those items of public affairs which affect them most greatly and to share with larger
bodies of government that control over those
matters of state which affect a broader region.

In the field of housing there seems to be no
question that a locality should have a very
strong voice and strong control over the location and quality of residential development.
It has a right to see that the residential development that takes place within its borders is
not injurious to public health and safety.
Home rule poses no problems for either side
on this issue. But, the question is home rule
for whom? Our (SAI) theory is that the town
that receives power from the state to control
its local affairs does so in the interests of the
entire citizenry of the state. It must, in its
laws, act so as to provide equal opportunity
under its laws for all the citizens of the
state. . . .

A township as the agency of the state and
operating under the constitutions of the state
and the United States may not under law, so
we believe, act in such a way as to guarantee
the protection of the law for a privileged section of the population; privileged by its wealth
or its previous entry into the community. We
think that home rule, and that includes zoning,
must be inclusionary, not exclusionary. Home
rule is for all the people and it is here that I
think we have our major debate. We think it is
highly improper for a township, acting in the
interests of the citizens of the state, to regulate the liberty of those persons who wish to
build homes in that township, by mandating a
certain price tag on their development. . . .

It cannot regulate housing development, and
the health, welfare, and safety factors surrounding it, in such a way as to have a direct
result of segregating the citizenry of the state
into classes of those who can afford the protection offered by the law and those who
cannot. . . .

Also, a distinction must be made concerning
the roles of private wealth and public law.
And then to distinguish in the law between
public regulation and public acquisition through
purchase. Now let me start with the distinction between law and wealth. It is our theory
that in our free enterprise or quasi-free enterprise society that a man's wealth enables him
to acquire the property he wishes. If a man
wishes to reside in a garden apartment, or a
town house, or on one, two, or 100 acres of
land and if he has the money to enable him to
make that choice, he should have that choice.
. . . This is what private wealth achieves. On
the other hand, it is our view that the public
law, which is employed to regulate the quality
of development in the community, must be used
to preserve opportunity for all citizens; that is
the first distinction. The second distinction is
that when the public seeks to control what
occurs within its community and seeks to enhance the environmental conditions, it operates
in one of two ways. First, it does so through
the use of its police power, which regulates
the liberty of individuals in terms of the desire
of the state to accord a minimum level of convenience, comfort, safety, and health to all
of its citizens. However, when the community
seeks to enhance the benfits of residency, or
when it seeks to accommodate desires for something that is necessarily above the minimum
standards of health and safety in the community,
it must use its right of eminent domain. That
is, it should pay for these amenities. For
example, when we wish to build a highway or
public library, we do not demand that the owner

of the land build them. We condemn or purchase
the land and we pay for it. . . .

If a town wishes a great deal of open space for
its public, it should make land available by acquiring it. The problem of the post-war period
in the suburbs is that communities have sought
to achieve through regulation what they properly
should achieve through purchase. And why? It
is because, as Oliver Wendell Holmes said,
governments tend to choose the cheaper way.
But there is a very dire consequence in limiting
liberty in order to avoid payment. It goes beyond the exclusion of racial and economic
minorities. It goes to the effect of the nature
of government and the degree of freedom it permits its members. Suburbs can have the amenities they want without regulation if suburbanites
are willing either through public purchase or
private purchase to achieve it. In that way it
would be possible, if desired, to see that land
is not developed. That is the direct way.

The indirection of suburban control over development in the post-war period has led to finding
devices that would restrict development to only
those classes of development that would reward
the town through high assessment of the land,
and structures built on the land, in such a way
as to guarantee that a community would receive
more in taxes than it had to pay in services or,
at least, to minimize the discrepancy between
the two. The town we are in (Mahwah) is an
excellent example of this. It is beautifully
operated to bring in new industry and generate
tax revenue. It has brought Ford and other industrial establishments to town and it has at
the same time acted effectively to prohibit the
people who work at Ford and other industries
to be able to buy houses in Mahwah. It has
accomplished this by large lot zoning. Even
the cheapest shack would be expensive if
built on an acre or two in Mahwah. The land
price is so high that the developer must place
a high price tag on his homes if he is to make

a profit. I do not mean to speak solely of Mahwah.
I use it as an example because it has effectively
been able to bring in high tax ratables and keep
out activities that would generate high service
cost to the community. And it is our belief that
this has done violence to home rule because it
has been a discriminatory home rule that they
have imposed. It has been a home rule that has
been operated on behalf of the privileged of our
society.

The Legal Assault on Exclusionary Zoning

The panel's objective in this area was not to give a case by case
analysis of contested zoning laws in New Jersey, rather to note
the legal bases on which zoning laws could be contested. [2] Mr.
Buchsbaum, who led this discussion, stated that there were three
general theories on which to contest zoning ordinances; they are
"social theory, " equal protection under the Fourteenth Amendment,
and freedom to travel. The "social theory" is of major importance
because it is the one that has been used most frequently. Mr.
Buchsbaum describes its evolution:

The New Jersey Zoning Enabling Act, which
embodies the "social theory" put forth by Paul
Davidoff in his discussion of home rule, sets
forth the numerous purposes of zoning; among
these are conservation of the health and safety
of the township and promotion of the general
welfare. And this is where, as a legal matter,
the controversy is raised. In the past, the public welfare has been construed to mean the public welfare of a township, or borough, or whatever the municipality happens to be; and this,
in a time of less population pressure and less
turmoil in the cities, worked out reasonably
well. A town could have one-acre zoning and
open space and it would not have an ill effect
on anyone else. This luxury is no longer available to us. As a consequence, the courts, in
reviewing zoning ordinances, have begun to consider not only whether they serve the needs and
objectives of the people of a particular township,
but whether they serve the needs of the region

or state as a whole. This is the big change that
is being created in the law. So when a provision
like one-acre zoning or a minimum-floor-size
law comes up for review, the court may say,
"Fine, I realize that you want to conserve some
open space in your town, and maybe one-acre
zoning has some effect in that regard, but
there are a lot of people who want to move into
your township. The kind of housing that can be
built with your zoning is extremely expensive,
which makes it prohibitive. Therefore, you
must rezone, and rezone in such a way as, perhaps, to sacrifice some of the things you may
like in order to promote the good of the entire
region." This has been the major thrust in the
New Jersey cases to date.

Mrs. Svarre noted in her presentation that this is exactly the
interpretation used by Judge Furman in the Madison Township
case. Paralleling Mr. Davidoff's discussion of home rule, Mr.
Buchsbaum stated that "equal protection under the law" was also
a basis for overturning exclusionary zoning laws. Townships that
zone out the poor or racial minorities are, in effect, violating the
Fourteenth Amendment of the U.S. Constitution. However, few
plaintiffs in New Jersey have used this as the major part of their
argument.[3] A third basis on which to contest zoning could be the
"right to travel." Mr. Buchsbaum stated that this included the
right to relocate one's residence in the place of one's choice.
Restrictive zoning prevents this, thus violating a right that has
been granted since the founding of the American Republic.[2]

The Moral Imperative

Mr. Erber stated that it is important to investigate the issues surrounding low-income housing in the suburbs from the vantage
points of judicial, political, and economic power. Interspersed
among these are the interests of many groups—suburban homeowners, real-estate concerns, politicians, and inner-city ethnic
constituencies, to name a few. All have definite self-interests
in any housing policy. Yet most do not recognize the consequences
that suburban housing policy is having on the cities and the poor
who inhabit them. We must enlighten all the parties involved in
this problem if we are to have the least chance of solving it.
Mr. Erber stated that environmentalists must be made to incorporate

a concern for the population that is already here into their "limits to growth" philosophy. Suburbanites must be made to realize that suburbanization "has turned our central cities into disemboweled remnants of what they once were." Americans must be made to realize that legal equality is not sufficient to solve this problem. "Equality of result" is essential.

Mr. Buchsbaum noted that legal rulings overturning zoning ordinances do not create low-income housing in the suburbs. They may set the stage for its development, but they in no way guarantee it. He also pointed out that the equation between zoning and the construction of low-income housing is not an exact one. He used the example of Long Island, where there is minimal large-lot zoning and, withal, very little low-income housing has been constructed. It can be added that enabling legislation, such as the creation of the Urban Development Corporation in New York, which has strong state powers to build public housing, has also proved to be of limited value.

In the final analysis, it will take a genuine public commitment to solve this problem. And this commitment will have to embody a morality imbedded in American democracy. Mr. Buchsbaum expressed it well when he stated:

> I'd like to know how many people would be here
> if there were a Board in the 1880s, 1890s, and
> early twentieth century passing on whether they
> deserved to be here or not. A lot of people came
> to this country with nothing much more than the
> shirt on their back, and no one said of them that
> they had to pass muster. There's something
> profoundly antithetical to the spirit of American
> democracy in forcing people to live in certain
> areas, to jump through economic hoops, or to
> be a certain kind of person. This is not how
> this country has grown great. Essentially, some-
> thing is wrong, as much as you want to talk
> about the legalities of the situation. As with
> desegregation, with reapportionment, and with
> a lot of other issues that have become legal
> issues, the ultimate solution for us is an ac-
> ceptance of a moral responsibility to resolve
> the problem. What do we want this country to
> be? As someone who has worked for the ACLU,
> I am reluctant to throw around the term

"patriotism, " but I believe it has some relevance
here. To me patriotism is caring for the good of
the whole country, not just your own tax rate, or
your own particular comfort, or that of the people
immediately around you. Try to understand that
the people in Newark, New York, and Paterson
who are living in a situation that is undesirable
are Americans, too.

Mr. Erber cautioned that our moral impetus must be tempered
with a pragmatism that understands that building low-income
housing in the suburbs will not be a panacea for all the problems
associated with the poor. He stated:

The victims of poverty live by the standards,
ethics, and views of property that we have condemned them, and shaped them, to live by.
Even in new towns such as Columbia, Maryland, [4] of which I am a resident, the movement
of people from deteriorated slum environments
to new towns does not bring with it, automatically, a solution to social problems that are
created in the cities. I think that, in facing
the problems of opening up the suburbs to people
with low incomes, we will have to face their
problems. The price we will have to pay to
accomplish it will be to retrace the steps that
have already been taken during the last two
decades toward separating our metropolitan
areas into the increasingly unrelated halves
of outer city (suburbs) and inner city.

Moving Toward Solutions

If the construction of low- and middle-income housing in the suburbs is to become a reality, the objections of the vested interests
involved will have to be placated. Perhaps the most important
interest group that must be addressed is the suburban homeowner.
Of major importance to this group of people is the local property
tax. This tax is used by suburban communities to provide essential
services and education. As Mrs. Svarre pointed out in her presentation, this puts tremendous pressure on the local community to
use fiscal zoning. This is partly reflected in the fact that 40 percent of the munipalities in Bergen County are zoned for one-half

acre development or more. That some towns are highly successful at fiscal zoning is demonstrated by the town of Mahwah, which has 161 million dollars in tax ratables. Only half of these ratables are attributed to individual homeowners.

The structure of the property tax is inherently inequitable. Some towns, because of fiscal zoning, can provide more funds per capita for education and city services. Unless there is some uniform system of financing education throughout the state, fiscal zoning will be a major barrier to opening up the suburbs for low-income development. The solution most commonly mentioned is a state income tax. However, this must wait for legislative approval. Some action is necessary because the State Supreme Court has ruled that the present system of financing education in the state is neither "thorough" nor "efficient," and it has mandated that the state institute a system that satisfies both of these criteria.

Regionalization of zoning was also discussed as a possible solution. Mrs. Svarre made mention of Governor Cahill's initiatives in this area. These have been incorporated into Assembly Bills 1419-22. She noted that:

> One of these bills, the Voluntary Balanced Housing Act, relates to the problem we are discussing today. Under this plan, the state will, every two years, draw up the housing needs of the state. These would be based on such considerations as job locations, environmental concerns, population, present housing trends, and housing needs. Then the amount of low- and moderate-income housing needed will be apportioned to the various counties. After hearings at the county level, the county planning board would apportion these requirements among the local communities. If, under the plan, the town chooses to comply, it will receive a certificate of compliance.

> Governor Cahill's approach is very pragmatic. What he is saying to these municipalities is, "If you go along with us and attempt to meet the housing needs of the region, we're going to protect you from Suburban Action." This approach will give the towns the opportunity to develop low- and moderate-income housing in

their own way. The governor is very interested
in protecting home rule. Yet he points out to
these communities that unless they use them
wisely, they may lose their home-rule powers
altogether.

Implied in regionalization of zoning is the concept of "fair
share" formulas, whereby each township will be asked to develop
so many units of low- and middle-income housing. The question
arises, is the concept of fair share enough? Mr. Davidoff
responded:

> No community has ever done all it could for any
> class of society. A community is an agency of
> the state. It must, at all times, be open in
> terms of where it has room for residential devel-
> opment for all of its citizenry. It cannot say,
> "We have carried our white man's burden far
> enough. We have built our share of low-income
> housing or elderly housing." There is never an
> end. Fair share is a good understanding of what
> it would mean, in our society, if we acted in
> an equitable way to end urban blight and related
> problems. But building new housing in the sub-
> urbs and in new communities would only be a
> beginning. At all times, if we are to have a
> just society, the community must be open to
> all citizens.

Mr. Erber continued the discussion of fair-share housing,
noting some of the places where it has been implemented and
showing its usefulness as a tool in the creation of low-income
housing in the suburbs. He stated:

> This is not just simply the moral concept that
> everybody should take a fair share of low-
> income housing. The concept has been devel-
> oped as an extension of regional planning in a
> number of metropolitan areas; beginning in
> Dayton, Ohio, where the Miami Regional Plan-
> ning Board has a constituency consisting of
> the city of Dayton and the surrounding suburban
> counties. The board had the job of selling the
> idea of fair-share housing, which one speaker

has called the "white man's burden. " I think
this has a very pejorative connotation, and I
would rather call it Metropolitan Planned Housing Allocation. . .Low-cost housing is being
built in the suburbs of Dayton under such a
provision. A number of other metropolitan
areas have followed Dayton's lead.

In the twin cities of Minneapolis and St. Paul,
the Metropolitan Planning Board has been
granted broad powers by the state legislature.
It has initiated a regional property tax and
allocates low-income housing in a more sophisticated way than Dayton's point system. It
takes into account factors such as access to
employment.

San Bernardino, California, now has such
planned housing allocation for all of San Bernardino County. The Washington metropolitan
area has also adopted a plan, though with
numerous shortcomings, and there are at least
a dozen other metropolitan fair-share plans
that are in various stages of development. So
this is a tool that has great potential. One of
the problems, of course, is that this particular solution is harder to get off the ground
since the Nixon Administration announced termination of all subsidized housing programs.
Without subsidized housing programs, fair-
share or planned-unit allocation becomes
rather meaningless.

Federally subsidized programs in the past have favored middle
income home buyers. While the FHA has guaranteed some 10 million mortgages in the suburbs (since 1949), only 800, 000 units of
low-income housing have been built. Most of these are of the
high-rise variety, similar to that of the disastrous Pruitt-Igoe
project in St. Louis. This policy should be turned around so as
to permit greater subsidization of low-income housing in the suburbs. Mr. Erber noted the current move away from this prospect
due to President Nixon's intention to replace subsidies with
housing allowances. He explained that this plan embodies the
"trickle down" theory, and he noted the likely consequences when
he stated:

This proposal [housing allowances] would permit
a person paying $90. 00 a month rent to obtain an
apartment of, let's say, $125. 00 a month. This
is supposed to help a person move up the
escalator. . . .

All I can see of this is that I think we are going
to finance the expansion of the ghetto and
hasten the process of turning our cities into
homes for the poor and the black and hasten the
white exodus to the suburbs. It will also strike
down fair-share and planned-unit allocation
on a metropolitan basis.

Mr. Davidoff carefully explained how government subsidies
for low-income housing could be used to build garden apartments
and town houses in the suburbs. In a brief overview of the Suburban Action Institute's proposed planned community, Ramapo
Mountain, Mr. Davidoff showed that through the use of innovative
building technologies, economies of scale, efficient use of land,
and the creative use of subsidies, low- and moderate-priced
homes could be delivered to needy consumers.

Another way of providing more housing to poor people is
through the rehabilitation of slum housing. However, it is 70-100
percent more costly to rehabilitate a building than to build a new
one. Even with rehabilitation of his building, a resident would
still live in a ghetto area that has few social amenities and a
shrinking job market. Mr. Erber noted that there were a number
of successful rehabilitation projects completed, but many of these
did not serve the interests of low-income people. Such an example
is the Georgetown section of Washington. Mr. Erber cautioned
that rehabilitation was a very risky and expensive venture and
that, before it is undertaken, a realistic cost-benefit analysis
should be made. A number of panelists agreed that rehabilitation
of housing in the central cities is only a partial solution to the
problem of meeting a metropolitan area's housing needs.

Conclusion

Almost 4 million urban households live in housing that is classified as substandard. Most of this housing is located in areas
with high social-morbidity statistics and a declining job market.
The creation of low-income housing in the suburbs is one way to
help alleviate this problem. The panel members noted the

complexities of the problem and the difficulty in implementing possible solutions. It was generally agreed, however, that open housing in the suburbs is a humanitarian concern that must come to be accepted by everyone. The need for such an attitude is essential for the preservation of social order in this nation.

References

1. Editors' note: Mahwah, New Jersey, along with three other towns in northern Bergen County (Ramsey, Upper Saddle River, and Saddle River) are now involved in a civil suit brought by the Urban League of Essex County and the North Jersey Community Union (Newark). The constitutionality of the zoning laws and land-use policies of each town is now before the New Jersey courts. The Urban League et al. asserts that the communities that, through their zoning laws, favor industry and large-plot residential development and restrict apartment houses are, as a result, excluding low- and moderate-income citizens from living in suburban communities. No judicial decision has been made at this date. Urban League of Essex County et al. v. Township of Mahwah et al., Superior Court of New Jersey, February 17, 1972.

2. Editors' note: Professor Jerome Rose's paper (III. H. 2) discusses all the major New Jersey cases on exclusionary zoning.

3. Editors' note: The only case that has used the "equal protection" argument as the major basis for its case is the one mentioned in Ref. 1.

4. Editors' note: Columbia, Maryland, is a totally new city. Many housing experts have argued that new towns such as this are a major way of providing balanced communities that contain representative percentages of groups found in the larger society.

H. PANEL

THE CHANGING NATURE OF ZONING LAW IN NEW JERSEY:
JUDICIAL DECISIONS

Members: Jerome G. Rose, Professor of Urban Planning at
Livingston College, Rutgers University, New
Brunswick, New Jersey

Daniel Bernstein, Attorney, Plainfield, New Jersey

Thomas Norman, Attorney, New Brunswick,
New Jersey

Michael J. Dwyer, Attorney, Ridgewood,
New Jersey

1. Introduction

This panel consisted of a summary and discussion of Professor
Jerome Rose's paper, "Judicial Trends in New Jersey Zoning Law:
The Balanced Community." This paper is reprinted in its entirety
because of its comprehensive treatment of recent significant
land-use decisions made in New Jersey courts.

Because New Jersey has had strong home rule, with a relatively weak state government, the challenges to local zoning
usually begin in one of the 568 municipal units. Many communities are now facing court suits on their local zoning ordinances.
Since the state has not, at this juncture, assumed a leadership
role in land-use-allocation legislation, those who are dissatisfied, such as builders and civil rights groups, have turned to the
courts to invalidate specific zoning laws, such as those that
restrict construction of apartments and low-income housing.
(See III. G, on low-income housing.)

In many of the recent cases, Professor Rose found that the
major concept that appears to be emerging from New Jersey court
decisions on zoning is that there is a need to have a "balanced
community." This concept, and what it means, is now being

131

considered by the Supreme Court of New Jersey in the Madison
Township case. In this case, the lower court held that the entire
town zoning ordinance was invalid because it failed to promote
a reasonably balanced community in accordance with the concept
of general welfare.

What does the court mean by balance? Rose suggested how
complex the court's definition of balance is in terms of guidelines for public policy. Does it refer to socioeconomic balance
or to fiscal balance? Or does it mean regional balance? If it
means socioeconomic balance, does it mean that each community
must allocate permits for housing construction on the basis of
current percentages of low-income families and racial-minority
representation in the state?

The courts in New Jersey are now major participants in the
policy-making process of land-use allocation. Dr. Rose indicated
that they will continue to show a willingness to decide questions
of land use until the state legislature begins to act. Since the
legislature has been reluctant to do so, he regarded this "as an
unfortunate development because the nature of the problem is one
that is best resolved by the kinds of political negotiation and
compromise on which a democratic legislative process is based."

2. Judicial Trends in New Jersey Zoning Law:
    The Balanced Community*

Jerome G. Rose
Professor of Urban Planning
Livingston College
Rutgers University
New Brunswick, New Jersey

Numerous judicial decisions in New Jersey have held that "the
essence of zoning is to provide a balanced and well-ordered
scheme of activity."[1] In 1971, in the Madison Township case, [2]
a superior court held that the entire zoning ordinance of the
municipality was invalid on the grounds that "it failed to promote
reasonably a balanced community in accordance with the general
welfare. . ."[3] Thus, a "balanced community" seems to have become a standard of the validity of zoning regulation that, like
motherhood, receives public support even though many engage in
private practices to avoid it.

The "balanced community" standard of zoning validity has
been accepted quietly and without controversy. There is a sub-
liminal appeal to things that are "balanced." Psychologically,
"balanced" means healthy and upright; just as "unbalanced"
means unhealthy and maladjusted. Legally, "balance" means
equity and fairness on the scales of justice. Politically, a
"balanced community" indicates that there is something for everyone—a basic tenet for political survival. With such appealing
connotations there is little wonder that planners and lawyers have
been attracted to the proposition that a balanced community is
not only a goal of zoning regulation but is in fact a standard by
which its validity may be determined.

The primary shortcoming of "balanced community" as a societal
goal and legal standard is that it has many different meanings
under different circumstances. For example, "balanced community"
may be defined to include socioeconomic balance, fiscal balance,

---

ecological balance, regional balance, and temporal balance. This paper will examine each one of these definitions and then will examine the role of the courts in enforcing this standard.

Socioeconomic Balance

Does the standard of a "balanced community" require each municipality to contain any given proportion of the low-income and racial-minority residents of the state? To what extent does this standard determine the validity of zoning ordinances?

Zoning ordinances have been used to prevent members of racial minorities and low-income families from moving from the central cities to suburban areas. The effect of such exclusionary zoning laws is to concentrate the poor and racial minorities in the cities and to restrict the use of the suburbs to middle- and upper-class residents. As a result, cities are required to undertake the higher social-welfare costs of the poor and thereby bear a greater proportion of the costs that, in all fairness, should be more equitably distributed within the state. In addition to the dangers inherent in geographic polarization by race and class, the socioeconomic imbalance created by exclusionary zoning tends to deny to the excluded groups the opportunity for better housing, better schools, greater employment opportunities, and better municipal services. Such exclusion may be regarded as contrary to the ideals of democracy and has been held to be contrary to the principles of the U. S. Constitution.

In the early days of zoning, the U. S. Supreme Court invalidated a municipal ordinance that zoned the city into racial districts and restricted the use and occupancy in each district to members of the prescribed race. [4] More recently the court has said that "legal restrictions which curtail the civil rights of a single racial group are immediately suspect. That is not to say that all such restrictions are unconstitutional. It is to say that courts must subject them to the most rigid scrutiny. "[5]

Although there are many similarities between community imbalance based on race and imbalance based on class or wealth, the courts have nevertheless tended to treat racial discrimination differently than discrimination against the poor. A number of reasons have been proposed[6] to explain this difference in judicial treatment: (1) Race is an inherited characteristic, beyond the ability of a person to change; (2) poverty, unlike race, is more a matter of degree than of kind; (3) current morality permits acceptance of distinctions based on wealth more readily than distinctions based on race.

In spite of the differences between racial and economic imbalance, it seems very clear, as the Supreme Court has observed, that evidence is available to show that discrimination against low-income groups is, to a large extent, discrimination against racial minorities, thereby requiring the ordinance to be "scrutinized with great care."[7] It is also true that some zoning ordinances operate to exclude many middle-income-class families from the suburbs as well, but as the court said on another occasion, "the reality is that the law's impact falls [hardest] on the minority."[8] Thus an examination of the validity of laws excluding the poor is equally pertinent to the issue of racial balance as it is to the issue of economic balance within a community.[9]

Interstate Exclusion

When a state attempts to exclude the poor from its jurisdiction, the U.S. Constitution may be invoked to invalidate such exclusion. In Edwards v. California[10] the Supreme Court held that the right to move from state to state is a constitutionally protected right under the Commerce Clause of the Constitution. Justice Douglas agreed with the decision of the majority but, in a concurring opinion, asserted that interstate travel is protected by the Constitution because it is one of the privileges and immunities of U.S. citizenship.[11] More recently, in Shapiro v. Thompson,[12] the Supreme Court invalidated the laws of several states that imposed a one-year residency requirement on applicants for welfare assistance. This time the court held that such restriction violated the Equal Protection Clause of the Fourteenth Amendment. In an opinion written by Mr. Justice Brennan, the court said:

> The purpose of deterring the immigration of indigents cannot serve as justification for the classification created by the one-year waiting period, since that purpose is constitutionally impermissible. . . . More fundamentally, a state may no more try to fence out those indigents who seek higher welfare benefits than it may try to fence out indigents generally.[13]

Intrastate Exclusion

For the past two decades zoning laws have been used extensively in New Jersey as a device by which some municipalities have sought to exclude the poor from other municipalities within the state. In a series of decisions, in a period from 1952 to 1963, the New Jersey Supreme Court has upheld such zoning devices to exclude the poor as minimum floor-space requirements, [14] minimum lot size requirements, [15] prohibition of construction of multifamily units, [16] prohibition of mobile homes on individual lots, [17] and prohibition of mobile-home parks anywhere in the township. [18]

In the past few years the courts seem to have moved away from this early line of decisions, and a judicial principle seems to be evolving from recent New Jersey decisions that zoning law may not be used to exclude people on the basis of wealth or socio-economic status.

In 1970, in DeSimone v. Greater Englewood Housing Corp., No. 1, [19] the New Jersey Supreme Court held, in an opinion written by Justice Hall, that

> Public or semi-public housing accommodations
> to provide safe, sanitary and decent housing,
> to relieve and replace substandard living con-
> ditions or to furnish housing for minority or
> underprivileged segments of the population out-
> side of ghetto areas is a "special reason"
> adequate to meet that requirement of N. J. S. A.
> 40:55-39(d) and to ground a use variance.

Justice Hall's statement apparently is designed to offer the alternative that public or semi-public housing for either minorities or the underprivileged segment of the population would suffice to meet the "special reason" requirement of the cited use variance provision.

In 1971, two Superior Court decisions enlarged upon this evolving concept. In the Madison Township case[20] the court held invalid a township zoning ordinance that sought to restrict multifamily construction to about 500 to 700 additional units, none of which could contain three or more bedrooms and which divided most of the remaining vacant land to zones requiring one- and two-acre-minimum lots with minimum floor space of 1, 500 square feet and 1, 600 square feet, respectively. In a decision written by Judge Furman the court held the ordinance invalid because it "fails to promote reasonably a balanced community in accordance with the general welfare." The court cited with approval a statement in a recent Pennsylvania decision:

> The question posed is whether the township can stand in the way of the natural forces which send out growing population into hitherto undeveloped areas in search of a comfortable place to live. We have concluded not. A zoning ordinance which primary purpose is to prevent the entrance of newcomers in order to avoid future burdens, economic or otherwise, upon the administration of public services and facilities cannot be held valid. [21]

Later in 1971 the Superior Court held invalid a Glassboro zoning ordinance requiring that new apartments contain at least 70 percent of the units with no more than one bedroom, no more than 25 percent with two bedrooms, and no more than 5 percent with three bedrooms, and also requiring such expensive amenities as a swimming pool or tennis court, central air conditioning, and automatic garbage disposal. [22] The court determined that the ordinance was designed to restrict the population to adults and to exclude children because of the municipal cost of education. In responding to that finding the court said:

> There is a right to be free from discrimination based on economic status. There is also a right to live as a family and not be subject to a limitation on the number of members of that family in order to reside any place. Such legal barriers would offend the equal protection mandates of the Constitution. [23]

Then, in 1972, the Superior Court held, in unequivocal terms, that a Mount Laurel zoning ordinance that prohibited multifamily dwellings, except on a farm for farmers, is invalid for the reason that such ordinance discriminates against the poor and deprives them of adequate housing and the opportunity to secure subsidized housing. [24] In a decision written by Judge Martino the court said that it would be an improper use of the zoning power "to build a wall against the poor income people." [25]

Thus, in the past two years, the New Jersey courts appear to have formulated a principle that a well-balanced community requires some undetermined amount of social balance and that zoning laws may not be used to exclude people of low income from the jurisdiction.

Fiscal Balance

Does the obligation of elected municipal officials to provide essential municipal services within the limits of available revenue permit the use of the zoning power to maintain its fiscal balance?

The limited sources of municipal revenue and the increasing costs of municipal services provide an annual challenge to responsible officials to find ways to achieve the fiscal balance required by law and political survival. In their effort to maintain fiscal balance municipal officials tend to stimulate industrial and commercial rather than residential development. The zoning power is used to exclude housing to limit the need for school construction and other costs made necessary by increased population.[26] The term "fiscal zoning" is applied to zoning laws enacted for this purpose.

One of the most frequently posed questions of zoning law today is whether fiscal zoning is valid. An analysis of the New Jersey decisions reveals that the answer to this question depends upon whether the court determines that the zoning power is used: (1) to increase ratables and revenue, or (2) to decrease residential development and municipal costs.

Fiscal zoning to increase revenue

When the court can characterize the purpose of the fiscal zoning as an effort to increase ratables and revenue, the law will be upheld as a proper exercise of the zoning power. This principle was stated in Ward v. Montgomery Tp.[27] as follows:

> The conclusion is inescapable that the township was hungry for tax revenue. Manifestly, its fiscal picture was such that a new source of income would serve the general economic welfare. Pursuit of that objective was entirely worthy of the attention of the municipal fathers. And its achievement through land use regulation will not warrant judicial condemnation as long as it

represents an otherwise valid exercise of the
statutory zoning authority. If the amendment
of the ordinance is compatible with and furthers
a legitimate comprehensive plan for the zoning
of the municipality within the contemplation of
the statute, N.J.S.A. 40:55-32, it is legally
unobjectionable. The fact that increased tax
revenue is intended to result therefrom, or
that an individual property owner may be bene-
fited incidentally does not justify a charge of
perversion of power. . . .

When Justice Hall was a member of the Superior Court, he
was called on to answer the question whether a municipality may
use its zoning power to achieve fiscal balance by encouraging
the use of land for industrial ratables. In Newark, etc., Cream
Co. v. Parsippany-Troy Hills Tp., [28] he responded by noting that
the exercise of the zoning power was not limited to measures designed to serve the public health, safety, and morals. The zoning
power may also be used for the public convenience and general
prosperity of the jurisdiction. Justice Hall then stated:

The essence of zoning is to provide a balanced
and well-ordered scheme for all activity deemed
essential to the particular municipality . . .
Subject to the rule of reason, the kind of community and the kind of balance is exclusively a
matter for local legislative determination . . .
I conclude that a zoning scheme seeking balanced
land use to obtain a sound municipal economy by
encouraging industry on which taxes may be
levied to help meet the deficit in the cost of
municipal services to home owners is a proper
exercise of the zoning power, subject always
to the reasonableness of the classification and
regulations enacted to achieve the end both
generally and with respect to particular property. [29]

Fiscal zoning to exclude residential development

In the past few years a number of New Jersey decisions have
distinguished exclusionary fiscal zoning from the revenue-raising
zoning cases cited above and have held fiscal zoning to exclude
residential development to be invalid. In the Madison Township

case[30] it was conceded that the underlying objective of the zoning law in question was fiscal zoning, designed to avoid school construction and other costs resulting from increased population. [31] The Superior Court agreed that the use of the zoning power to alleviate "the tax burden and harmful school congestion" was valid if done "reasonably and in furtherance of a comprehensive plan."[32] However, the court held that the use of the zoning power to stabilize the tax rate by the exclusion of new low- and moderate-incoming housing was an invalid exercise of the police power.

In the Glassboro case[33] where the zoning law restricted the number of bedrooms in a garden-apartment complex, the court rejected the argument that judicial sanction may be given to municipal efforts to avoid an increase in the tax burden. [34] Even though the testimony persuaded the court that the municipal cost of education of children in the proposed project exceeded the tax revenue to be derived therefrom, nevertheless the court held that the municipality could not validly use its zoning power to restrict its population to adults and to the exclusion of children. The court said:

> The effort to establish a well balanced community
> does not contemplate the limitation of the number
> in a family by regulating the type of housing. The
> attempt to equate the cost of education to the
> number of children allowed in a project or a
> community has no relation to zoning. The govern-
> mental cost must be an official concern but not
> to an extent that it determines who shall live
> in the municipality. [35]

A year later (1972) in the Mount Laurel case[36] involving a zoning ordinance prohibiting multifamily dwellings, Judge Martino reaffirmed the distinction between exclusionary fiscal zoning and revenue-raising fiscal zoning when he said:

> Local legislative bodies know better than to
> state that more low-income producing structures
> will mean a higher tax rate. This is what the
> courts have abhorred as fiscal zoning. . .
> What local governing body would raise an objec-
> tion to bringing a factory into a neighborhood
> because it would increase the population of
> the economically poor? While it may be an

argument that it would affect property values,
and while it is proper to zone in certain instances against factories, it is improper to
build a wall against the poor-income people. . .[37]

Thus the rule seems to have been established that fiscal
zoning for revenue increases may be valid but that fiscal zoning
to minimize municipal expenses by excluding people is invalid.
However, this principle may be more easily stated than applied.
The challenge of the courts during the next few years will be in
distinguishing between valid zoning amendments from residential
to light industrial[38] and invalid "insincere" industrial zoning
designed to exclude residential development.

Ecological Balance

Does the standard of a "balanced community" require each municipality to balance the ecological consequences of development
against the socioeconomic consequences of nondevelopment?

In recent years the courts have begun to recognize that
ecological and environment factors are entitled to greater weight
in creating the "balanced community" required for zoning validity.
This realization has been long in coming. In American history,
land development has been the essence of land-use policy. From
the Northwest Ordinance of 1787 to the Homestead Act of 1862,
to the large scale FHA mortgage insurance programs in aid of
home ownership in the 1950s, the objective of national land use
policy has been the development of land. Our property-tax system
accentuates this policy by assessing the value of vacant land for
tax purposes at its "highest and best use" for development. Thus,
in the absence of some form of tax relief[39] farmers, to avoid payment of high property taxes based on development value, are pres-
sured into selling their land for development. Only recently has
the goal of "urban development" been translated into the pejorative
"urban sprawl."[40] Only recently has consideration of the ecological consequences of development been weighed against the forces
of profit incentive, proprietary rights, municipal prerogative, and
social need.[41] When conflict arises between advocates of environmental protection and advocates of social need, i.e., low-
income housing, the encounter of these forces frequently produces
manifestations of acute ideological schizophrenia.

When this conflict reaches the courts, it usually takes the
form of an attack on the validity of floodplain zoning or

agricultural zoning. There are sufficient differences between the two to treat each separately.

Floodplain zoning

Floodplain zoning imposes restrictions on the use of lands that are useful in reducing flood levels by absorbing water from rains and runoff. To the extent that such land is covered with structures or paved surfaces, flooding and flood damage may be increased because the runoff is accelerated instead of being absorbed into the ground. Floodplain zoning also restricts the use of wetlands for the purpose of preserving its spongelike capacity to create a natural detention basin for flood waters in time of heavy rainfall.

The validity of such a zoning ordinance in New Jersey was considered in Morris County Land Improvement Co. v. Parsippany-Troy Hills Township. [42] In a decision written by Justice Hall, the New Jersey Supreme Court held zoning ordinances restricting the use of land for flood water detention purposes to be invalid because it constituted a taking of land for public purpose without just compensation. Although the court conceded that the determination of whether any zoning ordinance is a valid regulation or an invalid taking is always a matter of degree but that "there is no question that the line has been crossed when the purpose and practical effect of the regulation is to appropriate private property for a flood water basin or open space."[43] The court stated that public acquisition rather than regulation was required and pointed to the authority granted to governmental agencies to purchase or condemn property needed for flood control.[44]

Until recently, the Parsippany-Troy Hills case represented the prevailing judicial attitude in most states toward environmental zoning.[45] However, in 1972 the courts of a number of states have begun to recognize circumstances in which ecological considerations may outweigh the owner's right to develop his land. The courts in Massachusetts[46] and Wisconsin[47] have upheld the validity of laws that prohibit the draining, filling, and dredging of wetlands even though the owner is thereby prevented from developing his land. In New York, the Appellate Division upheld an ordinance that rezoned land from multiple family dwellings to single family residences because of the town's ecological need for new systems of water supply and sewage disposal. The court held that the long range ecological considerations outweighed the owner's proprietary rights.[48]

In New Jersey, one of the unanswered questions of floodplain zoning is the effect of the Parsippany-Troy Hills decision on the recently enacted Flood Plains legislation. [49] This new law provides two forms of control: (1) It directs the State Department of Environmental Protection to regulate development of land in floodways, and (2) directs municipalities to regulate development of land in flood fringe areas within one year or submit to state regulations. The Parsippany-Troy Hills decision invalidated the zoning ordinance on constitutional grounds, i.e., that the ordinance resulted in an unconstitutional taking of private property without just compensation. It is likely that eventually the New Jersey Supreme Court will be asked to rule on the validity of this legislation. It will be interesting to see what changes, if any, have taken place in the past decade in the judicial attitude toward ecological considerations in the constitutional balance of interests. [50]

Agricultural zoning

The second category of cases in which the proponents of environmental protection are pitted against the proponents of proprietary rights are the cases involving agricultural zoning. [51] This type of zoning ordinance restricts the use of land to agricultural uses for the purpose of limiting the cost of municipal services, protecting the scenic quality of open space, preserving ecological balance and postponing the intrusion of problems associated with increased population. Agricultural zoning is distinguishable from floodplain zoning in that land zoned for agricultural use retains economic use without which the regulation would be confiscatory and invalid. [52]

The New Jersey courts have not been called on to determine whether the limited use of land for agricultural purposes is a reasonable use of the land so as to avoid the charge that the restriction constitutes an unreasonable economic burden and is therefore confiscatory and void. The legal problem is somewhat complicated in New Jersey by the fact that a New Jersey farmer may escape the burden of real property taxation resulting from assessment based on development value. The Farmland Assessment Act[53] permits a farmer to have his land assessed as agricultural rather than potential development value. The farmer who continues to use his land for farming can hardly claim that he is deprived of its reasonable use. The speculator-purchaser of farmland who avails himself of the tax benefits of the Farmland Assessment Act may be stopped from arguing unreasonable economic burden because of the affirmation of agricultural use required by the Act. In spite of the arguments for validity of agricultural zoning made possible by the Farmland Assessment Act, it is very likely that the New Jersey courts will not uphold agricultural zoning where a high development value of the land imposes an unreasonable and disproportionate burden on the landowner in order to achieve a public purpose.

Once it is clearly established that agricultural zoning is not a valid means of preserving open space in the path of urban development, responsible government officials will become reconciled to the necessity of public acquisition of such land with the payment of just compensation. The New Jersey Green Acres Land Acquisition Act of 1961[54] is a step in the right direction. However, it is unlikely that sufficient public funds could be made available to acquire all the land required to fulfill the open space needs of the state. It is very likely that purchase of less than the full fee simple, i. e., the development right, will be necessary to maximize the impact of the government acquisition program. Even better than that, it may be possible to preserve open space without any cost to government and with compensation to owners of preserved open space land by requiring owners of developable land to purchase the development rights of owners of "preserved land." Legislation to establish such a system has been proposed in Maryland and is being prepared in New Jersey.[55]

Regional Balance

Does the standard of a balanced community in accordance with the general welfare require a municipality to consider the needs and welfare of all of the people of the region or of the state?[56]

In a few states the zoning enabling legislation imposes an express obligation on municipalities to consider regional needs.[57] In a number of states, including New Jersey, the courts appear to be developing the principle that even in the absence of specific legislative instructions, nevertheless there is an implied obligation of municipalities to consider regional needs when enacting zoning ordinances.[58]

The argument for an implied requirement to consider regional needs is based on the most prestigious of zoning precedent. In the landmark case of Village of Euclid v. Ambler Realty Co.[59] the U. S. Supreme Court upheld a municipal zoning law designed to prevent the encroachment of central city industry into a suburban community. While recognizing the power of the local government to exclude industrial use within its boundaries, the court declared that in the future there might be "cases where the general public interest would so far outweigh the interest of the municipality that the municipality would not be allowed to stand in the way."[60]

In the nearly fifty years that have elapsed since the Euclid case the prophecy contained therein has come to pass: aggregations of urban population have created problems of water supply, solid-waste disposal, air and water pollution, transportation, education, and land-use control that transcend municipal boundaries. Courts, particularly in New Jersey, have begun to recognize circumstances where the general public interest (i. e., regional or state interest) so far outweighs the interest of the municipality that local zoning laws will not be allowed to stand in the way.

In 1949 the New Jersey Supreme Court expressed an awareness of the problem when in Duffcon Concrete Products v. Cresskill[61] it said:

> What may be the most appropriate use of any
> particular property depends not only on all the
> conditions, physical, economic and social, pre-
> vailing within the municipality and its needs,
> present and reasonably prospective, but also
> on the nature of the entire region in which the
> municipality is located and the use to which the
> land in that region has been or may be put most
> advantageously. The effective development of
> a region should not and cannot be made to de-
> pend upon the adventitious location of municipal
> boundaries, often prescribed decades or even
> centuries ago, and based in many instances on
> considerations of geography, of commerce, or
> of politics that are no longer significant with
> respect to zoning [emphasis added].

Nine years later the New Jersey Supreme Court once again expressed its self-conscious awareness of the problem when it upheld a zoning ordinance excluding apartments from a munici-pality but expiated that there was no showing of regional needs.[62] The court said:

> It is quite another proposition to say that a
> municipality of 960 acres must accept uses it
> believes to be injurious, in order to satisfy the

requirements of a county. There, of course, is
no suggestion that a county is so developed that
Hasbrouck Heights is the last hope for a solution, and hence we do not have the question
whether under the existing statute the judiciary
could resolve a crisis of that kind. [63]

Then, in 1971, in the Madison Township case[64] the Superior
Court declared the township zoning ordinance invalid on the
grounds that it failed to promote reasonably a balanced community
in accordance with the general welfare of the entire region. [65]
The following year the Superior Court invalidated the Mount Laurel
Township zoning ordinance where there was a finding that "it was
the intention of the township committee to take care of the people
of Mt. Laurel Township but not make any area of Mt. Laurel a
home for the county."[66] The court cited with approval the statement from Duffcon that the municipality must consider regional
needs in determining the appropriate use of land within the
municipality.

Taken together, these decisions indicate that even in the
absence of express statutory instructions to consider regional
needs, the New Jersey courts may impose a judicial requirement
that municipal zoning laws be consistent with regional needs.

Temporal Balance

Does the standard of "a balanced community" recognize and sanction the uneven and intermittent stages in which municipal development proceeds in time?

Balance within a community is not static; it is always in a
dynamic and changing state. The forces of social, economic,
political, and physical change constantly interact on each other
along a continuum of time. Today's community balance may become
tomorrow's imbalance. Today's placid and fallow fields may become a center of tomorrow's teeming activity. All components of
community structure do not grow and develop with equal and uniform progress. Houses, streets, utilities, water supply, schools,
and recreational facilities do not emerge abruptly as a monolithic
community infrastructure in the required proportions of a balanced
community.

The urban planning process is designed to provide plans and
programs for rational and interrelated community growth. Zoning

laws are enacted to allocate land to meet the projected community needs on which the plans are based. Until recently, zoning laws have not been devised to coordinate the sequence of development to maintain a community balance during the process of development over a period of time.

In 1972 the New York Court of Appeals was called on to determine the validity of a zoning ordinance that required land development to proceed only in accordance with such a plan for sequential development and timed growth. [67] The zoning ordinance of the town of Ramapo in Rockland County, New York, was based on a comprehensive master plan for future growth and upon a capital budget providing for the location and sequence of capital improvements for a period of eighteen years. Special permits for development would be issued only when designated services or facilities, such as public sewer, drainage, schools, roads, firehouses, and parks were available. A point system was created to assign values to each such facility, and a permit would be issued only when fifteen development points were applicable to the proposed development.

The New York court upheld the system even though development of the land could be prevented for a period of up to eighteen years. The court conceded that an ordinance that permanently restricted the use of property so that it could not be used for any reasonable purpose would constitute an unconstitutional taking of the property. However, the court characterized the restriction of use for up to eighteen years as a temporary restriction and concluded that the property could be put to a reasonable use within a reasonable time.

The question whether the New Jersey courts would uphold an eighteen-year restriction of land use would be answered by Lomarch v. Mayor of Englewood. [68] In Lomarch the court held that an Official Map Act providing for a "freeze" on development of land for a one-year period would be an unconstitutional deprivation of property unless the owner was compensated for the "option" price of the "temporary taking." Based on this decision there is little reason to assume that the New Jersey court would accept the reasoning in the Ramapo case than an eighteen-year postponement of use in only a "temporary restriction" rather than a permanent deprivation; nor would the New Jersey court accept Ramapo's reasoning that the restriction is "substantial but not absolute."

Nevertheless, there is appeal to the argument that rational and comprehensive planning contemplates a process of development over a period of time and that it is reasonable to assume that the development will take place sequentially rather than all at once. Some land will be developed before others, and some land will not be "ripe" for development until community services and facilities are available. Therefore, it does not seem unreasonable to permit zoning law to regulate that development to take place in an orderly way.

The Court as a Balancing Agent

When a court determines that a municipality has failed to comply with the requirements of, or has exceeded the authority granted under, the zoning enabling legislation, it will find such exercise of power to be ultra vires and invalid. If the court finds that a municipal zoning ordinance imposes an unreasonable burden upon a person or unreasonably discriminates against him, the ordinance will be declared a violation of the due process clause or equal protection clause of the Fourteenth Amendment. In all cases the role of the court is negative. Its decision invalidates the ordinance but does not provide the affirmative measures necessary to create the desired "balance" in the community. This form of decision is in accordance with the traditional role of the judiciary in our governmental system.

Under the traditional view, it is the function of the legislature to formulate public policy and to enact laws to carry out this policy. The courts may not intervene in this process unless and until a real issue arises involving the application of those laws. As applied to an imagined "scale of community balance" the traditional role of the court would be only to remove those zoning laws that upset the balance. The courts may not add a new program or develop an affirmative plan to restore equilibrium.

This traditional role of the courts seems to be changing. Courts have begun to take a more active role in seeking community balance by requiring affirmative municipal action to redress the alleged legal wrong. Numerous federal courts have assumed this role in the past few years. In 1972 a New Jersey Superior Court adopted this role in prescribing its remedy.

The Gautreaux case[69] has attracted national attention because of the seven-year battle involving the Federal Court and the Chicago City Council. The court ordered the Chicago Housing

Authority to adopt a policy of site selection for public housing
that would place public housing in white communities in an effort
to achieve racial integration. The court directed the Chicago
Housing Authority to build integrated public housing on sites in
accordance with a detailed and comprehensive program and time
table. This order was affirmed by the Court of Appeals. The
Supreme Court denied certiorari. The Housing Authority was
unable to comply with this order because the Chicago City Council
refused to approve the sites for integrated public housing in white
areas. In April 1972, the court ordered the Housing Authority to
disregard the City Council requirements and to acquire the property for housing in the designated white sections of town.

In another public housing case[70] a federal district court
ordered county officials to join with the municipal authorities in
finding sites for public housing outside the central city. In its
decision the court said, "For better or worse, both by legislative
act and judicial decision, this nation is committed to a policy
of balanced and dispersed public housing [emphasis added]." On
appeal, the decision and remedy were upheld by the Court of
Appeals for the Fifth Circuit.[71] In another decision[72] municipal
officials were ordered to submit a plan that would equalize municipal services within the jurisdiction. In an earlier case[73] the
court ordered municipal officials to devise a plan to accommodate
the needs of low income families including public housing and
"requiring the exercise of the fiscal and eminent domain powers
of the city if such be necessary and reasonably feasible under
the law to accomplish the objective . . ." The city officials were
ordered to report back to court every three months to show progress in complying with the court order.

With this background and judicial precedent, the New Jersey
Superior Court in 1972 in the Mount Laurel case[74] ordered affirmative municipal action to eliminate the economic discrimination
perpetrated by the municipal zoning ordinance. The court ordered
the municipality to do four things: (1) undertake a study to determine the extent of the housing needs of the community; (2) determine the number of low and moderate income housing units
necessary to meet those needs; (3) develop a plan of implementation to accomplish that goal; and (4) report and describe any factors
that interfere with the implementation of the plan.

Thus, the courts seem to have undertaken the delicate and
difficult task of maintaining community balance that the legis-
latures have been reluctant to accept. This is an unfortunate

development because the nature of the problem is one that is best resolved by the kinds of political negotiation and compromise on which a democratic legislative process is based. The legislative process has defaulted on this critical issue, and as Governor Cahill predicted,[75] if the legislature fails to meet its responsibility, there will be no alternative but for the courts to step in and fill the void.

References

1. J. D. Construction Corp. v. Board of Adjustment of Freehold, 119 N. J. Super. 140, at 147 (1972); Kozesnik v. Montgomery Township, 24 N. J. 154, at 169 (1957); Berdan v. City of Paterson, 1 N. J. 199, at 204 (1948).

2. Oakwood at Madison, Inc. v. Township of Madison, 117 N. J. Super. 11 (1971).

3. Ibid., at 21.

4. Buchanan v. Warley, 245 U. S. 60 (1917). Although legal scholars have debated this point, this decision was based on the reasoning that the zoning ordinance constituted an unreasonable deprivation of the property of the white seller rather than a deprivation of the black purchaser's equal protection of the laws.

5. Korematsu v. United States, 323 U. S. 214 (1944).

6. See Note, "Exclusionary Zoning," 84 Harv. L. R. 1645, 1657 (1971).

7. Bolling v. Sharpe, 347 U. S. 497, 499 (1954).

8. Hunter v. Reickson, 393 U. S. 385, 391 (1969).

9. "Careful examination on our part is especially warranted where lines are drawn on the basis of wealth or race, two factors which would independently render a classification highly suspect and thereby demand a more exacting judicial inquiry." McDonald v. Board of Election Commissioners, 394 U. S. 802, 807 (1969).

10. 314 U. S. 160 (1941).

11. Ibid., at 177-186.

12. 394 U. S. 619 (1969).

13. Ibid., at 631.

14. Lionshead Lake Inc. v. Wayne Tp., 10 N.J. 165 (1952), app. dism 344 U.S. 919 (1953).

15. Fisher v. Bedminster Tp., 11 N.J. 194 (1952).

16. Fanale v. Hasbrouck Heights, 26 N.J. 320 (1958).

17. Napierkowski v. Gloucester Tp., 29 N.J. 481 (1959).

18. Vickers v. Gloucester Tp. Committee, 37 N.J. 232 (1962),

19. 56 N.J. 428 (1970).

20. Oakwood at Madison, Inc. v. Township of Madison, 117 N.J. Super. 11 (1971).

21. National Land and Investment Co. v. Kohn, 419 Pa. 504, 215 A. 2d 597 (1965).

22. Molino v. Mayor and Council of Borough of Glassboro, 116 N.J. 195 (1971).

23. Ibid., at 204.

24. Southern Burlington Co. NAACP v. Tp. of Mt. Laurel, 119 N.J. 164 (1972).

25. Ibid., at 176.

26. Gruber v. Mayor and Township Comm. of Raritan Tp., 39 N.J. 1; 9 (1962).

27. 28 N.J. 529, 535 (1959).

28. 47 N.J. Super. 306 (Law Div. 1957).

29. Ibid., at 328.

30. Supra, note 2.

31. Ibid., at 18.

32. Ibid., at 18.

33. Supra, note 22.

34. Ibid., at 203.

35. Ibid., at 203.

36. Supra, note 24.

37. Ibid., at 176.

38. Gruber v. Mayor and Township Comm. of Raritan Tp., supra, note 26.

39. Infra, note 53 and discussion pertaining thereto.

40. See note, "The Scope of State and Local Action in Environmental Land Use Regulation, " 13 Boston Col. Inc. & Com. L. R. 782 (1972).

41. On January 13, 1973, New Jersey Governor William Cahill suggested that we strike a balance between economic growth and sound environmental planning. In talking about the New Jersey coastal region he said:

> The area is under intense and constant development pressure which threatens to destroy its precious environmental assets. The pressure must be balanced against environmental demands. This balance cannot be achieved piecemeal, but must be accomplished on a region-wide basis [emphasis added]. New Jersey Environmental Times, Vol. 5, No. 3, Jan. 1973, pp. 1, 4.

42. 40 N. J. 539 (1963).

43. Ibid., at 555.

44. E. g., N. J. S. A. 58:16A-1 et seq. and N. J. S. A. 40:69-4. 1 et seq. See also New Jersey Green Acres Land Acquisition Act of 1961, N. J. S. A. 13:8A-1, et seq. for similar authority for open space, parks, playground and conservation purposes.

45. E. g., Vartelas v. Water Resources Comm'n., 146 Conn 650, 153 A. 2d 822 (1959).

46. Turnpike Realty Co. v. Town of Dedham, 72 Mass. 1303, 284 N. E. 2d 891 (1972).

47. Just v. Marinette County, 201 N. W. 2d 761 (Wis. 1972).

48. Nattin Realty Inc. v. Ludewig, 67 Misc. 2d 828 (Sup. Ct. 1971), aff'd. 40 A. D. 2d 535 (1) (2d Dep't. 1972).

49. Stat. N. J. Acts. Ch. 185 Public Laws of 1972, App'd. Dec. 14, 1972.

50. Although the decision was not based on this issue, Judge Furman felt obliged to recognize the relevance of ecological considerations in the Madison Township case. In the last substantive paragraph of the opinion in that case the court said:

Only engineering data and expert opinion and,
it may be, ecological data and expert opinion
could justify the ordinance under attack. These
were lacking both in the legislative process and
at the trial. The record fails to substantiate
that safeguarding against flood and surface
drainage problems and protection of the English-
town acquifer would be reasonably advanced by
the sweeping zoning revision into low population density districts along the four water
courses and elsewhere or the exclusionary
limitations on multi-family apartment units.

It would seem that from this day forward no zoning litigation
will be complete without the presentation of ecological
experts by both sides.

51. See note, "Protection of Environmental Quality in Nonmetro-
politan Regions by Limiting Development, " 57 Iowa L.R.
126, 143 (1971).

52. Katobimar Realty Co. v. Webster, 20 N.J. 114, 122, 118 A.
2d 824, 828 (1955); Morris County Land Improvement Co. v.
Parsippany-Troy Hills Tp., 40 N.J. 539 (1963).

53. N.J.S.A. 54:4-23.1.

54. N.J.S.A. 13:8A-1 et seq.

55. See Rose, "Development Rights Legislation May Change the
Name of the Real Estate Investment Game, " 1 Real Estate
Law Journal (Winter, 1973).

56. For a general discussion of this issue, see Walsh, "Are
Local Zoning Bodies Required by the Constitution to Consider
Regional Needs?" 3 Conn. L.R. 244 (1971).

57. E.g., Colo. Rev. Stat. Sec. 106-2-14 (1963); 9 Del. Code
Ann. Sec. 2603 (a) (1953).

58. In addition to the New Jersey decisions discussed herein
recent Pennsylvania decisions have required municipalities
to consider regional needs. E.g., in re Kit-Mar Builders,
439 Pa. 466, 268 A.2d 765 (1970); in re Girsh, 437 Pa. 237,
263 A.2d 395 (1970). For other citations see Walsh, supra,
note 56 at 247-250.

59. 272 U.S. 365 (1926).

60. Ibid., at 390. See Weinberg, "Regional Land Use Control: Prerequisite for Rational Planning," 46 N.Y.U.L.R. 786 (1971).

61. 1 N.J. 509, 513 (1949).

62. Fanale v. Borough of Hasbrouck Heights, 26 N.J. 320, 139 A. 2d 749 (1958).

63. Ibid., at 328; 139 A. 2d at 753-54.

64. Supra, note 2.

65. Ibid., at 20-21.

66. Supra, note 24 at 169.

67. Golden v. Ramapo, 30 N.Y. 2d 359, 334 N.Y.S. 2d 138 (1972).

68. 51 N.J. 108, 237 A. 2d 881 (1968).

69. Gautreaux v. Chicago Housing Authority, 296 F. Supp. 907, 304 F. Supp. 736 (N.D. Ill. 1969), aff'd. as to program of relief, 436 F. 2d 306 (7th Cir. 1970), cert. denied, 402 U.S. 992 (1971).

70. Crow v. Brown, 332 F. Supp. 382 (N.D. Ga. 1971).

71. Ibid., aff'd per curiam, 457 F. 2d 788 (5th Cir. 1972).

72. Hawkins v. Town of Shaw, 437 F. 2d 1286 (5th Cir. 1971).

73. Southern Alameda Spanish Speaking Organization (SASSO) v. City of Union City, California, 424 F. 2d 291 (9th Cir. 1970).

74. Supra, note 24.

75. New Horizons in Housing: A Special Message to the Legislature, William T. Cahill, Governor of New Jersey, p. 5 (March 27, 1972).

IV. THE SEARCH FOR SOLUTIONS

New Directions for Land Use Policy

A.   INTRODUCTION

The second day of the conference dealt with the search for possible solutions to land-use problems in a state rated as the most urban in the nation.

The three main speakers suggested policies and programs that could be significant in problem resolution. Professor D. Bennett Mazur, who chaired this part of the program, outlined the dimensions and complexity of the environmental land-use choices we now face.

Mr. Richard Galantowicz of the North Jersey Conservation Foundation, a private conservation organization, saw the issue as one of intense urgency, that unless local and state governments act to provide a balanced environment, which includes protection for the natural resources of our land as well as housing for the populace, the courts have shown a willingness to assume that policy-making function.

He stressed the need for each town to include a natural-resource inventory in its master plan. This would enable local officials to include environmental variables as well as the business and residential needs of the citizenry in their considerations of the advisability of future development.

In order to maximize land-use efficiency, community planning should include or consider the feasibility of new towns, cluster development, or planned unit development.

A relatively new concept for preserving land that has intrinsic natural value was described: the purchase of property-development rights, a system in which property ownership and development rights are dealt with as separate commodities.

He examined the concept of regional distribution of revenues derived from the lucrative ratables possessed by the more wealthy towns. This policy would decrease the competition for industrial properties between communities.

157

Sidney Willis, assistant commissioner for Planning and Housing in the New Jersey Department of Community Affairs, pointed out that local dependence on the property tax has resulted in policies that encourage industry and discourage low-income housing. Like Mr. Galantowicz, he urged balanced planning, with regional needs taking first priority. Each, of course, stressed different aspects of balanced planning; one stressed environmental, the other social needs.

Mr. Willis pointed out that the newly proposed community-planning law now under consideration by the New Jersey State Assembly would bring about better local and regional planning due to (a) the fostering of cooperation between the three layers of government and (b) the setting of qualitative standards and procedures for local planning and zoning boards.

Thomas O'Neil, of the New Jersey State Department of Environmental Protection, articulated the state's intense concern over the results of rapid unplanned, and environmentally destructive, economic growth, which has deeply scarred New Jersey. He cited numerous new laws and regulations that indicate the trend of greater state involvement in land allocation policies, which have been, up to now, almost the exclusive jurisdiction of local government.

One of the strongest components of the state's program is the movement toward regional planning. Regional planning is already a fact, or has been proposed for the Pinelands (south Jersey), the Tocks Island area (northwest Jersey), and the Skylands Region (north central Jersey) of the state.

Land-use practices in New Jersey have been detrimental to the physical environment. Few would disagree with the contention that New Jersey must profit by its past mistakes in its formulation of future land-use planning goals. While the solutions offered here are many and appealing, the economic, social, and political barriers to their implementation are formidable.

OPENING ADDRESS

Livingston Goodman

Mayor
Mahwah, New Jersey

On behalf of the Township of Mahwah, let me welcome you to
Mahwah this morning on the second day of the conference, simply
by saying that it probably is fitting that this is being held here at
this time. That we are here at Ramapo College demonstrates one
aspect of Mahwah's land-use program; that Ramapo is here at all
demonstrates one aspect of the way Mahwah believes the land
should be used. You may recall that when the college was looking
for a site in 1970, there were many towns in Bergen County that
were hostile, but Mahwah was not.

When President George Potter and Dr. Joseph LeMay first
discussed this conference with the Township Committee, we explained the unusual and delicate situation we find ourselves in
because of the litigation over zoning ordinances. For wholly
proper reasons as given by our attorneys, while the matter is being
readied for the courts, we are unable to discuss our land uses and
zoning as openly as we might like, especially in view of the many
erroneous things that we hear and see on television and read in
the newspapers. But despite this, we assured the college that
any discussion on the question of land usage and any effort directed
toward reasonable and workable solutions should be encouraged.
And while we would be unable to be participants, we would certainly be interested listeners, and there are many Mahwah
officials in the audience.

So I was asked to say a few words, according to Dr. LeMay,
to indicate "that the town is not being excluded from participation."
Yesterday's opening session, which I understand was covered in
the New York Times this morning on page one, was directed
toward land-use problems. Today's meetings are concerned with
the search for solutions. The program indicates there is an
impressive assortment of experts with impressive credentials.

159

Now we who are on the municipal level of this firing line of land usage very probably can learn much from them, and they can learn little from us because we are laymen. We are part-time volunteers We are not experts, and all too often, in the matter of zoning and land uses, we are involved with daily pressures; the daily questions; the minor subdivisions; the developers agreements; the site review plans; the complaints about nonconforming uses; the pressures for variances; the rewriting of building and plumbing codes; all of these things.

We don't often have a chance here in Mahwah to welcome and express a few of our thoughts with a group such as this on such an important topic. So if you will permit, I would like to give you one small picture of a section of this vast township. If you drove to Ramapo this morning along Route 17 and Route 202, you saw a very limited part of the town. You saw some commercial uses on Route 17. If you came down Ramapo Avenue or Darlington Avenue, you saw some residential uses, perhaps the County Park, which is another aspect of what the land is being used for, and then along Route 202 past Birch Farm, or the remainder of Birch Farm.

Now when I drove down this morning—I live in Cragmere, which is the residential section over in the eastern part of town where homes were built in the 1920s, by and large on 75 × 100 ft lots—I drove down the hill, through an underpass, went past one of our industrial parks along a residential area. I passed three brand-new homes on 50-foot lots. I passed another residential development that's new; thirteen homes on 75-foot lots. Went past the small town business center. Past our town park and pond, which, by the way, is being spoiled at the moment because the utility doesn't see fit to put its lines underground. Past a recreational field, a school, historic church, over Route 17. Again the commercial uses are there. Skirted the high school campus. Just to the south of the campus is a future 380-acre office park and multifamily residential section that we have just rezoned. And down through a residential area to Route 202. Along the river, past the farm, past some nice residences that are on one-acre lots. And thence to Ramapo College.

Now these are just some of the varied things that land is being used for in Mahwah, and let me assure you that that is just one small section of a 26-mile community that actually is made up of 7 different communities.

By reviewing these varied land uses in this one small corner of our 26-square-mile township, I haven't solved any problems, but I did give an accurate picture of one part of Mahwah, and here in our township sometimes it seems to us that the "in thing" today is to call us a one-acre or a two-acre community. We don't often see or read a full and accurate and fair description of the township. Even the Regional Plan Association, as you may know, fell into this on a recent television program and gave a very unfair portrayal of this township today.

So with those few remarks, which I think are pertinent if for no other reason than to give you a little picture of the township in which this important conference is being held, we are happy to welcome you, and we are taking away much of the information with us. I am sure that all of you will leave here at the end of today's meeting with more knowledge and more understanding than when you arrived yesterday, and for that small benefit I want to thank Ramapo College and the Northwest Bergen Board of Realtors.

C. FORMULATION OF THE PROBLEM

D. Bennett Mazur

Associate Professor
School of Human Environment
Ramapo College of New Jersey
Mahwah, New Jersey

The post World War II period has been marked by a phenomenon called urban sprawl. Our metropolitan places have erupted across the countryside in an unremitting pattern of decentralization that might be likened to butter melting on a hot plate. It has precipitated a crisis in the use of land and an assault on the environment. We are concerned with "solutions" to some of these overwhelming problems. Let us summarize these problems briefly. They are of extreme concern to us all.

We are concerned with the rapid consumption of open space by low-density development because it is inevitably followed by increased intensification of land use, and, with it, a resulting detrimental impact on our environment. We are concerned with the air and water pollution that comes from overburdening systems that were never meant to accommodate additional concentrations of activity and from development in places where no such systems exist.

We are concerned with the growing cost of local government, whose major source of revenue comes from taxing land and improvements thereon. This situation has resulted in the development of zoning strategies designed too often to minimize cost, as well as to maximize revenues, at the expense of other communities. We are also concerned with the struggle to maintain a reliable transportation system in the face of the ever-increasing volume of automobile travel and the dispersing of commuting travel patterns.

Finally, we are concerned with the declining fiscal viability of the central cities and older suburban areas and the associated problems of economic and, too often, racial segregation and polarization, with their concomitant problems of providing adequate housing stock and improvement of economic opportunities for all.

163

As the urban spread takes place, many qualitative changes are taking place within our environment, our economy, and our society. Many new stresses and strains are appearing to replace the older problems, and we are having difficulty in coping with them, or even understanding them, because we are trying to solve them by applications of the political traditions and institutions of past generations. Basically, we have an environment that is crying out for planned intervention and direction of development. Unfortunately, we live in a society that places a major emphasis on immediate gratification and consumption, a society that is accustomed to thinking of our resources and land as inexhaustible. I might add that this is a society that historically has been inimical to the concept of planning.

We live in a society that reveres an economic tradition of free enterprise and that acknowledges the wisdom of the market place as the most preferred of all means and methods for determining both the spatial arrangement of activities and the utilization of resources—which bestows on the entrepreneur and on the institution of private property prior rights to much that is of value.

This is a society of many small governments nested within a federal system. Therefore, fragmented decision-making has been built in, and the system is completely protected by all sorts of checks and balances. It's a system designed to guarantee a large portion of local participation at the expense of centralized efficiency. The assumption has always been that the many jurisdictions, each seeking to maximize its own well-being, will somehow arrive at some state of affairs that will be in the best interest of the majority and do the least harm to the minority. It has been alleged in the past that regional policy will best be served by the self-regarding, and often defensive, actions of the home-rule communities.

We know now that this is not always true. We know that allowing every municipality to do what it pleases will not result in a maximum of good but in regional anarchy instead. However, rest assured that it is the wish of planners to preserve the rights of local residents, in particular, to participate in decisions that affect them. We know, at least I hope we do, that leaving all matters to the marketplace will not necessarily result in the most efficient arrangements of things, but we do not want to destroy free enterprise or the institution of private property. We recognize, therefore, the need to constrain the system in some areas and to channel its productivity into desirable directions.

These words summarize the predicament of the policy-makers, who must formulate policy alternatives for elected officials. Thus we have the basic conflict between private and public claims to the use and development of property. We have the rights of the individual, or the smaller community, versus those of the larger community of which it is a part. We have to choose between a loosely coordinated, and hopefully equitable, local home-rule decision-making apparatus and a more highly centralized and efficient regional or state system. We also have the conflict, the seldom remarked conflict, between the rationally prepared plans of administrators and planners, based on what they think is technologically feasible, and the ideas of legislators, each representing different constituents and negotiating for them, and what they consider will be politically feasible. Somewhere in each of these conflicts there exists a reasonable middle ground. These are the dilemmas that face our policy-makers today as they approach the environmental problems precipitated by the changing face of our metropolitan area and as they seek solutions they feel will be politically palatable, legally sound, capable of being administered, and that will achieve the desired outcomes. In other words, policies that will work.

D. ENVIRONMENTAL CONSIDERATIONS

Richard Galantowicz

North Jersey Conservation Foundation
Morristown, New Jersey

My subject will be "Environmental Assessments, " and I am afraid
it will hit some of the sensitive areas of court cases, zoning,
and what have you. I think I would say at the outset that I am not
going to be particularly picking on Mahwah, and I am sure that
none of the other speakers is, either. This is a very general subject. Unfortunately, we have the dubious distinction, here in
Mahwah, of being right in the thick of it. I think the reason that
it's general is that any community in New Jersey, or probably any
community in the United States, could be in the same spot. I
don't think you're unique in your own particular laws here in the
town, and I would hope that the officials and the mayor, if he's
still here, will not think I am picking on Mahwah.

I'm with the North Jersey Conservation Foundation, working
on a project called "The Process of Environmental Assessments,
Options and Limits. " The project has to do with new approaches
to land-use planning that, hopefully, will then be implemented
into new zoning regulations. The reason we initiated this project
is simply because of the situation here in New Jersey. I'm sure
most of you know by now, after attending this conference, that
New Jersey has a few dubious distinctions, being the most
densely populated and the most urbanized state in the United
States. And I think that is why we are having the current upheaval
in zoning here. We have the two major crises of concern for environmental quality and, of course, our old friend, housing.

When we go right back to the beginning, zoning started, or
at least came to the forefront, around 1926, with the case of the
Village of Euclid, Ohio v. Ambler Realty. In that case it really
was a question of nuisance. Certain users were trying to come
into a residential area and the case was decided on that issue.
The nuisance, I think, concerned the introduction of industry and

apartments in a residential district. The courts found that zoning is a legal police power in the state and that power can be handed down to municipalities. So we see that zoning power in munici- palities is a right delegated from the state. And I think this is something we should keep in mind when we consider how home-rule-oriented municipalities in New Jersey are. I am sure some of the others will speak on that point more than I want to. Actually, since 1926 things haven't really changed that much as far as zoning goes. It has been a technique used by the towns to do what local citizens thought they wanted or really wanted. The problem now existing in Mahwah, and all over New Jersey, and in the court challenges to zoning, is simply that, as in the past, there really is no basis in fact for the zoning. The questions are, Why are certain placed zoned for one acre, why are some places zoned industrial, and why are some places zoned commercial. I think, in most cases, in the past they were zoned that way be- cause that's the way they were when zoning first was considered in the municipalities. Or, in some cases, it was simply, well, we'll make this side of the road a half acre and that side of the road two acres, or one acre, or whatever. The size of the lots really doesn't matter. What is being challenged in the courts, I believe, is why those particular zoning districts are the way they are. And that is what our project and what we are concerned with are.

The problem is that once these cases are taken to court, and the courts decide that the zoning is unconstitutional or arbitrary, whatever the legal terminology is, what happens then? We see that Madison and Mount Laurel, the two towns that have had their zonings overturned by the courts, were given a certain amount of time to come up with a new master plan, a new way to eliminate the defects of their original zoning. But the question is, how do you do that? What will make the new plan different from the old plan? I think that if you looked at some of these court decisions, you would see that the courts, for instance, are suggesting a few of the things that ought to be considered.

First of all is people. Obviously, if we didn't have any people, we wouldn't have any problems. So in terms of people it comes down to uses of the land, particularly housing, because that's what affects people the most in this day and age, and especially here in New Jersey.

Second is the matter of natural resources. We do have a tre- mendous concern for natural resources in our state, and in the whole country, and people are concerned about how to protect them. Then we run into the problem of how to protect certain natural resources and still provide the housing that we need.

Third, we have to consider money—especially here in New Jersey where we have another distinction of being a state that is heavily reliant on the property tax to finance its municipalities and, in particular, its school systems. The courts say we cannot zone our towns on the basis of fiscal considerations alone.

Fourth, we are going to have to consider the region—I suppose this is one of the major considerations here in Mahwah, and it certainly was in the Mt. Laurel case and probably similarly in Madison. That is to say, we just cannot put a wall around our community and decide what we want for the citizens that are here now. We have to consider where that municipality is located in a larger region, and that larger region not only includes a population region such as the New York Metropolitan area but also natural-resource regions—a particular river basin, a particular land form, or what have you.

So, we feel, and this is the approach of our project, that we are going to have to consider people, natural resources, and money. Since there isn't a word that really includes all those, we, like all good organizations, coined our own, which we call "socio-environomics." And we feel that the way to plan is to start off with what's there on the landscape, that is, the landscape itself.

Consider the natural resources. We feel the basis of any master plan has got to be some type of a natural resource inventory. This means that someone or some agency, whether it's your planner, your environmental commission, or your planning board, must go out into the community, or township, and see what you have. Look at the soils and their ability to accept water, whether it is the effluent from a sewage plant, or rain water, or water from the rooftops of houses, or what have you. Look at your land forms: the ridge tops, the hills, the steep slopes. Your water system: the streams and underground water supplies. Look at the underlying geology. What does that tell you about the land's ability to accept effluent from septic tanks? Important natural resources. You must know about all these things, but I think if you look at the master plans and some of the zoning ordinances that have been passed because of master plans, you will see that they really have no basis in fact. Since the environmental movement began, I have seen master plans that, on page 20, described and inventoried the natural resources, the land, landforms, floodplains,

and what have you, but then, on page 60, when they set forth the
proposed master plan, they put industrial sites in the floodplain,
or they put housing developments on the steep slopes—and it
looks to me as though whoever wrote page 60 never looked at
page 20. So we cannot just give lip service to natural resources.
We really have to consider them. And I think the important factor
that was brought out in one of the court cases, I believe it was
Madison, N.J., was that the town was trying to uphold its large-
lot zoning because of considerations for the natural resources.
Well, the court said that nowhere else in their master plan, nowhere else in their zoning regulations, did they even mention the
word environment or talk about ecology. There were no data what-
soever to uphold the fact that the particular area under contention
was in the floodplain. I believe it was kind of a smoke screen,
because whether the facts could be substantiated, whether it
really was a floodplain or not, is hardly the question when you
get into court. The fact is that they could not support their claim
on the basis of their master plan. Therein lies the point that we
have to consider. If we are going to have to talk about environmental issues, we must have the facts. And that is why the
natural resource inventory of any community is really the corner-
stone of your master plan.

The natural resource inventory will not tell you everything
you must know to create your plan but at least will give you some
idea as to the best, and the least desirable, places in town to
consider for development. However, you must consider the needs
of the people affected by the plan. If we still have enough time
and enough land in our town, we can satisfy the requirements of
the people and the land. We can put the people where they're
best suited, while avoiding future problems for them when they
come to live in that area.

Now the question of money and taxation is a hard one. It's a
tough one because we have a kind of unfortunate system here in
New Jersey that forces us to rely so heavily on property taxes for
the financing of municipal services. As a result, we have
really keen competition between communities for good ratables,
and obviously good ratables are ones that return a lot of taxes and
require few services. This is certainly the bind that most communities are caught in. This is why we have the attempt to preserve
large-lot zoning, which reduces the number of houses and, thereby,
reduces the number of people that have to be serviced. The question is whether this really works out. I think there's a lot of evidence to show that it really doesn't work out the way people think.

For one thing, if you invite industry to your town it provides a certain number of jobs, let's say a hundred. For each one of these new industrial jobs, new service jobs are created, which may be on a one to one ratio or even greater—so there's another one hundred jobs. Each of the two hundred workers supports a family of perhaps 2 or 3 or 4 people. Now instead of a hundred jobs, we are talking perhaps of 600 or 800 people. So we see what happens; there is a multiplier effect in industry. Even if you get the so-called good ratables — clean industry with a few highly paid people—you're bringing in a lot of people. This causes a lot of problems for your town, because it is people that require services, and it's the services that require municipal expenditures, and municipal expenditures create the need for taxes. So it's the people demanding services that create taxes, it's not the particular kind of industry or the particular kind of ratable. I think we should simply get off the ratable merry-go-round, by giving up the ratable argument, and start planning our communities in a way that is environmentally and socially sound. I would like to see the property tax revised, so that municipalities will end their competition for ratables. Then, perhaps, we'll see what other problems are really being covered up by the ratable fiscal issue. I think this is probably where the more difficult real problems lie, but as long as we're going to have this competition for ratables, they are going to be covered up, and we won't even be able to begin dealing with them.

The regional problem, I think, is going to become obvious with the Regional Plan Association's television series, whether all the facts in it are right or not. We do belong to a large region. Suburbs have a relation to urban areas, and they are going to have to work together. They are related not only in the sense that people working in urban areas live in suburban areas but also in the fact that, in many cases, urban, suburban, and rural areas provide the natural resources that permit a city to function. I'm not sure that more housing in suburban or rural areas is going to alleviate the problems of the cities. I think that with a natural resource inventory, and some of these other considerations, we might find out that there are some areas in our suburbs and rural areas that we will simply have to leave open if municipalities and urban centers are going to have the water, the food, and at least some semblance of clean air to maintain themselves. So it's a trade-off, and we're going to have to begin investigating the economic results of it.

As far as the solution to these problems goes, I'm not sure that anyone knows the answer. I think that we're going to have to begin looking at our community in terms of these social and environmental factors. Once we decide on the areas that should be developed, high level, truly competent planning is going to have to come into play. For example, we will have to use new development schemes. Most people are familiar with cluster development, but we will have to take it a step further, into planned residential development. In these communities houses will be built on smaller lots, but there will be some community facilities included, such as small commercial establishments, schools, and what have you. The next step to planned unit development will include not only a variety of housing: single detached houses on their individual single lots; attached housing, such as townhouses; apartments, both garden and high-risers, if the land calls for that; and a variety of industrial and commercial land uses. Of course the ultimate step in this series would be the development of a new town, a totally self-contained community.

Other new ideas are also on the horizon. Perhaps you'll be hearing more about them in the future; you may have heard of at least one already—the concept of the transfer of development right. This is a concept that requires the community to go through the master planning process, hopefully similar to the one I just described. In certain areas, the areas least suitable for development and those that have intrinsic natural value—aquifer recharge areas, floodplains, steep slopes, things such as that—are put in a preservation zone (you know, those little green blobs on the master-plan map that very seldom stay green) in today's methodology. The new process begins by defining preserve areas and areas suitable for development. People who own property in the preserve area are given development rights certificates, like stock certificates. As we know, land has many rights associated with it. One of these is the right to develop the property. We are suggesting that it will be necessary to separate the right of ownership from the right of development. Then, the person in the preservation area will get a transferable development certificate. A man who wants to develop property in a residential area will be able either to develop it at the density that has been determined by the master plan, or he will be able to go to someone in a preservation area and buy some of that person's development rights and apply the development rights to his land in the developable area. Perhaps this action will increase the density of use on the developable land, above the original density allowed by the plan, but an absolute maximum will also be set by the master plan. Basically, this is a device designed to protect the value of all private property and the environment. It forestalls a situation in which people whose land is suggested for preservation will say, "Well, you are preventing me from taking advantage of the full development potential value of that land" and will immediately take the town to court unless it wants to buy the land. The creation of development certificates gives the people in the preservation area a way to get full value from their land, the developer has a way to intensify land use elsewhere in the town, and the municipality gets its open space and housing. Use of this new technique is going to require some new legislation, which is just in the formative stages now, but I think you're going to be hearing more about it.

There are a lot of other possibilities, but I'll mention just one more. There is a program in the St. Paul-Minneapolis regional planning area whereby the communities are all combined into a region and work together in a set pattern. In that system, when a municipality gets a new ratable such as a new factory, 60 percent of the value of that ratable is retained by that municipality. But the other 40 percent goes toward general regional development and the regional good. Again, you can see that we could use such a system here in New Jersey to eliminate some of the competition among towns. This would allow industry to enter an area and not only benefit the specific municipality in which it locates but also to offset some of the cost that might accrue to other municipalities that did not get the industries but that are in the general area and, perhaps, share some of the cost incurred by the industry's presence. Any new planning, whether it's environmental planning leading to environmental zoning, as I've suggested, or any of the programs that are going to be mentioned after is going to require public and citizen involvement in the local government. Local government must become more responsive to the citizens, and citizens must, in turn, give local government much more help than they have in the past—the public must help the town authorities develop their plans. I think this is the only way that municipalities can be made responsive to the needs of the region and the state, while maintaining their home-rule policies. There have been indications from state and federal levels that if municipalities cannot handle their planning responsibilities, some of the authority of local governments will be assumed by larger units. If we want planning to remain at the local level, we must become involved.

E. LEGISLATIVE PROPOSALS FOR IMPROVED LAND USE

Sidney Willis

Assistant Commissioner of Planning and Housing
New Jersey Department of Community Affairs
Trenton, New Jersey

It appears from my perusal of the New York Times this morning and
the program format that a good deal of discussion has focused on
environmental protection of highly fragile land-use areas, the
floodplains, the wetlands, the coastal areas, and, as in Commissioner Sullivan's remarks of yesterday, on special regions of
the state—the Skylands and the Tocks Island region and some
other particularly vulnerable environmental areas. It appears, in
many instances, that the solutions to these problems lie in some
kind of a regional approach. In the remaining areas of the state,
however, the issues and solutions are much more complicated
because they revolve very much around the questions as to who
shall have a say, and to what extent, in the process of developing
land for the generation of jobs, housing, shopping, and other
land uses that serve existing and future populations. It was interesting that Dick Galantowicz mentioned the problem of local master
plans that contain sound technical material on page 20 and perhaps
tend to overlook this information on page 60. I'm a little sensitive
on that point, but I certainly would concede that his observation
is correct. That's the difference between the technicians telling
us what we ought to want to do and citizen participation in the
process of determining what a municipality actually will do. However, I think we need both inputs to arrive at viable conclusions.

I think the most complicated problems we have to deal with
are the daily decisions of the municipalities, counties, and the
state itself, which, to some extent, are directly regulatory but
also, to a great degree, simply happen. For example, a decision
is made to locate a facility in a particular location. The facility
has an impact on the value and on the potential use of adjacent
land, and it has an impact on the traffic on surrounding roads. In

some cases, roads must be widened but, in all cases, facilities must be in place. This process, which proceeds without direction, I'm afraid, results in what Mason Gross described yesterday as urban sprawl. Yet this very process, at the present time in New Jersey, has a greater effect on the overall environment than some of the more direct problems that we have been confronting in recent years. This is the daily environment within which all of us live, work, shop, and, except for special excursions to the shore or the mountains, to a large degree find our daily and weekly entertainment.

It is in this area that we have the greatest problems of wasteful sprawl and the imbalance in development to which I want to address some of my remarks. I have prepared a paper that discusses how we regulate this activity and the proposals that are, at the present time, in the legislature. They are designed to improve on, and to build upon, good legislation and, perhaps, to revise somewhat that which has not worked out well. Many people have called attention to the fact that we are here in Mahwah, and it is unfortunate that this particular community has been singled out to be the illustration of some of the problems faced everywhere in New Jersey, and not confined to Mahwah. The cases that are now in court, which I'm going to mention, refer to many municipalities and certainly not only Mahwah. I think it has been unfair that so much attention has been focused on this one municipality in our state because it's simply illustrative of the difficulties. Zoning problems have already emerged as among the most sensitive in New Jersey in the 1970s. However, I want to sort out a few viewpoints so you can look at zoning from the various perspectives of people who are involved in this problem on a daily basis. And when you look at it from different viewpoints, you don't come out with the same answer. Therefore, some variations, as between page 20 and page 60 of our local master plans, for example, is inevitable.

For example, one may view zoning from a position as a corporate or business leader. People who are in leadership positions, those who are influential within our government and who are very much concerned with the state and its present and future development, recognize that the continued industrial growth, development, and the prosperity on which much of the future of the state will depend cannot occur unless employees working in industries have a decent place to live in some reasonable proximity to the areas in which they are employed. The same people come home in the evening, and they change their hats and become municipal officials because New Jersey is characterized by part-time government activity, which, frankly, I think is one of our assets. When they think in their roles as municipal officials, it seems equally apparent to them that planning, zoning, and other development policies severely affect both the municipal revenue, under our property tax system, and expenses for public services, particularly schools. In fact, every measure designed to encourage industry and com merce and to discourage population, particularly moderate- and low-income population, growth seems, somehow, justified.

When we think about the same problem in our roles as business people, we are concerned with the continued effectiveness of the private-enterprise system. It seems apparent from that point of view, in housing at least, that the system is working badly and is made worse by planning and zoning for industry without concern for housing of employees. Or, zoning areas to favor one income group, but not all others.

When we think about this same problem in our roles as informed citizens, and that's the role I think we are all playing here today, we desire to maintain a large degree of local control over our own communities. We have to concede that the use of public powers, which tend to seek out ratables while avoiding responsibility to their employees, will result, even if unintentionally, in excluding whole classes of people from wide areas of the state. It becomes clear, then, that such practices must eventually be seriously challenged. We are aware that the demands of people not to be prevented from living where they work by public power—let me stress that word "public"—no matter how long deferred, will eventually make themselves felt through legitimate channels, through the courts, as is the case at the present time in New Jersey, in the legislature, and in state and national executive offices. Pressures for improved access to good housing, good jobs, and good public services are growing daily, and from a widening group of people. Planners, in their roles as technical persons and as citizen members of local planning boards, have known for a long time that the concept of zoning which was intended to control the use of private property by government, was some day going to run head-on into the idea of equal protection under the law, as guaranteed by the Constitution. This issue is now being raised in the cases of Madison Township, which has been mentioned here earlier, and Mt. Laurel, in Burlington County, and, to some extent, in a number of other cases. At this particular moment, the Madison and Mt. Laurel cases are before the state supreme court, have been heard by them, and are awaiting decision.

It is evident that if home rule and local zoning result in a pattern that discriminates against certain income groups, whether intentionally or not, or does not protect everyone equally, then we must either adjust the ground rules, or the power zones at local levels eventually will be nullified. I personally believe it would be far better to adjust the ground rules and to re-examine the constitutional purposes for the powers that we exercise. I also believe that we can do this without a great deal of disruption, requiring only proof of good will and good faith on the part of the three levels of government that are going to be involved.

In our department we've tried to anticipate some of these problems and to define some reasonable proposals, some of which have been laid before the legislature, which would help to adjust the system in the direction of a better balance in the use of land in regions while leaving the responsibilities for local actions in the hands of municipal officials. This is an attempt to achieve some kind of a balance and involves asking municipal officials to consider issues in terms of their regional impact. In the same way, they must begin to think of the needs of the area of which the municipality is a part and to make suitable decisions within this general guideline. Such decisions should be made without threat of penalty and without an enforcement machinery because they are based on a common understanding that if we can do the job that must be done (by becoming more responsive to the needs of all of the people), we will provide the courts with a basis for continuing to uphold local zoning ordinances and local master plans.

That will require some increase in statewide and county guidance; I'm not suggesting that it will not. But I believe that that kind of guidance can still be provided in some orderly way without mandatory overrides or enforcement machinery attached to it. That is the essence of several pieces of legislation that have been proposed and I fear are very largely misunderstood.

Let me say a word about the piece of legislation that I think is of primary importance. It is the proposed Community Planning Law introduced as A 1422 by Assemblyman Merck, a suburban legislator from Morris County. The aims of that bill are, among others, to streamline and to strengthen local planning. Eighty percent of the bill relates to streamlining local procedure, e.g., increasing the Board of Adjustment to seven members, providing for appeal procedures, determining how many days the municipality should have to review a subdivision ordinance, i.e., guiding municipalities through all the mechanics of the planning process. All the little

decisions add up to make a profound impact on our environment.
And that's what we're going to live with as the years go by. For
this reason, local procedure has been made the dominant part of
the proposed Community Planning Law. The final form of the legislation was ground out over a two-year period as a set of compromises among municipal attorneys, the federation of planning
officials, the league of municipalities, the builders association,
the industrial development people, and realtors, all of whom had
a slightly different idea, as I've tried to describe to you, of how
the world ought to be. We believe that the results are such that
everyone, generally, can live with. That's why we have the support of the League of Municipalities and why League members have
been writing to the legislature in order to call attention to the
fact that the official agencies of the municipalities have indeed
been promoting, sponsoring, and endorsing these legislative proposals. So when people say, "Oh, my God, home rule is is
going down the drain," I ask you to consider the sources of support for the legislation that we have put before the legislature.

A second purpose of the legislation is to establish a framework
for cooperative planning among and between the three levels of
government. Let me describe that a little bit because it is a key
to the proposal. At the state level, there is a state planning procedure, and there are decisions made by state departments that
subject land use to state regulation, interference, and control.
Decisions in this category relate directly to land usage with
regard to floodplains, wetlands, and other large areas of the state.
Then there are all the state decisions that affect the location of
the freeways, the expansion of rapid transit, and the development
of community colleges; all of these have a drastic effect on the
municipalities involved. The state, therefore, has a major part in
local development, but its plans and those of the municipalities
are not always in any way coordinated. I'd like to provide some
procedure under which there will be a state plan that municipalities
can look at in order to see what the state is providing for, or
intending to do, so that they can, in some orderly way, adjust or
object, if that's necessary.

The county planning operations as they exist at the present
time are the best hope for regionalism within the state. Now
that's not a popular thing to say in New Jersey. There are many
cases in which the municipalities would prefer that the county
would dry up and go away. Perhaps in some counties, at the
present time, it would not be a bad idea; nonetheless, there is a
role for this level of government because it is a little closer to

local conditions than Trenton and a little farther away than the Borough Hall. We need that in the state because, as has been pointed out, not every municipality in New Jersey is going to be able to answer environmental questions, such as those concerning stream management and solid waste disposal, for itself; it just is not physically possible. So a slightly larger area makes sense for solving some of these problems.

Finally, there's the municipal planning level where the daily decisions must continue to be made, simply because local officials are probably the only people who know what's going on. To develop an area effectively, the three planning levels must coordinate their activities, but at the present time they don't. We are convinced that the three planning jurisdictions can come together, first by providing for a formal planning procedure at the state level, which we do not have now, and then by requiring municipalities, in their local planning and zoning strategy decisions, to take policy positions with reference to the county and state plans. Now that doesn't mean that if the municipality thinks that development ought to proceed in a certain way, that's it. It simply means that the municipality, if it thinks that development ought to proceed in some other way, will set forth in its master plan why it believes its own plan is preferable. This must be done because, you can rest assured, from now on there will be litigation with regard to local decisions. You've got to have a master plan that sets forth the basis for the decisions that you have made. We were reminded this morning by one of your speakers that in the Madison Township case the municipality's lawyer said, "Oh, we're protecting the environment here." And the judge said, "Well, show it to me in the plan." But the explanation wasn't in the plan and, therefore, it didn't count. Their zoning was thrown out, and the case is now before state courts. We must begin to justify our zoning laws and to be specific about what we want them to accomplish. If we, at the local level, take issue with decisions made at the county and state level, we must formally set our reasons down in our zoning policy statement and incorporate them in the master plan. If reasons are justifiable, there is a good chance of their being upheld. If they are not, I think the courts will throw them out.

Now that's the kind of thing we think can be worked out cooperatively, leaving the vast majority of the decisions at the local level, with guidelines at the state level. Let me close by saying that we are cognizant that there are new requirements being placed on those of us who are concerned with the regulation and the use of lands. These requirements are very much a part of the new recognition of the impact of the decisions being made on the environment and of the close relationship between all of these factors and the health and welfare of our society. We are also aware of the demands—in many cases, legitimate demands—for a better housing situation within the state. There are many instances in which local zoning decisions are being severely tested and, very often, thrown out. We are proposing to strengthen the system so that it can withstand overly general criticisms by responding to the legitimate aspects of those criticisms. If we can do that jointly, with good will, I think we can continue to enjoy the advantages and benefits that local planning and local zoning can give to New Jersey. If we cannot, I fear that we will be subject to individual court decisions, throwing out this or that ordinance, and to continuing chaos for many municipalities. In northwest Bergen County, most of the action, or at least a great deal of the action, has been brought to the courts, causing continuous useless expenditures on court defense and wasting funds needed to respond to the legitimate needs of the community, which all of us know really do exist.

F.   GOVERNMENT COORDINATION

Thomas O'Neill

Executive Assistant to the Commissioner
New Jersey Department of Environmental Protection
Trenton, New Jersey

I will begin by repeating something you've all heard many times
before. Land use is the single most important factor in determining the quality of our life. That may seem a self-evident proposition, but if you look around, you will see that people act as though
they do not believe it. I drove up Route 17, from the Garden State
Parkway to Ramapo College, this morning and could not help notic-
ing that it presents a very interesting exercise in how the esthetics
of design should not be handled. Unfortunately, too much of our
state looks like that. This problem is more than a matter of
esthetics. Environmental design has an effect on the way we think,
the way we feel, and the way we interact with people. This is a
concept that isn't often expressed anymore. Another point that
deserves to be repeated is that land is a resource, and a limited
one. We are all dependent on the very complex set of natural resources that make up our environment, and land is
one of the most important of these resources. We make many competing demands on that set of resources, but we must balance all
these demands because the resource base is finite.

In the case of the wetlands, for example, the price paid for
these lands did not represent their true resource value. There is
a basic law in economics called the law of supply and demand;
it expresses the idea that the more limited something is, the
greater is its potential value. It follows from this proposition
that if there is only one of something then it may be infinitely
valuable. Only wetlands can perform their particular ecological
function. From a resource point of view, therefore, wetlands are
unique, and, by definition, infinitely valuable. Traditional use
of the wetlands has not reflected this concept, and we are now
faced with the logical consequence of its undervaluation: over-
use, damage to the environment, and, since our economic and

social systems are dependent on our environment, a deterioration in the quality of life.

Land is not only a natural resource, it is also a common resource. I use the word "common" in a special sense—something held by all, that is, in common. We may occupy the land but we don't own it, no matter who has title to it. We all really own the land conjointly. We also hold the land in trust for future genera- tions, and we only get to use it for a very brief period of time, as is true for all natural resources. There is an interesting article by Garrett Hardin, called "The Tragedy of the Commons," in which he explains why the use of any commonly held resource is difficult to regulate. In this case, the commons he referred to were the English pasture lands in the eighteenth century. Shep- herds used the pasture lands although they did not own them— nobody owned the pasture lands—to graze their flocks. Since no one owned the pasture lands, it was impossible to regulate the number of sheep allowed on them. Each shepherd who wanted to maximize his profit calculated that he would be better off if he increased the size of his flock. In areas where many shepherds using the pasture land made that same calculation, the number of sheep increased far beyond the ability of the grass to feed them. As a result of extensive overgrazing, the pasture land suffered greatly from the processes of erosion—sheep starved, shepherds suffered financially, and the land was devastated.

We still live with the tragedy of the commons; the competi- tion for tax ratables among the municipalities is comparable to the competition among eighteenth-century English shepherds for grazing land for sheep. The individual shepherds were short- sighted, just as the municipalities in competition for ratables are shortsighted. However, we really can't blame the people who are in that competition because they operate in a system that does not allow them to take a long-term view and that does not really recognize the legitimacy of actions taken to preserve the environ- ment. No shepherd would voluntarily reduce the size of his herd because he had no certainty that all the others would follow suit; therefore, none did so. We live in that same system; no munici- pality can really afford to withdraw voluntarily from the competition for ratables.

Now that we have talked about the theoretical basis of the land-use problem that confronts us, the tragedy of the commons, and the need to assure that the demands on our limited resource base are balanced, we should also mention the unity of the environment. We have 567 municipalities in this state, but we have only one environment. We cannot divide the environment up along political boundary lines; it's hard enough to divide it up along natural boundary lines, like stream beds or stream-flow areas. All these theoretical bases, the tragedy of the commons, the need for balance, and the unity of the environment, argue for moving greater land-use powers back to somewhat higher levels of government, which can have a wider grasp and a wider view over what is happening while retaining the necessity for local public input into the process. They also argue for the inclusion of environmental factors in planning.

Zoning ordinances are coming under attack as never before. It is apparent that the courts are not going to tolerate exclusionary zoning unless there's a compelling justification to limit the population of a particular area. Too often, people use the environment as a mask for bigotry, as a mask for the last man in syndrome, or as a mask for just keeping things the way they are. We don't intend to allow that. Last year, the Department of Environmental Protection intervened in one of the state's zoning cases. The department's intention was to identify the considerations a land-use plan and a zone ordinance must take into account if they are adequately to reflect environmental considerations. The brief in the Bedminster case has been widely distributed, and it serves as a guide to municipalities for the preparation of adequate plans and ordinances. That brief basically says that if you're going to claim environmental reasons for some kind of zoning, it had better be supported well, and it shows you how to support it. Even the best-equipped municipality cannot take into account all the effects of a particular project. Some of these effects will be felt far from the site of the project itself. Therefore, state and regional bodies are going to become more active in the land-use field, especially in the environmentally critical areas. Now these areas deserve and require a special degree of care because they transcend political boundaries. No political entity can make wise land-use decisions within these regions unless spill-over effects are considered. Local or even county governments, even if equipped with environmental information concerning their own area, cannot take these external effects into account. Therefore, shared responsibility for charting the future of these areas is required. The state must help ensure that these areas are used in environmentally sensible ways. The floodplains of the state are one such region now coming under state regulation. The municipalities are going to have a large role to play, and they should. The environmental commissions within the municipalities of the state are going to have a special role to play in protecting flood-prone lands. Under the new floodplains regislation, the state will regulate land use in the floodway, that area most frequently and most severely inundated. It will also publish guidelines for municipal protection of the less frequently inundated flood hazard areas. Municipalities must adopt a protective regulation for flood hazard areas within one year or the state will regulate them as well. In large part it's going to be up to environmental commissions to provide the expertise to draw up regulations that will be effective in protecting flood hazard areas throughout the state.

The coastal zone is another precious resource, the misuse of which can exact a very high price. The passage of Assembly Bill 1429, which is poetically named the Major Coastal Area Facilities Review Act, is our number-one legislative priority for this year. The tidally influenced zone embraced by that bill is very important both in ecological terms for the food chain and in terms of recreational potential because it's close to the water and faces tremendous industrial and commercial development pressures. If those pressures succeed in upsetting the balance of that area, then we won't have a valuable coast. This would adversely affect the number-one industry in the state, the tourist shore industry. Nor would we be able to maintain the fragile ecological balance in these tidally influenced areas. Balance is required, but it cannot be made on a piecemeal, individual municipal basis. Suppose every municipality on the coast said, "Well, we have to sit down and have a balanced land-use plan for our little area, so we'll devote half of it to industry and preserve half of it." That is obviously not the kind of balance we want. Half of each town devoted to industry means that the people of the next town will be swimming next to an oil refinery within the jurisdiction of the first. The kind of balance that must be achieved must be approached on a region-wide basis so that we can take into account the nature of the land throughout the entire region and balance it in such a way that the various uses will be compatible.

The rural area of Warren and Sussex counties, which would be affected by the Tocks Island project if it's completed, will form another critical environmental area. The Commissioner talked yesterday about the need to protect this region against the kind of intrusive and tawdry development that would ordinarily follow the completion of that project. We feel that the way to guard the unique areas of the state against adverse development pressures is to develop a regionalized system of planning. The state would participate in this system because the area is important not only to the people who live in it but also to the people of the entire state. Some of the municipalities in that area don't even have rudimentary zoning ordinances. The bill that is going to be introduced shortly is designed to set up a regional planning council, on which the state will be represented. Planning for the area will be based on an environmental design, which is a sophisticated type of natural-resource inventory. The master plan for the development of the area will then reflect the natural-resource constraints on that development; these constraints will be used as the basis for municipal zoning and planning and for the review of variance applications that are sure to arise. This is a new approach in the state. I don't know what success we're going to have with it the first time, but we think it's an important way to go in environmentally critical regions.

As Sid Willis said, most of the state is not in an environmentally critical region. Most of the state, therefore, is going to have to be governed by the kind of bill Sid talked about, A1422, which would produce a real step forward from the kind of planning that goes on now in municipalities. I think it is necessary to include in our master plans all the considerations that have to go into a zoning ordinance. The kinds of things I have been talking about here really only apply to a portion of the state, an environmentally critical portion but not, perhaps, the most socially critical portions. The Skylands Region, right next door to this area, is another critical zone which is coming under very intensive pressure as roads are built through it. Here we not only have a recreational problem, but the Skylands Region is a crucial watershed and supplies a good deal of the water for the major municipal areas a little to the south of us. Development in the area will threaten its water-supply capabilities if it is not placed in the right locations. Therefore, we're planning to introduce the same kind of legislation for Skyland as for Tocks Island, with a special eye here to preserving the essential features of the region, which, in this case, are its water supply functions and its recreational features.

Both public and private projects must be assessed from an environmental standpoint throughout the state. The new turnpike extension to the Jersey shore, the sports complex, and the meadowlands, have undergone intensive environmental scrutiny by the state. Other state projects may have an adverse impact on the environment and on the future plans of municipalities unless they are properly designed, located, and subjected to vigorous review. Governor Cahill mentioned in his 1973 Annual Message that he will soon be promulgating an executive order that will require an environmental review of all major projects built or funded by the state before they are allowed to proceed. All state construction projects, as the governor said, will probably have to prepare an environmental impact statement based on guidelines the governor will issue; the statements will then be reviewed by the Department of Environmental Protection, which will then advise the governor as to the degree of accuracy and completeness in that statement and on measures necessary to reduce the project's negative impact. The governor has already issued Executive Order 40, which establishes a State Planning Task Force that will also ensure that state projects are compatible with our guidelines for social and environmental progress. This Task Force will initiate the state planning program until the legislature acts to establish the permanent state planning council under A1422.

Our land-use system has worked for many years to the detriment of the environment, and the operation of the system has made us prisoners of the past. The system arose when America thought it had a limitless frontier to develop and did not recognize the limitations of the natural-resource base on which it is dependent to support life. When that outdated philosophical cowboy concept is associated with a tax system that bases government revenues on land use and with an economic system that rewards polluters rather than penalizes them, the result is incipient disaster.

The land-use measures Governor Cahill recommended to the legislature in his Annual Message, coupled with those already in force, are going to help make our system of land-use regulation more environmentally rational. In addition to affecting how the land is used we must also begin to seek ways to change the economic system so that its operation is more compatible with a sound environment. Economic and environmental considerations are often thought to be mutually exclusive, or at least competitive; in fact, however, they are not opposed but mutually reinforcing.

A polluter can be defined as one who inflicts costs on society by reducing the quality of the air, the land, or the water. He can range in character from a litterbug to a strip miner. Our economic system must be modified so that the environmental costs created by the polluter are paid for by him and by those who buy his products. We must build into the economic system incentives and disincentives to encourage all enterprises to operate in an environmentally sound fashion. Shaping the economic system is primarily the responsibility of the national government, but the states can serve as laboratories for change and can experiment more flexibly than can the national government. One of the things we're looking at, at the governor's request, is a way to modify the pressures for development that grow constantly in this state. Environmental impact review will help to ensure that the development that does occur is environmentally sound, but the economic system now rewards those who are involved in the conversion of the land and rewards them handsomely with speculative profit. The role of the speculator in the disappearance of open space and agricultural lands is well know. I think we now lose something over a farm a day in this state. The economic system rewards the speculator for ignoring the overarching social and environmental role played by the land he converts to less desirable uses. Our agricultural lands serve important social, economic, and environmental goals, yet we're losing them. During the period 1962 to 1972 New Jersey lost 6,200 farms. As a result, 1/2 million acres of agricultural land were converted to other uses. The Commission on the Future of Agriculture will soon be making recommendations concerning the preservation of these lands. We are considering recommendation of a surcharge that would recapture part of the speculative profit derived from dealing in open lands. This profit is unearned by the speculator because the increase in the value of the lands he buys and sells is due to the actions of others. Suppose a speculator goes out and buys a piece of land for a thousand dollars an acre. The state comes through with our tax dollars and builds a road beside it, which raises its value to $10,000 an acre. That value increase of $9,000 is a profit the speculator makes but it isn't due to his hard work; it's due to our tax dollars.

The proposed surcharge will serve as a disincentive to speculation by reducing the gains to be had from dealing in open and vacant lands. The purpose of the surcharge is to reduce wanton speculation and thus reduce the need for the ad hoc purchase of land for preservation. Speculation promotes shabby land use, harms the environment, and threatens to obliterate the state's agricultural community. The surcharge is designed to permit those who hold open lands for a short period of time to appreciate a reasonable profit on their investment, but it will recapture the speculative profit on short-term transactions. We will probably recommend that the funds generated from the surcharge be placed in a special fund for the preservation of open space and for the retirement of the Green Acres bond issue. There is an appealing element of social justice in this surcharge since those who play such an important role in destroying open space will provide the funds to preserve open space.

We have talked about environmentally critical areas, the state's participation in their development, and the importance of these areas to the whole state because this is the justification for state participation in the planning process. But most of the work, as Sidney Willis said, will still be up to the municipalities in most areas of the state. For these people, the state must first rationalize the planning system, as A1422 will do. We think it is necessary for every municipality involved in planning to have an environmental commission to conduct natural-resource inventories and to advise it on the kinds of environmental considerations it must contend with in order to develop a really sound master plan.

G. THE PROPOSED COMMUNITY PLANNING LAW
How Will it Affect Municipalities?[*]

Sidney L. Willis

Assistant Commissioner of Planning and Housing
New Jersey Department of Community Affairs
Trenton, New Jersey
and
Chairman of the drafting committee
that prepared the Community Planning Law

and

James R. Jager

Secretary to the drafting committee

On March 27, 1972, Governor William T. Cahill announced his
support of a new proposed Community Planning Law. [1] When enacted, this proposal will replace the myriad laws, amendments,
and court decisions that have enabled and guided municipal,
county, and state planning in New Jersey. The introduction of
this omnibus legislation in the New Jersey Legislature and its
eventual adoption will realize the completion of a two-year cooperative effort by the New Jersey State League of Municipalities,
the Federation of Planning Officials, the Department of Community
Affairs, and numerous concerned organizations. These efforts
have been stimulated by a growing alarm that the inadequacy of
the existing legal framework regulating land use to meet modern-
day sound development and environmental protection requirements
have led to court decisions that are rapidly eroding municipal
planning and zoning powers. In the absence of corrective action
by the legislature looms the prospect of the loss of regulatory
powers without safeguards against disorderly, unplanned suburban
sprawl.

---

[*]Reprinted by permission of the New Jersey State League of
Municipalities as it appeared in New Jersey Municipalities, June,
1972.

The proposed legislation was prepared by a drafting committee of attorneys and planners appointed by an advisory committee representing forty statewide organizations interested in new land-use legislation. The committee's overall objective was to completely rewrite earlier proposals for revising New Jersey's planning and zoning laws that had been pending over the last few years. The committee's recommended draft has been endorsed by the executive committee of the Federation of Planning Officials, the Land Use Law Study Committee of the New Jersey State League of Municipalities, and the New Jersey Association of Realtor Boards.

The article outlines the effect that the new law is expected to have on municipal planning boards and boards of adjustment. Over a period of years, local plans and ordinances will gradually be revised to meet the new standards. The procedural requirements will need to be implemented locally within 6 months of passage of the bill. Within two years thereafter, master plans and zoning ordinances will need to be revised or, as an alternative on the part of the municipality, the zoning ordinance will have to be certified by the state within two years. Thus, ample time will be allowed for municipalities to adjust to the new legislative requirements.

On introduction of the bill, a series of public meetings in various locations within the state have been arranged with the cooperation of the league. Information and assistance in applying the new law after enactment will be available from the Department of Community Affairs.

Streamlining the Process

A major objective of the Community Planning Law is to streamline the local planning process in order to cut out pointless red tape, thus conserving the time and energy of the citizen board members to better enable them to focus on the essentials of good planning. The governing body is seen as the final policy maker and as the reviewer of disputed decisions. The processing of applications for development and arranging full public hearings are the responsibilities of the expert boards. Insofar as possible, an application for development would receive one complete processing by either the planning board or the board of adjustment.

To this end, "special exceptions" have been re-termed "conditional uses" and placed under the purview of the planning board rather than the board of adjustment. In practice, the strong tendency had been to refer a special exception application to the planning board for basically site-plan review before the board of adjustment would pass on the application. However, there was no good reason for overburdening hard-pressed citizen boards with dual review when one concentrated review would suffice. Because in practice special-exception review required much the same expertise as site-plan review, this type of review was assigned to the planning board.

Toward this same goal of one review, the planning board would also be authorized in reviewing subdivisions, site plans, and conditional uses to grant variances from the zoning ordinance, except for use variances. Use variances are too significant a departure from the zoning ordinance to come under the jurisdiction of any other but the board of adjustment, a quasi-judicial body.

The existing legislation has permitted referral as well as approval planning boards in the review of subdivision applications and for the referral of use variances recommended by the board of adjustment to the governing body. However, it seems incongruous that the policy-making body should handle undisputed decisions on applications. If no interested party was disturbed by a decision of a board, then there was no reason to take up the time and divert the attention of the governing body.

Accordingly, all planning boards would approve or deny subdivisions, and the board of adjustment would approve or deny use variances without referring the application to the governing body. However, the drafting committee concluded that a quick administrative appeal by a dissatisfied interested party to the governing body should be allowed. At the same time, if the decision on one type of development application could be appealed to the governing body, then appeals should be permitted on all disputed approvals or denials. Thus, a dissatisfied interested party would also be authorized to appeal a decision on a hardship variance, a site plan, or a conditional use to the governing body. However, the governing body, just as an appellate court, would simply review the evidence in the record from below and hear the arguments of the contending parties before reaching a decision.

Both the governing body and the courts would be aided by the requirement that every hearing on an application for development be recorded by some means, i.e., stenographer, tape recorder, etc. Any interested party to aid his appeal could then obtain a transcript of the proceeding by agreeing to pay the cost of transcription from the recording. Thus, the administrative boards would no longer be bothered by remands of their decisions because of inadequate records on which to base appellate review.

Strengthening Local Planning

A second major objective of the Community Planning Law is to improve and strengthen local planning. The planning board is directed to include in the municipal master plan a specific policy statement as to how that master plan relates to the master plans of adjacent municipalities, the county master plan, and the state development plan. Thus, the planning board is reminded of the planning of the state, the county, and its neighbors as it formulates its own plan. In adopting a zoning ordinance, the municipal governing body is directed to the scheme of the land-use element of the municipal planning board's master plan, but it may elect to diverge from that scheme by a majority vote of its full membership for reasons stated in its minutes. Thus, the fundamental responsibility of elected officials for legally binding municipal policy is recognized, while at the same time, the comprehensive planning concept of the master plan must enter into the thinking of these officials.

Public improvements are also an important influence on land use. Accordingly, the proposed Community Planning Law makes provision for the governing body to authorize the planning board to prepare a six-year capital improvement program based on the municipal master plan. Should the governing body adopt that capital improvement program, the first year of it would constitute the capital budget for that year.

Local planning would be further strengthened by sufficient advance notice of the state's intentions in regard to new state facilities through the state development plan, a long-range capital improvement program and an official state map. These plans would be prepared and officially adopted by a state planning council consisting of citizens appointed by the governor and the heads of departments of the state government whose programs affect development. Municipal officials would have the opportunity to influence the state development plan and official state map at public hearings. In addition, state agencies not presently so obligated would be required to give notice of the proposed location of a new state building or road before an undue financial commitment had been made. Municipal and county planning boards would then have forty-five days in which to object to the proposed project. Once an objection had been filed, a state agency could not act contrary to this objection without notifying these boards of the reasons for doing so.

Local planning would also be encouraged by increased technical assistance. The state would be obligated to provide municipalities with a planning and land-use manual that would contain provisions for land-use control ordinances, sample procedures, and forms for their administration, and other explanatory material and data to aid municipalities in the preparation of master plans, capital improvement programs, and the administration of ordinances. Also, a municipality could request state review and certification of its master plan and land-use control ordinances for conformity to state standards for balanced development as established by a new state planning council.

New local planning powers would be added by the Community Planning Law. A new provision would permit the establishment of a design-control district for an area containing buildings of historical, architectural, or cultural merit. Environmental design standards could be established for these districts for the harmonious relating of proposed structures to the terrain and to existing buildings.

Another new power would be authorization to require a developer to contribute his pro-rata share of the cost of water, sewer, drainage, and street improvements outside his subdivision.

An additional authorization to municipalities would be the right to adopt by reference the standards for the control of erosion and sedimentation during construction as established by the State Soil Conservation Committee.

To ensure that municipal planning and its implementation are updated, the municipal planning board would be required to prepare a report every five years on the current adequacy of the master plan and ordinances implementing it. Thus, a municipality would not be permitted to issue a general prohibition of development in order to prepare new plans and ordinances. However, the municipality would still be allowed ample protection against unforseen changes through the right to establish a zoning ordinance not based on the land-use element of a master plan for any interim period of not more than two years. The proposed legislation includes revised and enlarged joint planning provisions to provide for municipal and county agreements to establish regional boards of adjustment and joint building inspectors and zoning officers as well as regional planning boards. The agreements would provide any regional boards and joint officers with their powers, while any remaining powers not delegated would continue as the respon- sibility of the boards or officers of the constituent municipalities or counties.

Clarification

Perhaps the most important modern advance in land-use controls is the planned unit-development concept that provides common open space and promotes imaginative design, employment close to place of residence, and potentially a balance of municipal cost-consuming and revenue-producing uses. The progress of this concept in New Jersey has been hampered by the ambiguity and questioned constitutionality of the existing enabling legis- lation. The drafting committee for the proposed Community Plan- ning Law has solved these problems with the hope that the new provisions will be more widely utilized.

One of the increasingly used forms of land-use control is site-plan review, which is presently allowed by a somewhat strained judicial interpretation of a brief statutory provision. Essentially this type of regulation lacks a statutory framework worthy of its importance. Site-plan-review standards would be limited to preservation of the landscape, adequate circulation and parking, drainage, screening, setbacks, and lighting; one- and two-family housing is excluded from this type of review. If additional standards are needed for a type of development, the zoning ordinance may provide for performance standards and con- ditional uses requiring special permits. In addition, the requiring of performance and maintenance guarantees for improvements would be specifically authorized by the proposed statute for both approved site plans and conditional uses.

An area of planning law most in need of elucidation is that of the rights of the developer upon receiving approval for a sub- division. The present statute guarantees him against changes in the "general terms and conditions" of tentative subdivision ap- proval for a period of three years. The proposed revision would specifically include within the "general terms and conditions" such items as use requirements; layout and design standards for streets, curbs and sidewalks; lot size; yard dimensions; and off- tract improvements. At the same time, the public interest would be amply protected against municipal oversight or change of con- ditions by allowing the municipality to modify by ordinance such general terms and conditions as relate to public health and safety.

The term of tentative approval, to be redubbed "preliminary approval, " could be extended by the planning board, which has not been allowed under court interpretation of the existing statute. Also, final approval would be assigned a term of two years with extensions by the planning board permitted. More generous periods and extensions for the effect of preliminary and final approval could be permitted by the planning board for larger developments.

In the interest of greater procedural clarity, time periods were assigned for the denial or approval of all types of development applications. The decision to grant or deny preliminary subdivision approval was allotted 95 days for a subdivision of more than ten lots, and 45 days for a subdivision of ten or fewer lots. The existing period for grant or denial of final subdivision approval was maintained at 45 days. The period for acting on conditional uses, termed "special exceptions" under existing law, and on variances is extended to 120 days from a previous maximum of 95 days; site-plan review would be given 45 days.

All these time periods would run from the date of the filing of a complete application and could be extended with the consent of the applicant. Failure to reach a decision within the period specified in the proposed statute or further period agreed to by the applicant would result in approval. However, it was felt that an applicant would prefer to agree to extending the time for decision if the municipal board was moderately diligent rather than be faced with a quick denial and a possibly time-consuming and costly court proceeding. The only exception would be for use variances, the most extraordinary form of land-use approval, for which failure to decide in the period allotted would be deemed a denial for purposes of appeal.

Other Major Powers

The state planning council would be authorized to devise "critical area" regulations for floodplains and to supplement local regulation for areas adjacent to airports, state highways, and other public facilities in order to protect the public investment. Municipalities would be authorized to administer these additional regulations at their option. In all instances, local boards of adjustment would have the responsibility of passing on applications for hardship variances from these state devised regulations.

The county planning provisions in existing law are incorporated in the proposed Community Planning Law. Additional experience under the 1968 revisions of the county provisions is necessary before the need for changes can be soundly evaluated.

The Blighted Areas Act is incorporated in the proposal to aid in the recompilation of Chapter 55 of Title 40 of the Revised Statutes into Title 40A of the New Jersey Statutes.

Conclusion

Generally, the proposed Community Planning Law is a reaffirmation of the principle that local boards, with increased but voluntary guidance, can continue to be relief upon to assure the orderly growth and development of New Jersey. Although some changes are necessary in local procedures, there is a remarkable stability in the existing system. Recommended revisions are built upon the experience of the past two decades, the court decisions that indicated weaknesses in the present statutes or have whittled away local powers, and the new characteristics of development as we are observing them at the present time in the state. In brief these trends are a move toward large-scale developments; the public's increasing demand for good neighborhood design as well as good individual house design; the need in communities for a variety of house types, sizes, and services to different income and age groups; and the environmental protection requirements that have required the development of houses to include simultaneously the development of elaborate and expensive public facilities and service systems. Planning in the future will need to take into account the full range of economic, social, architectural, and physical community factors. This places a large burden on those local boards and agencies that regulate development in the public interest.

The responsibility for making the new system for regulating land development work will rest more than ever before on locally appointed municipal boards. The bill being proposed is not a lifting of authority from one level of government to another, but a procedure for providing more useful guidance and standards based on statewide and regional needs to be translated into specific decisions by local boards and based on local circumstances. There are some who would recommend that the complexities of development in the next decades will be too much for local boards to cope with. This bill reaffirms confidence that local regulation with appropriate guidance can effectively do the job.

References

1.   Editors' note: This bill lapsed at the termination of the 1972/73 Legislature.   The local sections of the bill are being reworked under the aegis of the New Jersey State League of Municipalities as a separate bill, hopefully to be introduced into the New Jersey Legislature in the fall.

V. ALTERNATIVE MODELS FOR DEVELOPMENT

Two Case Studies

A. INTRODUCTION

Two governmental units have legal control over extensive areas
of open land in northern New Jersey, the Hackensack Meadowlands Development Commission, which has recently been given
jurisdiction over development in the Hackensack Meadowlands
by the state legislature, and the City of Newark, which has
owned the huge Pequannock Watershed area for many years. Both
Newark and the Hackensack Meadowlands Development Commission are developing land-use policies for the regions under their
control, and naturally these policies will affect almost all of the
citizens in the northern part of the state.

Chester P. Mattson, chief of the Environmental Programs and
Planning division of the Meadowlands Commission, discussed
the commission's general land-use planning concepts and its
zoning policies for the 20,000 acres of land under its administration. He asserted that the commission's zoning techniques
are regional and comprehensive in scope and that they are innovative because they do not separate environmental decisions from
the development process; in order to carry forward its concepts,
the commission has divided the region into a series of "Specially
Planned Areas (SPA)." If the design is successful, it may provide
a model that can be adapted in other regions.

The Pequannock watershed covers an area of more than 35,000
acres in northern New Jersey. Development plans for the area
were discussed by Mr. Terrence D. Moore of the city of Newark.
Newark, located about fifteen miles to the southeast of this area,
intends to develop 6,247 acres of land in the watershed according
to a development model based on the ideas of Professor Ian McHarg
of the University of Pennsylvania. Newark's plans for this area
will affect a number of communities in the north central part of
New Jersey and are, therefore, of regional significance.

Here, then, are two ambitious attempts at regional planning.
Their success is of vital importance to the furtherance of an
effective land-use policy for northern New Jersey.

203

B. INNOVATIVE ZONING AS AN ENVIRONMENTAL
   CONTROL TECHNIQUE
   The Hackensack Meadowlands

Chester P. Mattson

Chief of Environmental Programs and Planning
Hackensack Meadowlands Development Commission
Lyndhurst, New Jersey

The Hackensack Meadowlands Development Commission's zoning
ordinance is not theoretical: It is actual. It was adopted on
November 8, 1972, after a two-year developmental moratorium,
itself one of the (then) new environmental control tools, during
which moratorium contemplative action had a rarely offered opportunity to precede regulatory action.

The Hackensack Meadowlands, 9,600 acres of urban open
space, were combined in 1969 with 10,000 acres of urban development (this last number includes 2,220 acres of active and
inactive sanitary landfills) into the Hackensack Meadowlands
District. The legislature, in creating a Hackensack Meadowlands
Commission, directed that from this imponderable (but valuable)
land mix was to come, first, a master plan, and then a regulatory
zoning ordinance. The goals to be produced in this two-stage
process were listed as three:

1. To provide homes, jobs and recreation space for the region.

2. To preserve the delicate balance of nature and protect
against air and water pollution.

3. To solve one-third of the state's solid waste problem
caused daily by the then 26,000 tons (now 52,000) per day of
garbage emanating from 115 New Jersey municipalities and land-
ing in the Hackensack Meadowlands marshes.

In the Meadowlands—they lie 6 miles west of Times Square—
resides every environmental problem conceivably found in an urban
area. Not surprisingly, each problem is tied in some way to the

205

consuming power of a force called urbanization. I shall discuss
that force as the take-off point for my paper.

Urbanization and the Environment

Urbanization, the intensification of urban forms within the city
itself, the extension of those forms outward into the surrounding
hinterland, and now its doubling back to fill in the overlooked
pockets, is the vehicle that transmits the metropolitan variety of
our environmental problems. This urbanization phenomenon places
a terrible burden on the relatively small land base supporting all
this activity, on the narrow columns of air above our urban places,
and on the tiny ribbons of water that intersect the city's reaches.
For example, in densely populated areas, a river "dies"—it loses
its capacity to assimilate, disperse, dilute, and carry away the
wastes for the surrounding area. Then downstream it regenerates
(we do not come close to understanding how), then "dies" again
where it next encounters an urban center.

In cities built where major rivers meet the sea—logical places
for urban growth over thousands of years—the competition between
environmental resources and relentless urban forms is particularly
severe. The stakes are high.

How do we view this impinging of men and their instruments
of manufacture, communication, and trade on their biological
lifelines? Are its various showdowns most profitably seen as
traditional adversary procedures where intelligent men of all
persuasions fight it out until a resolution is forced? In what other
ways can the problem be described?

And how do we deal with the predicament, given that, as
usual in urban matters, the debate about how to think about problems is carried out while the solutions are attempted?

The mélange of possible solutions has become familiar to all
of us. Some of us withdraw physically from the urban environment
to rural enclaves in order better to deal with the difficult challenge
of living harmoniously with nature. Or perhaps just to escape the
urban cacophony for a while. The action strategy adopted is a
reduction in the concentration of people and a reduction in the
variety and number of tools used by the community in operations
performed on the environment. How most to value nature, how
least to offend it with complex onslaught is the thrust of this
"solution." Sometimes, in the frustrated extreme, it takes the
"no more" approach: no more people, no more housing, no more

highways, no more water contamination, no more disruption of disappearing habitat.

Another approach is to regulate people who are already concentrated at urban densities. Their capacity to destroy the environment must be reduced. Their automobiles, for example, must not be used as weapons in man's various campaigns to subdue nature. A third approach deals with the need to recycle our urban discards. Raised to a more abstract level, our urban-oriented propensities to consume need to be rethought. Each of the "things" we attach to ourselves is produced at some environmental cost. The urban phenomenon needs massive regulation and value transformation: This is the thrust of these two approaches.

A fourth approach is to declare nature out of bounds for humans until we can learn to conduct ourselves in ways that merit putting it back in bounds. The action strategies adopted involve ways to secure patches of the wild from human intervention. The mental strategies, as usual, are more elaborate. But, in general, nature and man are found incompatible, or nearly so, and man is construed as the enemy. Guilty is how we should feel about the perverseness of our urban habits. People gathered in cities are somehow evil—or at least the effects of the gathering are evil. People alone with nature are somehow virtuous, or at least the effects of the encounter are virtuous. A fifth approach is to reconstruct for observation the ways we think of ourselves in a world that includes nature. Most obvious in this realm is the recent rise to American consciousness of the defects in the "progress" construct. To build, to "move ahead," to conquer new frontiers, to place man's works where they formerly were not—these deeds were elevated in our past to the level of values. But complicating even an inquiry into the "progress" ethic is the irredeemable fact that we will have to keep building in the years ahead to replace the deteriorated structures in which so many of our people still live and in which they will work in order to survive, and then to consume, perhaps. But to develop in the environment is so easily to recreate the conditions and habits of mind that produced the environmental crisis.

Thinking about values is, itself, a value-laden enterprise: The process leaves plenty of room for contradiction. But, again, at this more abstract level, the man/environment question becomes one of rethinking the place urban man occupies in a constellation of natural, technological, and human forces. He is not, it seems, solely the creator of his social, technological, and natural environments; he is also their creation. Nor is he, it seems, solely in support or in opposition to society, his technology, his natural surroundings. He is always in some of these reciprocal postures, and sometimes in all of them. Urban life is complex because it is all of these things at once.

Well, these approaches—dispersal, regulation, value transformation, isolation, cogitation—only suggest the others that could be mentioned here. But they make a point. Common to each, as contradictory as are their various action strategies and mental strategies, are four categories: space, man living at urban concentrations, technology, and the biological environment. And common to each of these, because it is the place where they all happen, is the land.

Strategies for protecting the land are disappointingly few. You have heard some of them discussed here. The Hackensack Meadowlands, the land of which I would speak today, is metropolitan land, metropolitan land in close to the urban core, six miles from New York City (every urban planner's nightmare).

Impinging on the land is the growth phenomenon—itself, to environmentalists, the bête noir of modern civilization. I should like to talk a bit about growth, nine types of growth, specifically, in my next section. I feel that each needs to find space for thought in the minds of environmental planners. Each, I feel, also constitutes an aspect of urbanization.

Growth and the Environment

Growth in land absorption

Land absorption is not pandemic to the whole American countryside. Rather, its selective patterns affect those parts of that countryside impinged upon by population increase, mobility, and migration, the combined effects of these three being urban densities.

The first, population increase, I will reserve for a separate growth section.

Second, the migration, in the first half of this century, of a massive wave of people who were radically changing both their roots and their expectations. This process took two forms: the migration of whites out of Midwestern America's farm heartland to the country's rims. (From 1952 to 1960, possibly representing the last big outbound spurt, population in the American heartland decreased 27 percent.) With this entire outpouring came a great leap in economic productivity—literally the transformation of the American economy from agrarian to industrial; and two, the migration of blacks out of the rural South's sharecropped farmlands to the cities of the North and Northeast (later to the West). This second wave of migrants also participated in the industrializing of America. Of interest, these two waves of American internal migration vastly outstripped the earlier, massive European immigrations and the relentless western march that resulted therefrom. These two migrations have some steam left, but their major effects are now completed.

Third, there is mobility, which consists of an essentially social phenomenon characterized by more gradual upward movement defined in terms of different neighborhoods or better jobs (or both).

The three—population increase, migration, and mobility— have altered densities as their consequence, most dramatically seen in the growth of metropolitan areas, which at last count (Census 1970) numbered 243. I shall save comment on this phenomenon—growth of metropolitan areas—until the next section.

Crucial to note, however, is that within these aspects of land absorption, some patterns are observable:

1. Center cities are not uniformly increasing in size of population. In fact, many of our major older urban centers had attained their present population levels by 1890. It's not an increase in people that crowds our big cities; rather, it's the ever more elaborate technologies each of us wields as we compete for the now-limited urban space. (Our automobiles are the best example: but our computers, files, air conditioners, appliances, and trucks are others that come to mind, all of which consume energy while competing with us for space.)

2. Much of the country's land is not entering the urbanized land bank.

3. Suburban and exurban lands in the path of these density rearrangements have come under incredible environmental stress.

Sorting out the environmental problems created by density changes (themselves wrought by population increase, migration, and mobility) is step one in designing different land-use controls for different land-use impacts. Within a new, emerging relationship of people and their available land, we have irretrievably become an urban civilization. But we are not becoming a nation of cities. Only the people part (not the nation part) is headed there. By the year 2000, writes Russell Train, 85 percent of us will live in urban agglomerations of 1, 000, 000 or more, occupying perhaps between 10 and 20 percent of the country's land area. He further notes that one lesson we will have to have learned is how to live closer to each other, much closer.

Incredible exchanges characterize this landscape of urban/ environmental variables. Water is carried hundreds of miles to New York City's high densities from upstate's low densities. Trees cut in Wisconsin make shopping bags for Los Angeles' suburbanites. Idaho farmland puts potatoes on Boston supper tables; Gulf of Mexico oil heats metropolitan New Jersey homes; Pittsburgh steel wrinkles into unrecognizability in a Seattle auto accident. It is true that many Americans are self-supporting on small farms, but their relative number is small. The rest of us live under the pressures of unprecedented interdependence.

In determining balances at this scale, the carrying capacity of the country is the regional container for environmental transfer calculations.

Closer to home, the urbanizing energies within and without New Jersey (one-third of the country's population lives within 250 miles) threaten the state with total and reckless land absorption. Let me dramatize that point.

Professors Raymond DeBoer and Norman Williams, both of Rutgers University, have, between them, articulated with great precision the dimensions of New Jersey's land crunch. If New Jersey's 567 municipalities act out their zoning ordinances (over however few decades that this will require), the state's land-use mix will look like this:

1. One-third of the state will be in housing, 99.5 percent of it single-family, 77 percent of that on lots of one acre or more in size.

2. One-third of the state will be in transportation uses— predominantly highways and local roads.

Norman Williams points out that our cultural reflex of ensuring every home frontage on a road is more exclusionary in its effects than is the now-familiar one-acre minimum clause. Every suburban home, we insist, must come equipped with 200 feet of road, and with it 200 feet of sidewalk and 200 feet of gas, water, sewer, electricity, and phone corridor. The consequence? The second 33 1/3 percent of what's left of the state will be in travel corridors to get us home (to the first 33 1/3 percent).

3. The remaining one-third itself will be divided: two-thirds into commercial, industrial, public, and semipublic uses, and one-third open space. Sum: 10 percent of what we can now view as open land will still be open land when our 567 official zoning ordinances, if acted out, have run their course.

Everyone here knows, of course, that the first steps have been taken to stem this reckless expenditure of, and statement of intent to use, our remaining land. For example, the Wetlands Act, the Flood Plain Protection Act, and the Coastal Protection Act—these proud first-generation zoning tools—have been passed in the state legislature. But they are still in the moratorium stage, untested in their execution. Further, these same tools address the problem of growth through the construct of ecological scarcity. Keeping men away is their thrust.

For another example, study of various state land-use planning and zoning techniques is underway to better fortify us against the mad run on metropolitan land. So far, however, only the Hackensack Meadowlands Act is testing the power of the state on that part of the land that our population most intently covets—for their homes, jobs, garbage, and open space—in the inner metropolitan ring. That the "land" in this case is an estuary further complicates the task.

Growth in population

A second type of growth is growth in population. I should like to refer for a moment to the President's Commission on Population Growth and the American Future. Their report told us what now all of us in the room know: that from 1900 to 1970 population in this country rose dramatically from 76 to 205 million. The annual growth rate was erratic. It was 2.1 from 1900 to 1910— massive growth stimulated and increased somewhat by immigration. It dropped to 0.7 in the 1930s. It rose again to 1.9 during the baby boom of the 1950s and leveled off at 1.1 in 1971, when the report was issued.

I'd like to quote from the report:

> Among the reasons cited for the potential
> that still remains here in this Country for

greater growth is the preponderance of
youth in the population. The youngsters
born during the "baby boom" are reaching
adulthood today, finishing school, seeking jobs, developing careers, getting
married and having children of their own.
Even if immigration from abroad ceased
and couples had only two children on the
average—just enough to replace themselves, our population would continue
to grow for about 70 years.

The recently attained (sustainable?) replacement level will
yield us a national population of 350 million persons 100 years
from now. Conrad Taeuber informs us that "In the next years a
large number of persons will be reaching the age of family formation—the result of a large number of babies born between
1947 and 1961 . . . In 1961, we had 4.3 million births. These
babies will have reached 24 years of age by 1985 . . . and will
have begun contributing to the number of children."

In 1971, there were about 42 million persons between 20
and 34 years old. By 1980, the number will have gone up to
58 million. Unless the birth rate drops (it has shown signs of
doing this), the number of children under 5 in 1980 will be
greater than it is at present. There is more uncertainty about
the year 2000. A major slice of the population in that year—that
is, all the persons who will be under 27—are still to be born.

Spread City has a guaranteed future. Population is a long-
term problem that gets worse as the term gets longer.

Two lessons, it seems to me, obtain for New Jersey in this
report: one, that an increase in the national rate of population
growth will exacerbate New Jersey's land-use problems. Across
the nation, children already born or now nearing the child-
producing age pose the land-use problems we face; and two, that
smaller population growth won't relieve our land-absorption problems because, again, New Jersey's time frame is about 30 years.

These facts should not, of course, deflect our attention from
population growth as a major environmental issue. Quite the
contrary. A slower national population growth rate would reduce
some of the demands on our limited resources, and it would contribute, as well, to our efforts to solve problems by gaining us
some precious time, perhaps as early as 30 years from now.

But a smaller population will also result in a further decline in the growth of Gross National Product. I will reserve comment on that aspect of growth for a few minutes.

What are the lessons for the environmentalist/land-use planner? First, we must address ourselves to <u>expectations</u>, especially those of the youth already in or likely to migrate to metropolitan areas. I didn't say alter—that's for sociologists to ponder. I said address—that's more in line with what government is asked to do. What demands will we be forced to satisfy? What ones can we regulate out of existence? This latter strategy, as Prohibition taught us, is mighty difficult to bring off. As a matter of fact, no large-scale effort to educate for value change has yet succeeded in this country.

Further, Resources For the Future, in Washington, D.C., has some instructive thoughts on the "lessons." Over the next three decades, they assert, population <u>distribution</u> will be most important in terms of regional water supply, the agricultural land bank, and outdoor recreation facilities. But <u>economic growth</u> will be a bigger factor than population in the demands we will impose on nonfuel minerals; and technological growth will assert a bigger demand than population growth on our energy supplies. They sum up by saying that environmental quality over the next 30 years will be tied more to land absorption and emission reduction than to population growth, and that it will require more regulation of individual lives than Americans are accustomed to. That's an uncomfortable aspect of the urban/environmental dilemma that we tend not to discuss.

For land planners, the "lesson" is to try to shake out those aspects of the larger environmental puzzle that best lend themselves to land-use planning and zoning for solution. Finding where best to invest our necessarily differentiated efforts is the key to the enterprise.

Growth in metropolitan areas

A third type of growth—in many ways reflecting the power of urbanization—is growth, in number and size, of metropolitan areas. Here is where the thrust of the population explosion and redistribution of the last 70 years has gone. The census of 1970 reveals this pattern: The national population (it increased by 13.3 million from 1960 to 1970) includes 62 million people in center cities (an increase of 3 million over 1960); 74 million in suburbs (an increase of 19 million over 1960); and 67 million outside the metropolitan areas (this number changed little over the decade). While about 70 percent of the U.S. population is now concentrated in metropolitan areas, 85 percent is expected to reside there in the year 2000. In that year, writes Russell Train, more than 6 out of every 10 Americans will live in cities of 1 million or more (compared to 4 of 10 who live there now). If people are the enemy, we are already living in the enemy's camp. Obviously, these settlement patterns hold the most serious consequences for land use and pollution emissions control.

Combining the figures for center cities and suburbs, it is seen that fully two-thirds of our population lives today in metropolitan areas, where, it should be noted, three-fourths of our bank deposits and industrial jobs are located. And, in metropolitan area expansion, both in number and in size, a significant fact about home building has materialized. In 1969, a watershed was reached after a 20-year climb: over half of all housing starts were in apartments. We are becoming a nation of apartment and condominium dwellers.

In the 243 metropolitan areas—which according to the census definition have a city of more than 50,000 at their core—80 percent of all work trips are by automobile. In the suburbs, the number is 96 percent. Reflecting this pattern (and the governmental influence of its participants), in 1970, public sector expenditures for transportation by all units of government totaled 25.5 billion dollars, of which 21.5 billion were for roads and streets. Of interest, 13 cents of the average American (1970) consumer dollar went for transportation. Mobility is our watchword.

In addition to daily migrations, the average American family moves every 5 years, most frequently (a) within the concentric rings of the same metropolitan area, or (b) to a "better spot" on another ring of a different metropolitan area. We don't regulate migration in this country—another indication of how constitutionally protected values, central to our way of life, confound solutions to environmental problems.

Following this largest segment of American migration—including the march to dwelling units in the suburban portions of the metropolitan areas—has been the migration of jobs, not only office and commercial jobs but more recently of the manufacturing and chemical industry jobs as well. Low- and moderate-cost housing are the slowest of the migrators. Reverse commuters are the evidence of this.

The truck—it increased in registered abundance from 4.8 million in 1948 to 20.5 million in 1973—has been a major beneficiary of the federal highway construction subsidy (90 percent), which produced the 41,000-mile Interstate Highway system. In winning the battle (over railroads) for migrational flexibility, the truck has become a rolling assembly line. The 15,100 motor-carrier companies respond to markets that now require timeliness, that experience fluctuation, and that demand door-to-door service— the hallmarks of a consumer society. Many industries, in fact, have their components delivered overnight for assembly the next day.

The Hackensack Meadowlands District—the heartland of the New York-New Jersey metropolitan area's warehouse and distribution capability (43 percent of this metropolitan region's truck bays are located here)—is testimony to this transportation development.

Nationally, trains still handle the heavy materials and other basic products that move long distances and that are keyed to steady flow. Indicating the centrality of its location, the Hackensack Meadowlands District also contains the biggest concentration of railyards in the northeast, making it, potentially, a natural interface between automobiles and mass-transit facilities.

As I noted earlier, metropolitan growth is also describable in terms of density. Let me comment further on that. Population changes by counties (1960-1970) are instructive. (See Conrad Taeuber, An Overview of the Problem of Density.) They show us, for example, that the migration is not random and pervasive. It flows in clusters: subnucleation is the word demographers use in description. Writes Taeuber:

> From 1960 to 1970, about 1,367 or more
> than 2/5 of the (nation's) counties lost
> population. Another 995 counties gained
> at a rate less than the national average,
> and only 773 gained at more than the
> national average . . . Gains and losses
> were unevenly distributed . . . For about
> 2/3 of the 1,367 counties which lost pop-
> ulation during the decade of the 1960's,
> this was the continuation of a trend which
> had also been observed during the 1950's
> and 1940's . . . It is fair to conclude that

in a substantial number of counties,
covering a rather large land area, there
have been declines in density in the
last decade.

Some other patterns in the metropolitan growth phenomenon
are also instructive. In all states the number of housing units
increased more rapidly than the number of persons. Increases in
density, naturally, are reflected in increases in the number of
housing units per unit of land. But housing-density increases do
not necessarily reflect growing population: they also reflect
changing life styles.

For sorting out what environmental problems are best
addressed where, however, no statistic to me is so telling as
this one: in 1960, about 70 percent of the population lived on
about 1 percent of the country's land area.

The black population now is proportionately more heavily
concentrated in the metropolitan areas than is the white population (74 percent of blacks, but only 68 percent of whites).
Further, 80 percent of the blacks, but only 40 percent of the
whites in these metropolitan areas live within the central cities.

Beyond the statistics, however, the metropolitan area phenomenon has gotten us to a new kind of urban society—a sub-
nucleated world of housing developments, shopping centers,
industrial parks, and service industries—all tied together by
autos and expressways, and (except for key components) increasingly oblivious to the urban core. So homogenizing has been the
effect of subnucleation that, for example, regional cultural differences have nearly disappeared. Corporation migration based
on the regional difference preferences of its officers stopped in
the late 1940s. Television English is rapidly (save in New Jersey
and New England) subverting our beautiful local dialects.

This new urban/metropolitan system is operational, but at
incredible cost. In dollars (one kind of cost), the cost of trans-
porting everything to everywhere makes life extremely expensive.
Chain stores, perhaps to make advertising possible, charge the
same rate for articles delivered at different cost to different shopping centers. The litany of environmental costs has already been
recited today. Further, in "operational" costs, the system is as

fragile as it is interdependent. A 20-minute strike by New York City bridge-tenders can paralyze 10 million people, yet another consequence of the dispersed society. An oil slick can wipe out an entire city's beachfront, paralyzing simultaneously and instantaneously its fishing industry and its beaches. One car running a city light and getting caught at midintersection immediately renders drivers blocks away motionless. We are irretrievably and inextricably connected to each other in thousands of invisible ways.

Ecologically, the central city, at the core of this system, presents a depressing model. The closer one gets to the core, less wealth (it migrated) is called on to produce more services (the region's sewage treatment, for example). The city's metabolism is badly disrupted: its daily intakes of air, water, fuel, raw materials, and construction materials are not matched, in any ecologically reasonable way, by its daily discharges of heat, emissions, sewage, solid waste, demolition rubble. It looks, for all intents and purposes, like a dead-end machine that has as its goal the consumption of the biosphere.

Worse, the demands on good citizenship are almost impossible to bear. Gone are the days when, by voting, you accomplished your duty as a citizen. Now you must join three environment groups, and at least one consumer group, to be a respectable cocktail-party conversationist (say less to make your influence felt). Our whole sacred American history of calculated indifference to government has given way to a recently born clamorous insistence that government produce our expectations. Which gets me to my fourth and fifth categories of growth:

Growth in the special district; growth in governmental expectations

Robert Wood has classified suburbia, now the largest population-growth area, as a "holdout against modern culture." Middle Americans, he argues, themselves both participants and consumers (by day) in modern industrial civilization's hallmark, the large organization (corporate, financial, educational, legal, and institutional), retire at night to communities where small, personalized government is their watchword. "Keep government localized, small, and accountable" argue these advocates of a fragmented, uncoordinated metropolis. And fragmented and uncoordinated it remains. As a new service is desired, a new unit is created. At present, the nation has over 100,000 units of government, comprising water-supply districts, housing agencies, public-works boards, museum boards, cemetery boards, parking authorities, traffic authorities, airport authorities, redevelopment agencies, police and fire commissions, sewerage commissions, school boards, library districts, water commissions, park boards, recreation boards, health boards, hospital boards, etc., etc., etc. In the San Francisco Bay area—9 counties—there are 500 government jurisdictions! In New York City there are over 1,400— Robert Wood catalogued them over 10 years ago in a classic study.

Little wonder that zoning, competing with all these, has had its tribulations. If a government official touched bases with all his pertinent counterparts in other agencies, he would spend his life in the basepaths. The trouble is, of course, that urban life is _not_ fragmented and uncoordinated. Interdependence and complexity are its hallmarks. And while keeping government accountably small, we ask for ever more benefits. Now we want government to rescue the environment.

Growth in technology

A sixth kind of growth is the kind of growth that you hear about when you talk to technologists—the growth in the "mass energy nimbus." As I noted earlier, population growth is not the chief problem of center city; Philadelphia attained its present level of population—about 1 million people—in 1890. So did Boston—with about 650,000 souls, not all of them Irish. The big period of population growth in many of our older cities ended over 70 years ago. What makes those cities and the newer ones more crowded today is not the greater number of people clustered together, but something that May Ways called the indelicate elephant of technology and energy that each of us carries around in front of us—a kind of mass-energy nimbus. The machinery for our thoughts, our production, and our communication takes up a good deal more space than we do. It also uses energy and raw-material resources. Technology is what typifies the modern industrial city, imposing on us its own urban/industrial growth phenomenon.

Barry Commoner has commented on the nature of this growing mass-energy nimbus and its effects. He has shown us that the kinds of turns taken by industrial growth since 1946 have been counterecological. We have developed—with a big advertising boost—a need for, and a supply of, such industrial products and by-products as chemicals, herbicides, insecticides, oil transport technology, supersonic aviation, and nuclear power generation. Chlorine, for example, is an important ingredient in the production of synthetic fibers. The dacron shirt I have on is counterecological in that mercury is an important material in chlorine production.

Commoner's point of view is this—if the public doesn't reject these processes, it is accepting them. As resources encounter scarcity, partly because of technological growth, demands for new resource materials will call for the introduction of newer technologies before we know enough about how they work. Use of phosphate substitutes in detergents is as good an example as any.

In yet another way, the problem compounds itself—which gets me to a seventh kind of growth ignored, at their peril, by environmental planners:

Growth in relative ignorance

We are, each generation of us, more ignorant than the preceding generation, in that each of us in each new generation is capable of knowing a smaller percentage of the total amount of knowledge available to know. That's a frightening fact about knowledge. Knowledge doubles in volume every ten years; thus, each of us can know less and less of the total—the growth in relative ignorance. Specialization, crucial to excellence, is the enemy.

Decline in the growth rate of Gross National Product (GNP)

The decline in the growth rate of the GNP is not to be overlooked in its consequences for environmental and urban planners. We are, in real dollars, more than twice as rich as our grandfathers. This increase in wealth has not come to millions of us, but to those so favored the key has been in the productivity increases that have come with the transition from an agrarian to an industrial society. Put simply, fewer people, using machines, can feed the rest of us at less cost than without machines, thus at greater productivity. Ninety percent of us used to farm the land, many at subsistence. That number is now 6 percent, freeing 84 percent of us to live at a higher living standard in urbanized areas. The economists are available to tell us, however, that the leap was essentially a one-time phenomenon. Relatively tiny productivity leaps are what remain.

Kenneth Boulding observed that we have come to a turning point in our ability to continue to increase productivity. GNP is still increasing, but its rate of increase has slowed. To an expanding population, one that has been able to see the poor get richer without the rich getting poorer, the writing is on the wall. Zero economic growth, seen by some as a goal that will reduce environmental carnage, will also force enormous adjustments in social values. Not only must the standard of living decline under this strategy, but the poor must get poorer unless massive income redistribution is simultaneously effected. Environmentalists will find few friends in this new zero growth venture. Dr. Boulding also sees in this strategy a repressing effect on innovation, another important American value. Innovation always carries risk, and risk invariably requires seed money, derived either from profits or from taxes on profits.

In the progressive state (the bad old days), economic conflicts were resolved by progress, itself. But some important arguments are now being offered for the pressing need for more successful conflict management (government?) and less adversary activity in a contracting economy—where ever-expanding goals (including the expensive environmental ones) become more disruptive as the absence of ever-expanding wealth makes the competition deadlier. A harbinger of this problem is seen in the expansion in the economy of the less-productive service sector (as education, government, service industries).

Early perceptions of this economic condition have produced among some in our society a brooding sense about the inevitability (in the next 50 years or so) of radical changes—in our technology, our social systems, our culture, and our self-image. It will be a difficult transition to make, and it is the subject of the last type of growth I wish to talk about, accompanying our transition toward knowing we occupy a small, closed, tightly crowded, limited spaceship: Earth.

Growth in better perceptions of ourselves

Ever so rapidly, man's place among society, technology, and nature has changed. Ever so slowly, his perception of these changes has matured. Two people whose words inspire me have been writing about this transition—Victor G. Ferkiss (Technological Man: The Myth and the Reality) and Dr. Elton Morrison at Yale (Men, Machines and Modern Times). These gentlemen articulate very precisely what many, I include myself, have

intuitively groped for—that man has become a participant in a
network of systems. Morrison wrote:

> Whereas before man appeared in an adver-
> sary position, organizing his technology
> to reduce the strong points in obstructive
> nature; in the future he will increasingly
> appear as one agency working within an
> intricately interconnected total system of
> his own devising.

He is not solely the creator of social, technological, and natural
environments; he is also their creation. Nor is he solely in support or in opposition to his society, his technology, and his
natural surroundings.

Morrison, in a review of Ferkiss' work, also wrote:

> To make the new technological environ-
> ment work better, human beings must
> acquire three new understandings. First,
> that men are not so much in an adversary
> condition against nature, as they are a
> working part of it. Second, that in the
> system of mind-body-machinery-society-
> nature, everything connects and interacts.
> This is a very important point to Mr. Ferkiss:
> the effects of acts and decisions in any
> one place are transferred inevitably through-
> out the system in which everything does
> connect. And finally, man must, therefore,
> recognize that the shape given the total
> system derives from what happens within
> the totality and not from the action of some
> tinkering agency—Fate, Fortune, God—up
> or out there.

To summarize this section on growth and to structure my final
section on zoning, I'll pose this question: If environmental problems are inextricably tied to the various facets and degrees of
urbanization and growth—and I believe them most advantageously
seen that way in terms of their solutions—what are our choices?

Taking a part of the question, first, our choices in "urban policy"—itself only recently argued as a valid enterprise for governmental attention—are, themselves, few. Some were discussed in this conference. In fact, if I may again cite Robert Wood, the policies available for the mind to tinker with seem to come down to about five:

1. We should not let the small towns die; they are the heartblood of America. Zoning has recently become a tool of the advocates of this "urban" strategy (raising, with some, the specter of zoning as inept, illegal, and immoral). The small towns that are dying—there are thousands—try to lure industry in. Those that are thriving (or have recently stopped thriving) try to keep new residents out. Voluntary migration thwarts them all.

2. Let the lines go where they will. This is also called the "extension of the rings" theory, or "spread city," wherein metropolitan areas keep expanding outward at their periphery while simultaneously doubling back to fill in the overlooked pockets. William H. White (The Last Landscape) sees this as so real that we had best make the most of it as it happens. York Willbern sees it as inevitable, and finds government policy largely irrelevant. Raymond Vernon, on the other hand, thinks that workable government strategies could make the process not only bearable but perhaps even felicitous. And Lewis Mumford decries spread city, arguing for what I'll call the third urban strategy being discussed these days:

3. Preserve the decaying core cities (an urban strategy sometimes favored by environmentalists who have successfully escaped to the country). Urbanists and governmental specialists have as yet found no way to accomplish this strategy at any scale, although certainly heroic and expensive attempts have been made—through public housing, urban renewal, community action programs, the war on poverty, and model cities. Revenue sharing is the latest venture, designed apparently to keep the suburbanites contentedly at bay while the city folk are given some desperately needed help. Lewis Mumford, again, calls our cities the glory of our civilization, and urges gigantic efforts at reclamation, matching, at least, the mammoth highway and housing subsidies extending to the suburbs over the last 25 years. Others, less sanguine about the cities than Mumford, say that the new breed of mayors seeking to lure back wealth and glory to the city are having a love affair with an urban ghost.

4. Build new cities. One hundred new cities of a million people each are needed in the next 30 years (3 a year . . .) and can perhaps be built with corporate financing, says the Rockefeller report. This, easily the most popularly discussed urban strategy, is also the most expensive, perhaps the least feasible. We have but a few "new towns," more suburban than urban, to show for all this talk—and no new cities.

5. Oil the squeaky wheel. The political response constitutes that time-tested governmental strategy that I trust will be with us for a long time. In fact, if it isn't, we shall have to inquire where our democratic institutions went. We should be more charitable about this approach than we are—politics is one of the precious few ways we have of settling differences in a complicated society with any real measure of accountability (even though throwing out the mayor, who never had a chance anyway, is a great American urban political pastime). In most cases, the more "accountable" a governmental unit gets (i. e., the smaller and more decentralized its task), the less of the total puzzle there is for it to be accountable for. My biases are showing. But to indulge in an aside, I would hate to see the environmental movement become criticizable as a holdout against modern culture, fragmenting, as has the metropolis, into a thousand small issue-oriented groups, soon discovering themselves in competition with one another.

These five apparent choices in urban policy are instructive—crucial, I would argue here today—to the framing of environmental land use policies for urban areas. At any rate, that is the assertion I bring to this conference.

And in many ways that's what I think the Hackensack Meadowlands Development Commission's Zoning Ordinance is about. So let me describe it, framing it with my announced topic:

Innovative Zoning as an Environmental Control Technique

Innovative zoning is inextricably tied to urbanization. In fact, this tool, traditionally passive in nature, depends on urbanization to activate its categories. This has been its curse. Zoning, grounded in the police power, and thus in a definition of the "public interest," has relied for its success on the forces that invariably have destroyed it.

But it is new judicial and legislative definitions of the public interest that, I feel, make land planning and zoning worthy of a new investment in thought, action, and even, perhaps, hope.

The Hackensack Meadowlands Act (Chapter 404 of the Statutes of New Jersey) is an example of the new legislation. To begin with, it incorporated, in 1969, a now-famous phrase, the "delicate balance of nature"—which phrase, in its inclusion as one of the goals assigned the Meadowlands Commission, forces a new look at all the other phrases. It thrusts environmental issues into that total arena of urban issues that, in their acting out, produce the environmental crisis.

Growth in land absorption has already characterized the Meadowlands. In November 1972, at the end of a two-year development moratorium, the land use chart of the Meadowlands looked like this:

	Acres
Active sanitary landfill	481
Inactive sanitary landfill	1,741
Clean fill	949
Transportation	2,955
Utilities*	786
Industrial development	2,384
Commercial development	254
Residential development	206
Marsh conservation (N. J. Turnpike)	85
Public park	15
Airport	438
Quarry (Snake Hill)	115
Marinas	42
Vacant buildings and buildings under construction	133
TOTAL	10,584

*Two power generating stations, 5 sewage treatment plants.

Some urban planners have called the Hackensack Meadowlands an official "ugliness zone, " i. e. , a place where, consciously, the unaesthetic aspects of urban life—garbage dumps, fuel-storage tanks, power-generating stations, massive highway corridors and connectives, water pollution outfalls, etc.—have been exiled.

The Zoning Ordinance is both stern and adaptive in the face of these land use realities. For example, four transportation centers are called for—all at rail and highway interfaces, and each to be produced or significantly aided by private capital. The incentive is this: a private developer gets to build high-rise office buildings if he also builds a transportation center. Permit me an aside, here. The trade-offs are mind bending. Some say that all office buildings should (somehow) go to revitalize the decaying core cities; not, say, to the Hackensack Meadowlands or to the more distant suburbs. We see the need, however, for private capital to produce a transit-based transportation system that "picks off" suburban commuters and whisks them into New York City, Jersey City, and Newark. In order to get clean air, however, we see also contemplated a regulating of automobile traffic to New York City, which runs the risk of driving away more of the office-building workers (and their management) who now drive to existing core-city office buildings. It seems you need revenue-producing office buildings (at transportation centers) to save office buildings (in core cities).

Traditional zoning, to continue, has terrible timing and phasing problems. When will these dreams painted on the zoning map ever occur? In what order? At what cost in municipal services? In traditional zoning situations, the money-making zones along the highway are snapped up first by retail stores, shops, MacDonalds', and gas stations. Then, when other land uses don't materialize ("clean" industry, luxury homes on five acres), concessions are made to permit variances. A municipal zoning ordinance is only realistic as a control tool when its variances are few.

The Hackensack Meadowlands Development Commission's Zoning Ordinance approaches these problems of phasing by requiring, through the establishment of large comprehensive zones called "Specially Planned Areas" (SPA), that both project-scale and land-use variety must be planned and developed simultaneously. No one here, for example, gets to build only a snazzy suburban-type shopping center, make a fortune, and then depart leaving a trail of highway expenses, unpredictable residential growth, and perhaps also decay of the downtown area five miles away.

To solve the classic metropolitan problem of dozens of small-parcel landowners building their various castles at privately determined heterogeneous moments, a prospective developer of an SPA must aggregate 80 percent of the land, possibly through the formation of a management group of the owners of that much of the land area in the zone, and come up with an agreed-upon general plan for the entire SPA. The developer need not develop a whole SPA (there are 14 of them, varying in size from 100 to 450 acres) at once, but his plan for the entire area must precede his development of any phased portion of it. Each phased portion must provide a proper proportion of the needed services (schools, libraries, mass transit systems, day care centers, etc.). The developer need not, himself, provide all of these services, but he must show the Commission that they will arrive on line when his buildings open.

The developer gets to build at high densities, as well, clustering his required roads and services, and maximizing his profit so that the "public interest"-type uses he is required to produce do not, in fact, regulate him out of existence—a style of government regulation that is environmentally popular in some circles but that just happens to be unconstitutional.

This technique, as you can see, is not automatically exportable to other areas. In fact, it depends for its plausibility on the fact that land values here are already high—that land ownership has already gone through a five- to ten-step speculator phase since the early 1950s and is now in the hands of people who will develop it to make their profits and justify their tax rates rather than sell to yet another speculator. (If I may be permitted another aside, environmental planners have to wonder a bit at why real estate firms, who seek and draw off the money values that urbanized or urbanizing location produces here, enjoy such unscrutinized respectability in our society. Somehow, the dollar value—its "windfall" characteristic—of the land should contribute to the later environmental costs that attend the development, particularly those that attend the production of open space, not just pass to and from those who have the cash to sit on land that urbanization is pushing upward in dollar value. Urbanization is society-wide in its pervasive effects, yet its financial benefits pass to so relatively few.)

In terms of environmental controls—to me the most exciting aspect of the SPAs—public open space is required, and this open space, because the Meadowlands constitute a marsh/estuarine ecosystem, must first be identified through the completion of a comprehensive Environmental Impact Assessment procedure—requiring the completion of three types of resource inventories: biological (vegetation, water quality, air quality, wildlife habitat, etc.); life-support systems (energy supply, water supply); and services (sewer systems, transit systems, etc.).

This assessment procedure, itself, is grounded in another environmentally innovative tool: an official and adopted Open Space Map, which maps the area of highest ecological value and highest strategic recreational location that a developer must protect or develop while constructing his (much) more profitable projects on the remaining land. In less strategic cases, the developer must work with the Commission staff to apportion the regional open spaces (wetland, recreational parkland, canoe trails, boardwalks, landscaped areas) and clustered development areas to best advantage. There is no prejudgment, however, of where all the regional open spaces are to be located. We want developers, architects, and environmental scientists, the best that we can find, to come up with their own versions for our analysis of how best to utilize a 400-acre tract in pursuit of interlocking goals. In this way, we are plowing new ground in the zoning process—attempting to overcome, through a mixture of comprehensiveness and flexibility, the disastrous effects of fragmented decisions, private and public, which characterize our metropolitan areas.

Both of these environmental instruments, the Environmental Impact Assessment and the Open Space Map, and a third, the Wetlands Order, are uniquely tied to the Zoning Ordinance—making environmental decisions not separate from but totally integrated with the developmental process, and giving regulatory stature to the legislative goal "to protect the delicate balance of nature. "

Rounding out the environmental aspects of the Zoning Ordinance's procedures is the incorporation, in the zones and the SPAs, of Environmental Performance Standards regulating, before construction (rather than after), emissions (air pollution, water pollutants, noise, radioactivity, etc.) produced in an industrial society.

An Environmental Design Committee, called for in the Ordinance, made up of at least seven members from the professional fields of ecology, architecture, and planning, will review the general plan for an SPA when the commission's Development Board seeks that advice. This permits government, usually an outgunned and weak partner in the urbanization process, to get the benefit of some very careful professional scrutiny of the proposals it receives.

Another innovation in the Zoning Ordinance is the requirement that every new tenant must come to the Meadowlands Commission for a land-use permit. This is an important environmental control. A traditional jurisdiction one can find in zoning law is that new land uses must be approved by the zoning board. In the Meadowlands, however, when a new tenant moves in, even if the use stays the same, a new land-use permit must be procured. Then we send out our environmental crew to correct existing problems, such as those involving water and air pollution emissions.

A final environmental component to the Zoning Ordinance is one that is new to this state, but one that has been discussed at length across the nation in the last two years — property tax sharing. How can towns get out from under the burdens of a property-tax system that forces them to fill up their remaining land with ratables to foot the soaring cost of municipal services: fire, police, schools, solid waste, etc. ?

The practice of tax sharing is not new; it is, for example, common in our various income-tax schemes. Federal tax money from one section of the country provides other sections with disaster relief, housing subsidies, law-enforcement subsidies, legal aid, or food stamps—the whole firmament of federal programs. Or state taxes—state income taxes—provide state police protection, state university educations, state highway construction, state health inspections, and state water-pollution inspection, for example.

In the Hackensack Meadowlands, this revenue-distribution principle is applied to municipal property-tax revenues. No money goes to the commission, however. May I repeat that? No money goes to the commission, however.

Essentially, towns "saddled" with zones that require big open-space areas (thus "deprived" of space-eating tax ratables) are compensated, through a sharing formula, from revenues derived from clustered, profitable development that occurs in other municipalities in the District. The formula operates at small scale at first. In 1973, for example, only 10 percent of the Meadowlands tax ratables go to the pool for redistribution. The 14 towns each keep 90 percent of their taxes garnered from the Meadowlands. Over 12 years, at 4 percent per year, the

pool gradually increases to 50 percent—at which point the percentage stops growing. This tool, designed to mitigate the fragmented, chaotic rush for ratables within our "region," serves
also as a key environmental control. In yet another way, environmental goals are integrated into the urbanization process.

I have had room for only a thumbnail sketch today. In summary, what we believe to be key environmental controls are
imposed on the urbanization process itself in the Meadowlands
Zoning Ordinance. Severe restraint on growth, as well, is evidenced by the fact that our Open Space Plan calls for an open
space bank of 6,140 acres to be carved from the 10,000 acres
still open. It will be no easy task—believe me—and there is no
one agency that can guarantee its success.

The last thing I want to do is tell you why I'm hopeful about
this place. I'm hopeful because the system that we produced,
which got us into this mess (the system of growth, measured in
the nine parameters that I chose to discuss), was largely inad-
vertent. It wasn't venal; it wasn't intended; it happened quickly.
Its instrumental urbanized effects were on the ground by 1890.
Its industrial and secondary migrational effects came after. Most
significantly, to my mind, it has taken us quite a while to come
to grips with what's been working on the land for a long time to
make things the way they are now.

Second, the system that we produced, the metropolitan system, happened in the presence of values that are good values. A
man's home is his castle. His property rights are important. His
right as an individual to migrate is an important American right—
but one that has induced some difficult byproducts in metropolitan
growth. The public interest, a crucial democratic value, has
traditionally protected the individual from the group. A more
crowded world now forces a new look at this vital value. The
adversary system—the core of our legal system and of many of
our democratic institutions—has sanctified individual expression
in law. But as our society has become more vulnerable to the
effective use of this model (New York City's bridge tenders come
to mind), this adversary model needs, I feel, to be rescrutinized—
with love.

Certainly, then, there is no indication that the values we
have held throughout the construction of this system have been
poor values. As a matter of fact, their persistence over the next
decades should be our primary political goal. But from an envi-

ronmental perspective, I think we need to come around to seeing the problem better than we have before. Complexity is upon us.

As you can see, I have not come here today suggesting something for you to "try" in the environmental zoning realm. Rather, I have sought two directions: one, to provide a rough-cut framework—the growth framework—into which new ideas can be set; and second, to offer for your scrutiny a tool—the Hackensack Meadowlands Development Commission's Zoning Ordinance— which is already in existence. Needless to say, I'm proud and excited to be in on that venture.

One cannot be an environmentalist at the Hackensack Meadowlands Development Commission and be against development. Further, I submit that one cannot be a member of the "no more" school of environmentalism and participate in the discussion of land use as an environmental control technique.

Even further, there are things that we need to bring, partially through zoning, into being. We need to rethink how our homes, jobs, highways, and open spaces will be produced and intermingled. We need desperately to rethink and reshape the force of urbanization; itself, I feel, soon to become our overriding environmental concern.

One shouldn't sum up complex topics. But if I had to, I'd say: Urbanization is comprehensive; growth is comprehensive; land absorption is comprehensive; it's time zoning was.

Have you looked at your local zoning ordinance lately?

C. THE NEWARK WATERSHED STUDY

Terrence D. Moore

Executive Director
Newark Watershed Conservation and Development Corporation
Newark, New Jersey

Introduction

The purity of the water that Newark now
enjoys was made a matter of record over
a hundred years ago, when Alexander
Hamilton sought to learn where the purest
and softest water in all the States then
established was to be had. . . . So, under
his direction, the government employed a
number of American and English chemists
to go over the entire area of the States,
examining the streams. In the report made
by the chemists, it was found that the
waters of the Pequannock Watershed in
this State were declared to be the purest.

So reported Frank J. Urquhart in his book, A Short History of Newark,
published in 1916.[1] The area he was referring to had recently been
acquired by the city of Newark as a new source of water supply.
This same area was the subject of a year-long policy study con-
ducted by the Office of Newark Studies of Rutgers University.

Newark's Pequannock watershed is located in parts of Morris,
Passaic, and Sussex counties, approximately 35 miles northwest
of Newark. It is approximately 63.7 square miles in area and
forms portions of six separate municipalities. These are Rockaway,
Jefferson, and Kinnelon in Morris County; Hardyston and Vernon
in Sussex County; and West Milford in Passaic County. Newark's
holdings comprise 86 percent of the entire drainage area, or
35,000 acres. The remaining property is held under private

231

ownership and scattered throughout the watershed. The area contains five reservoirs supplying one-half of the city's water resources.

The main transportation access to the property is via New Jersey State Highway 23. Three county roads also traverse the area from north to south. Although rail lines exist, none are currently in use.

The watershed is astride the Reading Prong of the New England Physiographic Province, geologically a complex area; it contains mainly precambrian rocks and infolded paleozoics. The Reading Prong is more commonly referred to as the "Appalachian Highlands" in northwestern New Jersey and southeastern New York.

Terrain in the watershed is rugged and glacially scoured. Slopes often exceed 25 percent and valleys tend to be narrow and steep-sided, rising from 200 to 800 feet from floor of valley to summit of parallel, flat-topped ridges. The many clear lakes and ponds, green valleys, magnificent rock outcroppings, gorges, mountains, and forest cover combine to make the Pequannock watershed an area of great scenic beauty. Wildlife inhabiting the virtually undeveloped area include deer, woodchucks, squirrels, rabbits, and small rodents, snakes (including rattlers and copperheads), and many birds. Among the latter are hawks, grouse, and turkey vultures.

Historically, the area was the scene of early colonial iron mines and forges. A few structures remain from this bygone era.

In May of 1971, at the request of the city, the Office of Newark Studies began an analysis of the property to determine alternative uses that the watershed might serve. The city pays approximately $1.5 million annually in property taxes, a figure that has increased rapidly over the past few years. The city, mindful of this economic burden, wished to develop a policy that would conserve critical areas of the property while reducing its yearly outflow of dollars. Funds to conduct the study were secured from the Ford Foundation and the New Jersey Department of Community Affairs.

During the course of the study, vast amounts of data concerning the watershed, the six municipalities, and the three counties were collected and analyzed. The data can be broken down into three major categories of analysis: property acquisition and taxation; economics, including regional and market studies; and physical, including engineering and ecological analyses.

Property acquisition and taxation

The study of property acquisition and taxation involved an examination of the watershed's role in the history of the six municipalities, a detailed analysis of property acquisition over time, and computation of Newark's changing tax burden coming from watershed properties.

Property-acquisition analysis included detailed surveys of city records and deed recordings within the three counties. The data were computerized during the course of the study and provide information regarding acreage, date of acquisition, deed recording, conveyance method, etc. The availability of such data enabled the staff to gain a deeper understanding of the watershed and the growing presence of Newark in the area since the turn of the century. A historical study was also undertaken to provide an insight into Newark's role in the history of the region. As such, the future policy could be judged within the framework of knowledge of the past.

The analysis of taxation of watershed properties included the collection of data relating to assessed valuation, tax payments over time, development of composite tax maps, and the awareness that within a five-year period Newark's watershed taxes had quadrupled in many communities. Past and current municipal service costs in each of the municipalities were also studied. These studies provided a framework for measuring the impact of a new policy on the six municipalities and on Newark's continuing watershed taxation prospects.

Economic analyses

The economic analyses performed during the course of the study examined the three-county (Morris, Passaic, and Sussex) area with an emphasis on the six municipalities encompassing the watershed. This information concerned population, housing, transportation, industry and employment, and other trends between 1960 and 1970. Trends were then projected to 1980, taking into consideration conditions that would promote or hinder growth, such as the availability of central water and sewerage systems, etc. A series of market analyses were also performed on possible development activities within the watershed.

The findings of these analyses showed an area undergoing rapid urbanization and an intensive commercial recreation industry. Vernon township, with the development of major ski areas, the

TABLE 1.
Natural Features* – Pequannock Watershed

Feature	Acres	Characteristics	Critical/Less than critical
Prime watersheds	19,993	Sub-watersheds draining directly into lakes, reservoirs	Critical
Wetlands	3,108	Floodplains and swamps	Critical
Prime agricultural lands	638	Class I - Soils that have few limitations that restrict their use for cultivation (deep, well drained, nearly level)	Critical with potential uses for forestry, agriculture, etc.
		Class II - Soils that have some limitations that reduce the choice of plants or that require moderate conservation practices	
Severe limitations for septic effluent disposal	4,306	Shallow depth to seasonal high water table, bedrock and slow permeability	Critical
Steep slopes	2,001	25%+ slopes	Critical
Primary developable	6,247	Soils, slope allowable, minimum impact on ecology under controlled conditions	Less than critical

*Natural features are mapped.

Source: Rahenkamp, Sachs, Wells Associates, 1972

Playboy Club, and other facilities, was indicative of this growth. In the classical relationship, urbanization was increasing land values and, therefore, municipal services and taxes.

The economic studies provided an understanding of what had occurred in the area during the past decade, what issues and developments were affecting present growth, and finally, what changes could be expected in the future. This understanding of the past, the present, and the future provided a framework for developing a policy with an awareness of what was occurring around the watershed.

Physical analyses

The physical analyses of the watershed (a central focus in the study) included the development of data and maps concerning soils, slope, forest cover, geology, micro-climate, wildlife, and other natural factors of the property. A natural determinant approach, similar to that developed by Professor Ian McHarg,[2] was followed. This approach produces a series of overlays or composite maps that allow a determination of which properties within a given area are of critical ecological concern and which properties are conducive to intelligent development.

In the case of the watershed, a natural determinants map (i.e., a composite of soils, slope, covering, and geological data) was developed to define areas that are critical, either for the water-supply system or for other ecological reasons, and areas that could undergo various forms of development. This approach was used because of an overriding concern that the policy should not be detrimental to the property.

The analysis of natural determinants (Table 1) showed that approximately 19,993 acres of the total 35,000 should be defined as critical to the water-supply system. These are made up mostly of lands that drain directly into the five reservoirs and constitute the subwatersheds of the Pequannock system. An additional 4,300 acres were determined to be critical because of soil conditions and not conducive to development. Another 2,000 acres are critical because of slopes in excess of 25 percent. Finally, wetlands (floodplains and swamps), also critical, amounted to 3,100 acres. The analysis concluded that approximately 6,247 acres of remaining land would be conductive to various forms of development under strictly controlled conditions.

The framework for a policy, then, became a combination of the awareness of the history of the watershed, an understanding of the impact of Newark's presence, knowledge of recent and future development trends, and last, extensive knowledge of the physical characteristics and ecological limitations of the property itself.

Criteria for a Policy

Criteria for the development of a policy for the Pequannock watershed may be defined as the objectives of an optimal policy. These were first developed as assumptions concerning the desirability of actions that the city might take in the future disposition of the watershed. Later, these were formalized as the general criteria on which the policy would be based and are as follows:

1. The policy should not have an adverse effect on the quality or quantity of the existing water supply system.

2. The policy should result in an efficient use of the Pequannock watershed so that its full potential as a resource of the city of Newark may be realized.

3. The policy should produce direct benefits to the people of Newark.

4. The policy should enable the city to decrease the amount of taxes being directly paid by Newark on watershed property to the six municipalities.

5. The policy should not have an adverse effect on the ecology of the Pequannock watershed.

6. The policy should not result in undesirable land-use patterns or economic imbalance in the six municipalities surrounding the watershed.

7. The policy should be in the best interests of the city of Newark and the state of New Jersey.

With the formulation of the criteria, a number of alternative policies previously discussed in the city were evaluated. These included continuation of the present policy of total conservation, sale of the water-supply system, and sale of all or selected portions of the watershed to private or public interests. As these were evaluated, it became clear that none conformed with the policy criteria; therefore, a new policy must be designed. With full recognizance of the vast amount of data at hand, a new policy was designed with the guidance provided by the policy criteria.

The Revised Policy

The revised policy is offered with full recognition that it does not constitute a detailed land-use plan. Rather, it is a direction for the city of Newark to follow in its future disposition of the Pequannock watershed. As such, the policy must be viewed as a first step in a continuing planning process.

The study recommends that the city of Newark pursue a policy allowing protective development and multipurpose use of the Pequannock watershed. It concludes that such a policy will allow the city to retain vast acreage (80 percent) in an undeveloped state, promote efficient use of the property, diminish the existing and future tax burden, increase revenues, and provide direct benefits to the people of Newark.

As indicated earlier, approximately 6, 247 acres were found to be suitable for controlled development. The study recommends that the acreage be leased for private development, developed by the city, or joint ventured through intermediate structures. Possible land uses include public and private commercial recreation, housing, and limited commercial and industrial development.

Lease arrangements with private developers would provide an appropriate fee for the use of the land, payment of taxes by the user, and in many cases retention of a percentage of the gross receipts of the development by the city of Newark. Economic studies indicate clearly that a demand for such use of the Pequannock watershed exists. All development of this nature would be guided by a detailed land-use plan, special development controls and standards, and individual environmental impact analysis.

Approximately 19, 993 acres were determined to be critical for water supply purposes. While this acreage would be excluded from the development indicated above, it can be used for various public recreation and educational purposes. Such use should also be determined by an overall conservation and development plan.

The remaining 9, 000 acres may be leased to public or private nonprofit organizations for public open space or recreation and educational uses. Payment would be used to defray taxes. Conservation easements may also be applied to critical acreage to restrict future development.

The policy, which allows development of 20 percent of the land under controlled conditions, conserves 80 percent of the

TABLE 2.
Compatibility of Natural and Man-Made Features

| | | Natural determinants | | | | | | |
| | | Water drainage | | | Slope | | | |
Potential land use Pequannock watershed		Prime watershed	Swamp marsh	Floodplain	0-8%	8-15%	15-25%	25%+
Conservation-water supply areas		+	+	+	+	+	+	+
Fish and wildlife preservation		+	+	+	+	+	+	+
Recreation	Public — City park organization	-	-	+	+	+	-	-
	Camp grounds	-	-	-	+	o	-	-
	Nature center	o	-	-	+	+	-	-
	Wilderness areas	+	+	+	+	+	+	+
	State parks	-	-	+	+	+	-	-
	Private — Golf courses	o	-	+	+	+	+	-
	Camp ground	-	-	-	+	o	-	-
	Fee fishing	o	-	+	+	+	+	+
	Winter sport facilities	o	-	-	+	+	+	-
	Hotel resorts	-	-	-	+	o	-	-
	Theme parks	-	-	-	+	o	-	-
	Conference center	-	-	-	+	o	-	-
Agriculture	Truck farms	o	-	o	+	o	-	-
	Tree farms	+	-	-	+	+	o	-
Residential	Low density	-	-	-	+	+	+	-
	Medium density	-	-	-	+	+	o	-
	High density	-	-	-	+	o	-	-
Institution	Special use	-	-	-	+	o	-	-
Commercial	Coordinated (neighborhood)	-	-	-	+	o	-	-
	Highway	-	-	-	+	-	-	-
	Office/research	-	-	-	+	o	-	-
Industrial	Light industry	-	-	-	+	-	-	-
	Heavy industry	-	-	-	+	-	-	-

Source: Rahenkamp, Sachs, Wells and Associates - 1972.

with Potential Land Uses—Pequannock Watershed

| (restrictions to land use) | | | | Physical services required | | | | | Social facilities and services required | | |
| Vegetation | | Soil | Climate | Utilities | | | Roads | | | | |
Forest/woodland	Meadow/open	Prime agriculture	Frost pocket	Public water	Public sewer	On-site sewer	Major roads	Minor roads	School	Fire	Police
+	+	+	+	-	-	-	-	-	-	-	-
+	+	+	+	-	-	-	-	-	-	-	-
+	+	o	+	+	-	+	+	+	-	-	+
+	+	o	+	+	-	+	-	+	-	-	-
o	+	o	+	+	-	+	-	+	-	-	-
+	+	+	+	-	-	-	-	o	-	-	-
+	+	o	+	+	-	+	+	+	-	-	+
+	+	+	+	o	-	o	-	+	-	-	-
o	+	o	o	-	-	+	-	+	-	-	-
+	+	+	+	-	-	-	-	+	-	-	-
o	+	+	+	o	-	o	-	+	-	-	-
o	+	-	-	+	+	-	-	+	-	+	o
o	+	-	+	+	o	+	+	o	-	+	o
o	+	-	-	+	o	+	-	+	-	+	o
+	+	+	+	-	-	-	-	+	-	-	-
+	+	+	+	-	-	-	-	+	-	-	-
+	+	o	-	-	-	+	-	+	+	+	o
o	+	-	-	+	+	-	o	+	+	+	+
-	+	-	-	+	+	-	+	+	+	+	+
o	-	-	-	+	+	-	-	+	-	+	o
-	+	-	-	+	+	-	+	-	-	+	+
-	+	-	-	+	o	+	+	-	-	+	+
-	+	-	-	+	+	-	+	-	-	+	+
-	+	-	-	+	o	+	+	-	-	+	+
-	+	-	-	+	o	+	+	-	-	+	+

Compatible +, Possibly compatible o, Incompatible -

property in open space and recreation use. When matched against the policy criteria, it offers a constructive alternative to the city of Newark. The future of the watershed may be seen as a center for tourist and commercial recreation and limited housing and industrial uses. Of utmost importance is the conservation of 29, 000 acres, which is made possible by the revenues derived from leases.

Continued Planning

The study strongly recommended the establishment of a continued planning capability for the Pequannock watershed. The need for such planning need not be detailed here.

An overall conservation and development plan should be based on the natural capacity of the watershed to absorb development. As such it must evolve from a continued ecological inventory and evaluation, the development of an economic model, and, perhaps most importantly, the design of development controls and standards tailored to the Pequannock watershed. Such a system for planning was included in the study. Of prime concern is the desire to program development that is compatible with the natural characteristics of a development site. A methodology for this is indicated in Table 2. Various development activities are judged as either compatible or incompatible with a series of natural determinants. Using a similar model, sites can be selected that will promote "safe development," i. e. , development that is sensitive to the land.

Administration

The study also recommended the creation of a Newark Watershed Conservation and Development Corporation. A nonprofit corporation, this unit would contract with the city to provide administrative, planning, conservation, and development services. It would develop a master plan, design development controls and standards, and implement the plan by negotiating the appropriate leases. The corporation would be governed by a board of directors appointed by the mayor of Newark with confirmation by the Municipal Council.

Present Status of the Policy

In October of 1972, the Newark Municipal Council adopted all of the recommendations of the study. In June 1973, the council approved the creation of the Newark Watershed Conservation and Development Corporation. This is presently being created.

The city has also received a grant from the U.S. Department of Housing and Urban Development for the conduct of an overall conservation and development plan for the Pequannock watershed. Such a plan is currently underway and will be administered by the corporation as soon as it becomes operational.

The product of this large undertaking is expected to begin a new era for the Pequannock watershed. The planning process is not one that has been widely used in New Jersey. It represents not the philosophy of the bulldozer and rapid urbanization but that of sensitive land use and orderly growth. It is strongly believed that the process will result in major benefits to the people of Newark, the state, and the six municipalities encompassing the watershed.

Mayor Kenneth A. Gibson, at a conference during which the study was released, stated the city's commitment to the Pequannock watershed in the following manner:

> I have often been quoted as saying, "wherever America's cities are going, Newark will get there first." Today, I say with great confidence and no small amount of pride, that in the quest for intelligent and sensitive land use in the state of New Jersey, the city of Newark will lead the way.

References

1. Frank J. Urquhart, A Short History of Newark, Baker Printing Company, Newark, New Jersey, 1916.

2. Ian McHarg, Design With Nature, Natural History Press, Doubleday and Co., Garden City, Long Island, New York, 1971.

VI. NEW ARCHITECTURAL MODELS

THE NEED FOR PARKS AND OPEN SPACE

Luciano Miceli

Miceli Weed Kulik
Landscape Architects
East Rutherford, New Jersey

The flight from the cities to the suburbs in pursuit of a better life is common. The present overcrowdedness in the city, the difficulty of getting around, the decay of neighborhoods and the new monumental scale of things sure do not permit people to comfortably exist in a balanced environment.

In the meanwhile, forested hills, babbling brooks, and verdant valleys, clean and safe schools, and spacious dwellings located at the edges of the metropolis and beyond, create an appealing image to many urbanites. With whetted appetites they pioneer to the suburbs in search of a better life, only to find that the quality of their new existence is also deficient. Lack of a workable growth structure, depletion and waste of the open space resource, and the monotony of sprawl are often the realities of the suburban environment. Ironically, the natural amenities sought are consumed by the transplants.

The ideal city and the ideal suburb are probably one in the same. Human ecology—the relationship of man the animal to his territory—has no recognized title or geographic description. A balanced community, an "eco-neighborhood," is an environment in which there exists harmony among natural and man-made elements. Energy, sewage, food and water supply, social exchange, and other systems must be relevantly linked. Today we are beginning to recognize the fragility of the chain of life while pursuing the planning and remodeling of our communities.

The value of open space as the protoplasm of life, as the breathing space for our communities, is significant. In cities, suburbs, and rural areas, land must be protected so as to ensure its natural viability. As population densities increase, so do

245

FIG. 1. Soils map. Bridgewater Township, New Jersey.

the demands for open space to relieve overburdened natural systems and to provide recreation opportunities.

Included among the priorities of our times are the tasks of
reintroducing open space into our cities and structuring a workable land-use pattern for our suburban and rural communities.

The following example, from the Open Space Plan for Bridgewater Township, New Jersey, is representative of the open space,
park, and recreation planning projects of Miceli Weed Kulik.

Open Space Plan, Bridgewater Township, New Jersey

Bridgewater Township comprises a 32 square mile land area in the
central portion of Somerset County, New Jersey. The predominant
land use is residential, with over 80 percent of developed land
used for that purpose. The 1970 population was 30,325, and it
has been predicted that by the year two thousand as many as
50,000 people will reside there. Arterial highway routes 78, 22,
287, 202, and 206 transsect the Township.

Land character is accentuated by two Watchung Mountain
ranges that span the Township northwest to southeast. The Raritan
River and the North Branch of the Raritan form the southern and
western edges of Bridgewater (see Fig. 1).

Planning Objectives

In our planning, we have identified the most naturally significant areas and proposed that they be protected—or withdrawn
from the pool of "developable" land.

The molding of an open-space system can effectively help
to preserve the environmental image and natural viability of
Bridgewater Township. Three areas where open space will serve
functional purposes are recreation, conservation, and shaping
development.

Valuable resources such as forests, wetlands, lakes, and
streams can be conserved in open spaces. Most conservation
areas can also be used for recreation. While these areas are
vitally important in protecting against soil erosion, aiding in
soil retention of water, and preventing rapid surface water runoff, their natural beauty makes them ideal locations for such uses
as hiking and riding trails, for fishing and camping areas, and
for laboratories for environmental education.

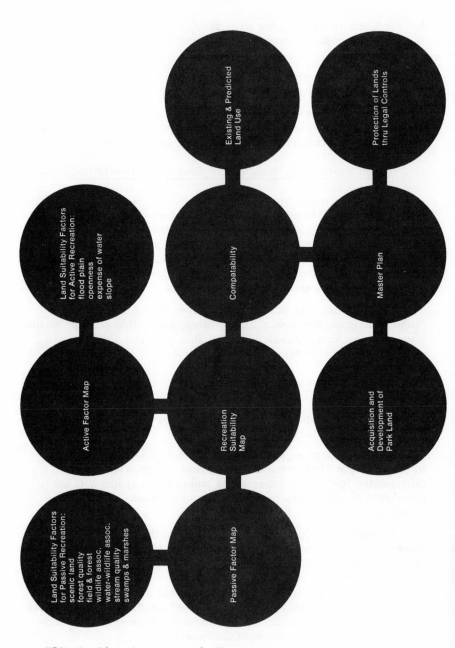

FIG. 2. Planning approach diagram.

The use of open space to shape development becomes increasingly important as population densities rise. Green spaces are needed not only to separate individual dwellings but also to buffer one community from another. In this way, we can prevent continuous monotonous growth and preserve the integrity of our villages.

Purposes of the Open Space Plan

1. To provide adequate open space to satisfy the needs of present and predicted populations (see Fig. 2).

2. To provide recreation opportunities for present and predicted population.

3. To help maintain viability of natural systems.

4. To mold a flexible plan, which stresses strategy rather than finality, so as to be able to cope with changing situations over a significant time span.

Methodology

The planning approach diagram illustrates how significant natural land characteristics are inventoried and existing and predicted land-use situations considered in formulating a planning strategy. The resultant is a two-faceted plan, including both a plan for acquisition and development of park land and a strategy for controlling land use through a series of legal devices.

The Suitability of Land for Active Recreation Use

Relatively flat and open lands are most suitable for the active forms of recreation. Floodplain land, openness as opposed to forested land are significant considerations. Expanse of water is desirable, and flatter land is more suitable than steep slopes. Ski slopes and sled runs are obvious exceptions and can be considered independently.

Data have been gleaned from various sources —soils maps, aerial photographs, geological surveys, Corps of Engineers reports, various state and local agencies, and our own aerial and field reconnaissance (see Fig. 3).

FIG. 3. The suitability of land for active recreation use.   Floodpl

Openness

Expanse of wat

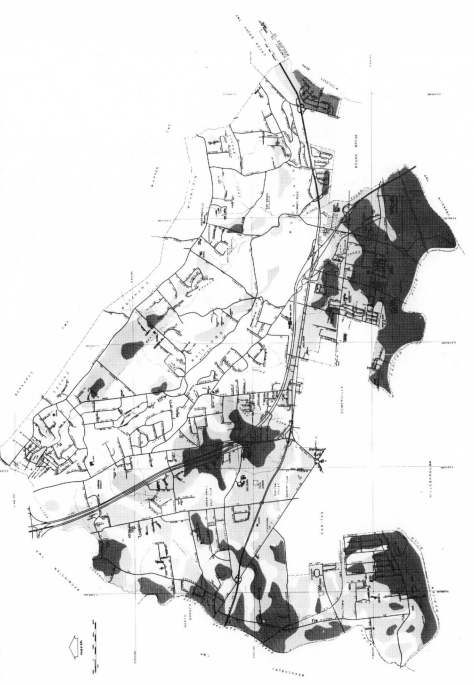

Slope

Active Recreation Composite Map

The composite mosaic map which results from the super-imposition of each independent factor, one upon the other, illustrates comparative values of the land for active recreation use. The darker the tone, the greater the value (see Fig. 4).

FIG. 4. Active recreation composite map.

The Suitability of Land for Passive Recreation Use

Land characteristics desirable for passive forms of recreation include water wildlife associations, stream quality, viable swamps and marshes, scenic land, forest quality, field and forest wildlife associations (see Fig. 5).

Passive Recreation Composite Map

The composite mosaic map which results from the super-imposition of each independent passive factor, one upon the other, illustrates comparative values of the land for passive recreation use. The darker the tone the greater the value (see Fig. 6).

FIG. 5. The suitability of land for passive recreation use.

Water wildlife associations

Stream qual

Swamps and marshes

Scenic la

Forest quality

261

Field and forest wildlife associatio

262

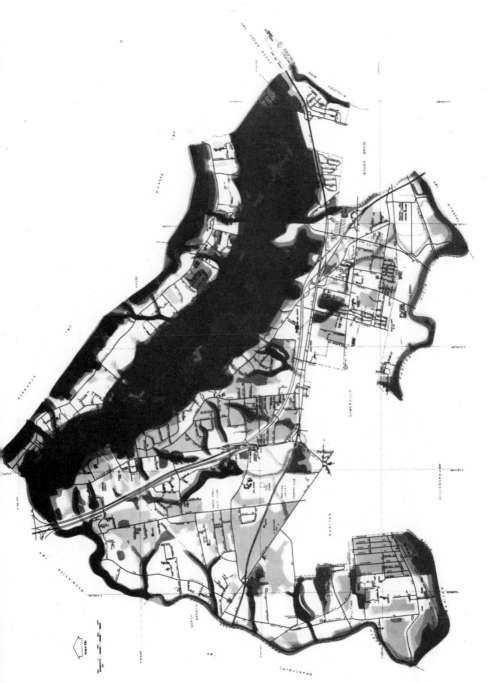

FIG. 6. Passive recreation composite map.

263

Recreation Suitability Map

A graphic representation of the suitability of township land for general recreation use is obtained by combining the active and passive composite maps into a single chart (see Fig. 7). The vast range of tones indicate the degree of suitability. The darker the tone, the greater the suitability of the land for recreation and conservation uses. Conversely, the lighter the tone, the greater the suitability of the land for development.

The composite maps become tools that aid in the selection of land for acquisition, in the planning of legal controls for land protection, and for evaluating future land use proposals.

The recreation suitability map and existing and predicted land uses are evaluated jointly to formulate the master plan. Land uses, neighborhood characteristics, population characteristics, school and other recreation facilities are considered.

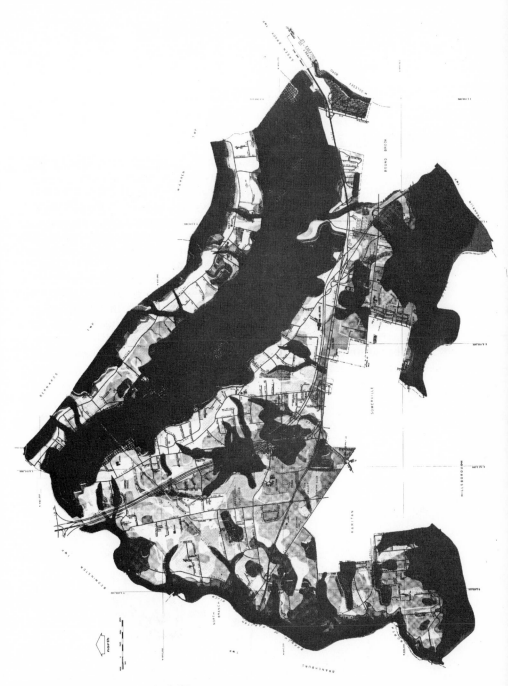

FIG. 7. Recreation suitability map.

Hierarchy of Parks

A network of open spaces planned to satisfy the varied parks and open-space needs of the community is woven into the land-use fabric. The hierarchy may include block parks, the smallest and most frequent park, geared to service people in the vicinity of their homes; neighborhood parks, which often relate to elementary schools and service neighborhood level needs; community parks, which often relate to high schools and provide major recreation facilities on a community level; special parks, which contain specialized core facilities such as recreation centers, environmental education facilities, swimming pools and ice rinks; linkage ways, trails for hiking, bicycling, etc., that link one community facility to another, and major open spaces, which are the natural preserves of the system. The following illustrations represent an approach to park development suitable for adoption by many communities (see Fig. 8).

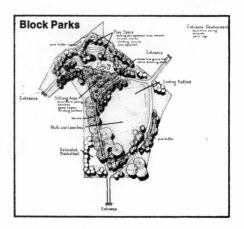

FIG. 8. Hierarchy of parks.

Linkage Way

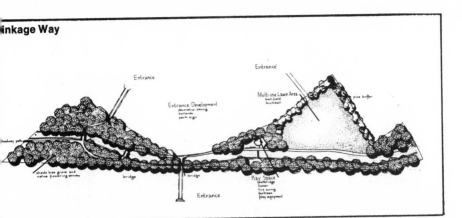

Neighborhood Parks

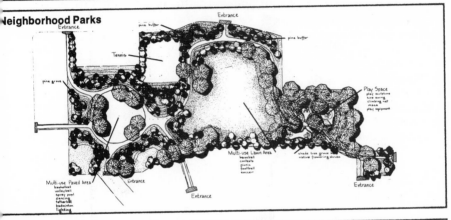

Community Park

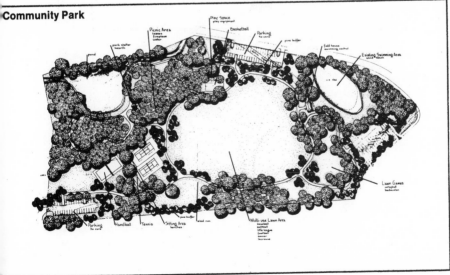

Master Plan

The master plan delineates areas for park and open-space use
(see Fig. 9). A range of legal devices will protect remaining
floodplain and steep slopes. Various ordinances for sign control, street tree planting, etc., are included in the overall considerations. Clustering of housing units is advocated to more
efficiently utilize the open space resource.

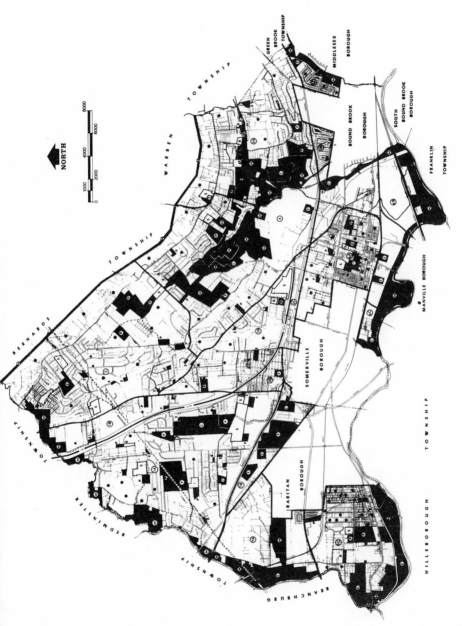

FIG. 9. Master plan.

INDEX

This index contains both author and subject listings. Numbers in brackets are reference numbers and indicate that an author's work is referred to although his name is not cited in the text. Underlined numbers give the page on which the complete reference is listed.